A Reaction to
Messianic Missionaries

A Reaction to
Messianic Missionaries

by
Rabbanit Michal Simani

ISBN-13: 978-0-9890160-4-9
ISBN-10: 0-9890160-4-8

Published by
Third House Publishing
United States of America.

Dedicated to

"The devout, the upright, and the perfect ones;
The holy congregations who gave their lives for the
Sanctification of the Name –
Who were beloved and pleasant in their lifetime
and in their death were not parted [from G-d]"

Contents

Part I: Wolves in sheep's clothing

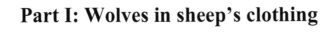

Greetings,

To those Jews who have been persuaded by friendship with Christian individuals, a well-organized program of their many institutions, or any of the various Messianic "Jewish" organizations –

Certainly, you are intelligent, strong-willed individuals, who are of good character. It is because of your many beautiful characteristics that this situation causes me such intense concern. If you would be so kind to grant a few minutes of your time, I shall attempt to explain why your situation worries me so much. The following are my honest thoughts and feelings; and I hope you will receive them in the same caring spirit as they are offered. I ask only that you sit with me and view these issues through my eyes.

All three of our sons were born in Jerusalem. One was born between Rosh Hashanah and Yom Kippur. For this reason, I did not accompany my husband to pray at the *Kotel* that Yom Kippur morning. When they returned, he told me that a young man, dressed as a religious Jew, approached him and began a conversation. He was shocked when this fellow tried to convince him that he no longer needed to fast on Kippur because the Mashiaḥ had already come. I was livid that Christian missionaries would be so callous and sordid as to proselytize at our holiest site on our holiest day. To entice a Jew to sin on Yom Kippur is a very serious crime.

Determined to write the "ultimate" rebuttal to missionaries, I began organizing my thoughts and researching all available material. Let it suffice to say that the joys of building a Jewish home and nurturing our contribution to the next generation superseded that venture. However, I never forgot my commitment.

Recently, I heard of the deep inroads that Christians, disguised as Jews, have made during those years. I felt very ashamed. Yes, I said that they are Christians who have cloaked themselves in traditional Jewish apparel. I realize that you have been convinced otherwise, but I challenge you to hear my disputation. If you find fault with it, then we can discuss it further.

While gleaming the most up-to-date data on these missionary programs, I found that the "Jews-for-Jesus" organization is using the words and image of the Rambam as well as other great sagas on their website. I cannot sit in silence any longer. I feel compelled to speak out. It is not my intent to demean any other religious path. Yet, enough is enough – it is time for us to stand up to anti-Jewish missionaries. Just in case you are not aware, let's begin with a few words regarding their background.

This book was written by a Jew for the benefit of other Jews, which includes all of the various denominations of Judaism, the Karites, and Beni Noah groups. If you are a devout Christian, who was not born to or a sincere ger of (convert to) one of groups, then you probably will not enjoy this work and, therefore, should not read it.

I-1 The Messianic Jewish Movement

In 1866, Christians established an organization specifically for evangelizing Jews, called the Hebrew Christian Alliance and Prayer Union of Great Britain. Jews, who had been lured away from Torah, joined them and worked towards spreading this concept in other countries. In 1915, Jewish apostates in the United States created the Hebrew Christian Alliance of America (HCAA). In 1924, Joseph H. Cohn persuaded the mission board to change the name to the American Board of Missions to the Jews (ABMJ). By his death in 1953, all of these organizations followed the doctrines of Evangelical Christianity, but their targets were exclusively Jews.

Still, there remained a tinge of discontent among many who felt that they were being forced to become Gentiles. They missed certain elements of their culture and wanted to retain familiar traditions while still enjoying the benefits of being Christians. They tried many avenues with some success. However, the turning point in their struggles came with Israel's stunning victory in the Six-Day War. They saw in this the fulfillment of Biblical prophecies. On this point, I agree with them. Suddenly they felt proud of their Jewish heritage. But, instead of returning to their Torah roots, they decided to reshape their Christian beliefs and life into a more Jewish style.

Part I. Wolves in sheep's clothing

This movement was spearheaded by Martin Chernoff and his wife Joanna, who started a home-based, Jewish-style church with a restructured form of worship. As time went by, their numbers increased, and they added more Jewish elements. This was not well received by their sponsor, the HVAA, who felt that they were becoming "too Jewish." In 1973, they were joined by the evangelist, Moishe Rosen, who created and headed the organization known as "Jews for Jesus" (JfJ) until his death in 2010.

After the turn of this century, Mark Kinzer founded an online graduate school, the "Messianic Jewish Theological Institute" (MJTI) in San Diego, California. Dr. Kinzer received his Ph.D. in Near Eastern Studies from the University of Michigan (1995), and his rabbinical ordination from the Union of Messianic Jewish Congregations (2001). Their purpose is to provide their leaders and laity with degrees to better promote their doctrines. Under Kinzer's influence, their religious leaders began using the title of "rabbis". In their programs, their students are instructed on how to dress, speak and behave as their authentic, Orthodox Jewish counterparts. Kinzer is driven by a desire to have his brand of Christianity recognized as an authentic branch of Orthodox Judaism.[1]

---

1 https://www.oneforisrael.org/bible-based-teaching-from-israel/messianic-judaism-messianic-jews/

The *Chosen People Ministries* (CPM) and the more recent branch, *Jews for Jesus* (JfJ), were established by Jewish apostates during the 20th century.[2] As Glaser states, the CPM designed and set in motion a major proselytizing campaign using the words of the prophet Isaiah as the spearhead to penetrate deep into the spiritual heart of Judaism both internationally and in our ancestral homeland, the State of Israel.

This does not surprise us, but it does disturb us. From its inception, Christianity has used every device and tactic imaginable to debilitate the faith of Avraham, Itzhaq, Yaacov, Yosef, Moshe, David, and the generations of prophets and sagas who followed them. This has caused us immeasurable pain. One Torah observant Jew, whom I happened to meet long ago, aptly described the words of missionaries as "candy-coated poison". Forgive my dismay, but the recent news reports have been extremely alarming.

An American evangelical Christian, who was born to a Methodist mother and Protestant father, disguised himself and his family of five as ultra-Orthodox Jews. While living in Jerusalem for fifteen years, he founded a religious seminary called *Yarim Ha'Am*, "quietly disseminating a Judaized version of Christianity and ordaining Christian 'rabbis' to further spread the gospel." He posed not only as an Orthodox rabbi but also as a *kohen* (a Jew of priestly descent) while working as a scribe and mohel. His wife also

---

2 Add here foundational data of these sects.

5

lied to the community by claiming to be the daughter of Holocaust survivors. [3]

Michael Dawson, a Lutheran by birth and heritage, and his wife, Summer, whose lineage was traced back to baptismal records in Mexico, were married in a Lutheran Church in 1995. After changing their name to Isaacson, they deceived several Jewish communities across the USA, claiming to be halakically Jewish by birth. Summer claimed to have Marrano heritage. They deceived a rabbi in Dallas, Texas, convincing him to perform a Jewish wedding for them. They moved about, collecting documentation to make Aliyah to Israel as an Orthodox Jewish family, and planning to join one of the many "sleeper cells" of fake religious Jews there. "It's very important that they [clandestine Christians] all become rabbis, that they all have beards and *peyot* like they have to be full-on *Hareidi* [ultra-orthodox Jews]. It's very important that they all have this look, they do this dance, and yet they don't." Michael and his son, Calev, misrepresenting themselves as Orthodox rabbis, performed sacred rituals that include supervising the preparation of kosher food, writing holy scrolls, washing the dead, as well as conducting weddings, divorces, and even conversions. [4]

---

3 https://www.thejc.com/news/israel/exclusive-unmasked-the-christian-missionary-who-went-undercover-as-an-orthodox-rabbi-1.516346 accessed 4/21/2022.
4 https://www.thejc.com/news/uk/exposed-sleeper-cell-of-evangelical-christians-posing-as-orthodox-rabbis-1.521679 accessed 4/21/2022.

These two examples are only a handful of snow from the surface of the imperialistic, Messianic iceberg. A large percentage of Messianic "Jews" were born Christians. Masked by a mendacious pretense of embracing Judaism, they undergo conversions, most often Orthodox ones. This tactic veils their true intent – to burrow their way into Judaism and Christianize it from within. I cannot think of a more fitting description for them than wolves-in-sheep's-clothing. When confronted, they express an urgency to convert Jews to Christianity, by any means possible, to hasten the "Second Coming" of their god.

One such deceiver, who was born to Christian parents, protested that he was not being deceptive. He simply wanted the Jewish people to recognize "Yeshua as their Moshiach" since he was so totally convinced that he was. He added: "Messianic believers choose to observe Jewish worship, as Yeshua did when He was here on earth, and we choose to identify with the Jewish people." But, they dress their culture and religious concepts in our traditions to deceive the young and uneducated among us. This imperialism at its worst.

It must be emphasized that the vast majority of Christians are sincerely good, caring people who respect the rights of all people to live by their own traditions and religious precepts. Of course, Glazer and other missionaries do not concern themselves with the suffering that they inflict on our people. On the contrary, they are fully confident that their tactics will please their god and win them greater rewards in the afterlife.

Since they have entitled their latest offensive against us the *Isaiah 53 Campaign*, then we have no choice but to view it as aggression – a spiritual, cultural attack. In my personal opinion, they can be liked in this sense to Amalek from the time of the Exodus. Like Amalek, whose intent was the physical annihilation of our people, they attack the weakest among us, those who are struggling spiritually and are often in the midst of a personal or religious identity crisis.

Messianic missionaries, regardless of their parentage, promote non-Jewish concepts clothed as Torah teaching. As an illustration of how this happens, we can take a custom practiced by a great many Ashkenazi Jews today who bake the symbolic *shlissel* challah on the Shabbat immediately following the holiday of Passover. Rabbi Berger, the founder of the AishDas Society,[5] informs us that those who follow this custom say that it is mentioned in the writings of Avraham Yehoshua Heshel (1748-1825), in the Ta'amei ha-Minhagim (1891), or some Torah scripture. However, this is not true. There is not one clear Jewish source for *shlissel* challah, nor is it in the Tannaitic, Amoraitic, Savoraitic, Gaonic, or Rishonic literature.

---

5 https://aspaqlaria.aishdas.org/media/speakers_resume.pdf

Among Christians, this same custom is called the "Easter" or "Paschal's" bread, which is baked with keys, and *shlissel,* inside. The connection is that the early keys resembled a cross. It is unclear how Jewish women were enticed into adopting this custom. Yet, to reason that since some Jews follow a custom, then it must be an authentic Jewish custom is an example of, what Rabbi Micha Berger terms, "reverse engineering".[6] Both he and Rabbi Bentzion Kravitz of Jew for Judaism quote Rabbi Yaakov Kranz (1741–1804), the Maggid (Preacher) of Dubno's parable of one happening upon an arrow stuck in a tree only to fine that the archer had painted each target around the arrow, and then joyfully declares that the arrow hit the bullseye. This is an excellent analogy for Christology in general. Wrapping a foreign tradition in Jewish guise does not transform it into a *Jewish* tradition or teaching.

This is an excellent analogy for the development of the Christian Text (CT) – aka the "New Testament". It, like the *shlissel* challah, is a hybrid. The authors of the CT preserved their most cherished concepts and customs by encasing them in a Jewish crust. Yet this has never fooled us into accepting them as authentic Torah. Thus, reverse engineering was the earliest, primary device

---

6 Jameel@Muqata, Shlissel (Key) Challah: The Loaf of Idolatry? (JewishPress.com: 28 Nisan 5782 – April 29, 2022). https://www.jewishpress.com/blogs/muqata/shlissel-key-challah-the-loaf-of-idolatry-3/2022/04/29/

deployed by early anti-Jewish missionaries in their initial offensive against Judaism.

Now, I realize that you have been told that these individuals and organizations are entirely Jewish, not Christian. But, please bear with me a little longer.

I-2 The Isaiah 53 Campaign

"We, as Jews, totally accept that there are multiple ways to believe in God," said Ruth Guggenheim, executive director of Jews for Judaism. "If we accept all of the different denominations, why not accept a belief in Yeshua?"

Younger individuals, explained Guggenheim, are understandably more accepting of pluralism, alternative lifestyles, and belief systems.

"They don't understand the distinction between Hebrew Christians [often referred to as Messianic Jews] and Judaism," said Guggenheim. "As long as it is wrapped in Jewish terminology, they have challenged us and said, 'What's wrong with it?'"

"I would say most of the younger generation is secular," wrote Dr. Mitch Glaser, president of *Chosen People Ministries* in a recent email communication to his email list, which was obtained by the Baltimore Jewish Times. In his email, he talks about preparing to bring the Isaiah 53 campaign to Israel, to target young Israelis who are "becoming more and more spiritually minded. ... It is time for young Israelis to hear the Gospel[7] in a way they can understand, and we must make Jesus more accessible to them."

He continued: "The Isaiah 53 campaign is distinctly Jewish; no one in Israel would ever think that the prophet Isaiah is anything but Jewish! We are

---

7 *Gospel* is a Christian term originating from German, meaning "G-d's word or story"; it replaced the ancient, polytheistic Greek term *mythos* that referred to the "true story of the G-ds".

presenting the Jewish Messiah through a Jewish prophet who is well-known to Israelis."[8]

During two millennia of waging physical and spiritual "warfare" against us, imperialistic missionaries have continuously attempted to derail our faith. In this effort, they have employed an array of devices to which we can apply the analogy of "Improvised Explosive Devices" (IEDs). Their current offensive is perhaps more organized and better funded, with the possible exception of the Inquisition. It must be kept in mind that even though the IEDs they have manufactured from passages of Isaiah, the Rambam, and the Kabbalah are mere illusions; yet, even the crudest constructed spiritual IED is capable of ripping apart a Jewish home. It is to mend the shredded hearts of mothers and fathers, sisters and brothers, who have already suffered so much at the calloused hands of the nations, that we now engage these aggressors. That is the purpose of this thesis: to identify those devices and defuse them.

The most essential, indispensable weapon in the anti-Jewish missionary's arsenal is "cherry-picking" scriptures. Once a passage has been taken out of context, they feel free to manipulate it until it appears to support their ancestral belief system. The force of this explosive device is best disarmed by widening the lens to

---

8 These excerpts from the Baltimore Jewish Times, were written by Erin Clare and published on June 20, 2013, accessed on April 4, 2022, at https://www.jewishtimes.com/fusion-of-faiths/

reveal the full meaning of the passage. Another device is when they joyfully identify certain truths that we share in common. By offering a hand of friendship, they convince many to lower their guard. They then trigger the device by proposing connections between legitimate scripture and pre-Christian, *avodah zarah* (idolatrous) concepts. Since they target the young and the lonely, this tactic has succeeded in confusing many, especially secular Jews.

One of the oldest accusations used against us is the assertion that Jews altered the scriptural texts, for the alleged purpose of removing evidence supporting Christian doctrine. Ultimately, it was repeated in the Quran, where their faithful are still taught that Jews expunged all references to Moḥammed from our Torah. This canonized slander is still propagated today. An anti-Jewish missionary once told me that the rabbis had removed the entire chapter of Isaiah 53 from the Tanach in an attempt to undermine Christianity. She was dismayed when I demonstrated that she had been misinformed.

Messianic missionaries, who are engaged in the *Isaiah 53 Campaign,* are more sophisticated and better versed in our scriptures. Their methodology is demonstrated throughout the JfJ website. They have very carefully constructed their published material to lead the reader down a specific path, which gradually constricts their understanding of the text, mentally herding our lost sheep into their spiritual trap. Then let's begin our frontline defense against them with an analysis of Isaiah.

There was a time that Judaism was also a missionary religion.[9] In 90 CE, emperor Domitian, the son of Vespasian and brother of Titus, put to death any Roman who had converted, to Judaism. (Suetonius: D. XII., 2) Our rabbis considered this so appalling that they forbade proselytizing by Jews. This *halaha* is still in force today, though I have heard that some Reform Jewish groups have chosen not to follow it. Still, Judaism respects the right of others to follow their traditional paths without concerns that we will attempt to destroy their families.

Let me pause here to clarify an essentially Jewish teaching. When Hashem[10] created man, He declared that his creation was not just good; it was *very good*. Since all people are descendants of Adam and Eva, it follows that all people are good. However, human behavior can be very bad. Thus, we acknowledge that people of other faiths are just as good as we Jews are. However, our experiences with the behavior of other religious groups have often been profoundly disappointing. More often than not, the atrocities inflicted upon our People over the past 2000 years were

---

9 William. G. Braude, Jewish Proselyting in the First Five Centuries of the Common Era: the Age of the Tannaim and Amoraim; (Providence: Brown University Press, 1940), pp. 11-25.

10 The Name of G-d – yod, he, vav, he – is sacred. We do not write in out except in religious text; instead, we replace it with ’ה in Hebrew texts and with "Hashem" in English.

incited by derogatory, inflammatory characterization of Jews recorded in their sacred texts.

The Torah instructs us to not be tale-bearers. Gossiping and maliciously bearing false witness against another is always destructive, but it is ghastly when the slander is canonized and taught to the very young. The following analysis compares and contrasts Jewish and Christian perspectives of Biblical texts. It is most regrettable that Christian and Muslim despotic missionaries have, by their inability to respect our right to live in peace – free of physical, cultural, and spiritual aggression – have brought us to the point of taking this self-defensive stance.

I-3 The Campaign Strategy

The JfJ website[11] is much more sophisticated than I had expected. It is well written and the flow demonstrates a solid, strategic construction and thought progression. It flows effortlessly with a nice balance of personal testimonials and philosophical discussions. I was impressed by the diversity of Jewish sources they quote, which we will explore as they become relevant. Overall, the pages offer a thought-provoking experience. After examining their material on Isaiah, there was a discernable pattern. Below is an outline of the material and a counter-argument for the Messianic missionary perspective.

First, we are informed that the rabbis have a "dilemma" with Isaiah 53. This is the first gate into which the site visitor is herded – the first narrowing of the perspective. The reader is forewarned that the rabbis, having lost sight of the true meaning of the passages, are confused. After tossing about a few excerpts from the passage, they ask the reader, "Who is this chapter speaking about?" Answering their own question, they explain: "The words are clear—the passage tells of an outstanding Servant of the Lord whose visage is marred and is afflicted and stricken;" and, not giving the reader too much time for independent thought, they add: "The text presents the Suffering Servant of the Lord *who dies as a korban*, a

---

11 https://jewsforjesus.org/ accessed between February and April 2022.

recompense for guilt." This is a very important gate through which the visitor's views must be herded. They know that the concept of the servant's suffering as *korban-Adam* (*i.e.* a human sacrifice) must be firmly established in the mind of the young Jewish reader, because, although this is an essential tenant of Christianity, it is foreign to Judaism.

Now that they have weakened the influence of the rabbis and slipped in the first Christianization of the text, they continue: "*Our* ancient commentators with one accord noted that the context clearly speaks of God's[12] Anointed One, the Messiah." Repeatedly, they emphasize that they are Jews, just like the reader, and as such, they simply present the text as anyone would read it if they had not been misled by the "confused" rabbis. This pattern of progressively narrowing the perspective, demeaning the rabbis, and inserting alien religious concepts and customs is repeated throughout the website.

I found it interesting that they draw the reader's attention to Sanhedrin 98b and Zohar II 212a, where the Mashiah is identified as a leper. This is very strange because nowhere in the Christian Texts (CTs) is their god presented as suffering from that horrible disease. Nowhere does it describe

---

[12] As an expression of reverence, Orthodox Jews refrain from writing the term "God" as "G-d".

17

him as having any disease or infirmity. Yet, it is recorded that Ḥezekiah's great grandfather was a leper, and it is possible that he also had contracted the disease.

Having established that the earlier rabbis considered that the Isaiah passages referred to the Mashiaḥ as an individual, they then turn to Rashi (Rabbi Shlomo Itzchaki, 1040-1105) and other Medieval rabbis who interpreted Isaiah as referring to the people of Israel collectively. The rationale that these missionaries give for Rashi's interpretation is that it was an emotional, "knee-jerk" reaction. We are informed that he "lived at a time when a degenerated medieval distortion of Christianity was practiced. He wanted to preserve the Jewish people from accepting "*such* a faith". This plants in the reader's mind that Christian anti-Semitism is simply a perversion of an otherwise caring and accepting religion.

This explanation left me wondering – what then should we do with the CT verses that refer to Jews as blind, evil, hypocrites, vipers, serpents, liars, murderers, and the *sons of Satan*? (Matthew 3:7; 6:2,5,16; 12:34; 15:7; 16:3; 22:18; 23:13-15, 23-33; 24:51. Mark 7:6-9. Luke 3:7; 11:44, 46-48, 52, 54; 12:1, 56. John 8:44, 12:42) It appears quite clear that the Christians of Rashi's time were only responding to the canonized slander skillfully interwoven in their sacred texts. Really. Have the horrors of two millennia of oppression, theft, rape, kidnapping of children, and mass murder simply been a misunderstanding that resulted in the perversion of a kind and gentle Christian doctrine? Or, has it been a weapon deliberately wielded for cultural conquest?

Messianic missionaries on the JfJ website present themselves as championing the Suffering Servant as an individual Mashiaḥ, as though the rabbis have rejected this view. This is a gross misrepresentation. They seem particularly hostile to Rashi's view that these verses refer to Israel as a nation. By switching roles and casting themselves as the champion of scripture, they feel that they have taken the high ground and are now posited to reveal the "true" meaning of the text. From our viewpoint, the focus of these despotic missionaries is too myopic. They view the Scriptures through a very narrow lens. They survey every verse with two goals –confirming the divinity of their god, Yeshu,[13] and the supersedure of their beliefs over all others. We could never accept their interpretations because they skewed the meaning of our scriptures to advance a foreign belief system. By contrast, we are prepared to present to you a wider, more inclusive perspective of the serious issues that separate Israel and Christians.

When considering translations, we must remember that the verses in Isaiah are poetic passages composed roughly 2,722 years

---

13 We can only refer to him as Yeshu and not by any of the names used by Christians, because they have deified and worship him. G-d grant that someday soon this situation will change.

ago. Historians often point out that it is a very difficult task to "get into the head" of ancient people. For this reason, we give more credit to those who have dedicated a lifetime to studying these texts. The rabbis' distinct advantage is an unbroken, multi-generational scholastic dedication reaches back to the days of Isaiah.

For the Masoretic Text, we use that of the online Jewish Publication Society (JPS)[14] and the ArtScroll Stone Edition (ASE)[15], which is not currently available online. In Judaism, there are two dominant perspectives of Isaiah 53. The JPS translation focuses solely on the Suffering Servant. The ASE's focus is that Israel (*i.e.* the entire Jewish People) is collectively the Suffering Servant.

To offset the accusation that the rabbis tampered with Isaiah 53, the Septuagint (LXX) text are included.[16] The LXX was the first translation of the Hebrew Scriptures into Greek. It was made in Alexandria, Egypt about 283 BCE (Before the Common Era). It was used by Greek-speaking Jews until the ascension of Christianity in the late second through the early fourth centuries Common Era (CE). Under emperor Constantine, Orthodox Christianity was defined at the Council of Nicaea in 325 CE. Thus,

---

14 https://mechon-mamre.org/p/pt/pt0.htm
15 Tanach – the Torah, Prophets, Writings: the twenty-four books of the Bible Newly translated and annotated, 2nd edition, editor Rabbi Nosson Scherman (New York: Mesorah Publications, ltd., 1997).
16 https://www.ellopos.net/elpenor/greek-texts/septuagint/

some 608 years after its first edition, monks set down to "correct" it, as well as the various copies of the Christian Texts (CT) that did not reflect the new orthodox doctrine. This fact is well known to scholars. The result of these "corrections" are their current scriptures. Parts of the LXX had been amended by early Christians during the century preceding Constantine. For this reason, the rabbis began promoting their translations, *targums*, of the Hebrew into Greek and Aramaic beginning in about 100 CE. The LXX presented below is that persevered by the Christian Church. Representing the CT, we present the King James Version (KJV),[17] the New International Version (NIV),[18] and portions found on the JfJ website. Please note that *all* translations bear the "fingerprint" of the location, historical period, cultural background, and personal biases of the translator. Interestingly, most of the differences between the translations of Isaiah 53 are stylistic; but each demonstrates its distinctive doctrinal fingerprints.

We suppose that each reader is intelligent, and thus, fully capable of reaching meaningful conclusions without being dictated to. It is not my place to tell anyone what to believe. Unlike the Messianic missionaries, I will not twist the meaning to manipulate your thinking. My methodology, throughout this work, is a

---

17 http://thekingsbible.com/
18 https://www.biblestudytools.com/niv/

straightforward compare and contrast analysis of our ancestral Torah-based scriptural exegesis with those of JfJ missionaries.

To demonstrate the flexibility of Hebrew terminology, I have provided for your benefit an etymological exposition based on Ernest Klein's *Comprehensive Etymological Dictionary of the Hebrew Language* (EDH)[19]. **The EDH entries below are *not* meant as *translations* of the verses**. Only an expert in Biblical Hebrew can accomplish that goal. They are simply provided as **a study aid** and to demonstrate the interconnectedness of the other various translations.

---

19 Ernest Klein, A Comprehensive Etymological Dictionary of the Hebrew Language for Readers of English (Jerusalem Carta: University of Ḥaifa, 1987).

I-4 Isaiah 53 יְשַׁעְיָהוּ

I-4.1 Verse 1

א מִי הֶאֱמִין לִשְׁמֻעָתֵנוּ; וּזְרוֹעַ ה', עַל-מִי נִגְלָתָה.

EDH: 1. Who <u>believed/trusted (2nd per. sing.)</u> our <u>report/tradition/decision</u>; Hashem will <u>sow/scatter</u> it, unto whom <u>has it/he been revealed/disclosed</u>?

JPS: 1. 'Who would have believed our report? And to whom hath the arm of the LORD been revealed?

ASV: 1. Who would believe what we have heard? For whom has the arm of Hashem been revealed?

LXX: 1. Κυριε, τίς ἐπίστευσε τῇ ἀκοῇ ἡμῶν; καὶ ὁ βραχίων Κυρίου τίνι ἀπεκαλύφθη;
1. O Lord, who has believed our report? And to whom has the arm of the Lord been revealed?

KJV: 1. Who hath believed our report? and to whom is the arm of the LORD revealed?

NIV: 1. Who has believed our message and to whom has the arm of the LORD been revealed?

JfJ: 1. Who has believed what he has heard from us? And to whom has the arm of the LORD been revealed?

The first part of Isaiah 53:1 provides foreshadowing that the following message is amazing and difficult to believe. The footnotes in ArtScroll Stone Version (ASV) of the Masoretic Text (MT) explain: "This is a prophecy foretelling what the nations and their kings will exclaim when they witness Israel's rejuvenation. The nations will contrast their former scornful attitude toward the Jews (vv. 1-3) with their new realization of Israel's grandeur (vv 4-7)."

The JFJ website mocks: "Many Jewish interpreters take 'us' in this verse to mean the Gentile nations and understand the passage to speak of the value of Israel's suffering on behalf of the nations of the world. The idea is that the Gentiles are exclaiming, "Wow! The Jewish people are suffering on our behalf! Who knew?!" Then the reader is told that "us" refers to those "who disbelieved God's word", which, of course, could only indicate "G-d's people" (*i.e.* Israel) and not foreign nations. Amazing! The JfJ flaunts that *it* is a Jewish organization that teaches the true Jewish faith. Yet, they begin with an anti-Semitic proposition. All Jews – past, present, and future – who do not see their divine Messiah in these verses are all faithless ingrates.

They inform us that the phrase "what he has heard from us" is parallel to "the arm of the Lord". However, the original Hebrew does not contain the word "arm". The poetic imagery is of Hashem as a planter, who scatters seed by hand as he walks through a field. It's the Greek translation that *interprets* this imagery and shifts the focus to the strong-arm motif. The actual text is telling us that the subsequent message has purposefully been scattered far and wide by G-d.

Our rabbis teach that every passage must be understood through four perspectives: the simple/basic meaning of the words, the allegorical/symbolic, the philosophical, and the mystical. For the basic perspective, it is possible that initially, this passage was a eulogy spoken by Isaiah at the death of King Hezekiah. Rashi's suggestion that the entire People of Israel is the Suffering Servant is an allegorical perspective. The philosophical perspective is from the views of Sa'adya haGoan and the Rambam on the Mashiaḥ ben Yosef and Mashiaḥ ben David.[20] The mystical perspective is based on the concept of the Messianic Age. As Jews, we are free to believe any, all, or none of these.

---

20 A fuller explanation of the Mashiaḥ ben Yosef and Mashiaḥ ben David will be presented in Part II.

I-4.2 Verse 2

ב וַיַּעַל כַּיּוֹנֵק לְפָנָיו, וְכַשֹּׁרֶשׁ מֵאֶרֶץ צִיָּה--לֹא-תֹאַר לוֹ, וְלֹא הָדָר
וְנִרְאֵהוּ וְלֹא-מַרְאֶה וְנֶחְמְדֵהוּ.

EDH: 2. He <u>arose/was uplifted</u> like a <u>suckling child/young plant</u>
before him, and like a root from a dry <u>land/country</u> – no
<u>form/figure/appearance</u> of him did we see and no
<u>sight/view/appearance/vision</u> [that] we should <u>desire/love</u>.

JPS: 2. For he shot up right forth as a sapling, and as a root out of dry
ground; he had no form nor comeliness, that we should look upon
him, nor beauty that we should delight in him.

ASV: 2. Formerly he grew like a sapling or like a root from arid
ground; he had neither form nor grandeur; we saw him, but without
such visage that we could desire him.

LXX: 2. ἀνηγγείλαμεν ὡς παιδίον ἐναντίον αὐτοῦ, ὡς ῥίζα ἐν γῇ
διψώσῃ. οὐκ ἔστιν εἶδος αὐτῷ οὐδὲ δόξα· καὶ εἴδομεν αὐτόν, καὶ οὐκ
εἶχεν εἶδος οὐδὲ κάλλος·
2. We brought a report as of a child before him; he is as a root in a
thirsty land: he has no form nor comeliness; and we saw him, but he
had no form nor beauty.

KJV: 2. For he shall grow up before him as a tender plant, and as a
root out of a dry ground: he hath no form nor comeliness; and when
we shall see him, there is no beauty that we should desire him.

NIV: 2. He grew up before him like a tender shoot, and like a root out of dry ground. He had no beauty or majesty to attract us to him, nothing in his appearance that we should desire him.

JfJ: 2. For he grew up before him like a young plant, and like a root out of dry ground; he had no form or majesty that we should look at him, and no beauty that we should desire him.

It is no secret that both Christians and Moslems have, throughout the centuries, mocked and ridiculed Jews as crooked in face, form and character. However, in an odd way this offer additional support for the ASV position that the Suffering Servant represents the Jewish people. The physical appearance of both have been ridiculed.

We agree with the JfJ authors that these two verses introduce the Suffering Servant, and this is also how the Jewish Publication Society (JPS) translates it. Yet, we also find support for a simple, basic interpretation for Isaiah 53 as a eulogy for the righteous Ḥezekiah, and this is the perspective that will be presented below.[21]

Isaiah tells us that "he had no form nor comeliness, that we should look upon him, nor beauty that we should delight in him." From this, we understand that King Ḥezekiah suffered from some

---

[21] Often

form of disfigurement. It could have been the result of a disease or birth defect that caused him to be rejected by his father. Ahaz refused to nurture Ḥezekiah. Hence, his childhood is described as a hard, dry environment. All commentators see the term "before him" as referring to G-d; however, it could refer to Ahaz, who rejected the child as a possible heir.

At this point, JfJ introduces the reader to what they call the "prophetic perfect" and explains that the verses use Hebrew verbs that are *normally* translated in the past tense "but that grammatically can apply to future events." This statement either demonstrates a poor understanding of Biblical/Classical Hebrew or is again leading the sheep to the slaughter. The "*waw* consecutive" is characteristic of not only ancient Hebrew but also other ancient Semitic languages.[22] This is not the place to attempt a lesson on this subject, so, let it suffice to state that placing a *waw* (usually pronounced *vav* today) before a verb switches its tense from future to past or from past to future. This verse begins with וַיַּעַל, where יַעַל means "he will arise/be uplifted" but the ו transforms the verb into "he arose/was uplifted".

I-4.3 Verse 3

---

22 J. Weingreen, A Practical Grammar for Classical Hebrew (Oxford: Oxford University Press, 1959) pp. 90-95, 114, 252.

ג נִבְזֶה וַחֲדַל אִישִׁים אִישׁ מַכְאֹבוֹת וִידוּעַ חֹלִי; וּכְמַסְתֵּר פָּנִים מִמֶּנּוּ,
נִבְזֶה וְלֹא חֲשַׁבְנֻהוּ.

EDH: 3. A man <u>despised/contemptible/distasteful</u> <u>formed/figured/appearance</u> of men of suffering and knew illness; As [one who] <u>hides/conceals</u> a face from us, <u>despised/contemptible/distasteful</u> and we did not <u>think of/account for</u>.

JPS: 3. He was despised, and forsaken of men, a man of pains, and acquainted with disease, and as one from whom men hide their face: he was despised, and we esteemed him not.

ASV: 3. He was despised and isolated from men, a man of pains and accustomed to illness. As one from whom we would hide our faces; he was despised, and we had no regard for him.

LXX: 3. ἀλλὰ τὸ εἶδος αὐτοῦ ἄτιμον καὶ ἐκλεῖπον παρὰ πάντας τοὺς υἱοὺς τῶν ἀνθρώπων· ἄνθρωπος ἐν πληγῇ ὢν καὶ εἰδὼς φέρειν μαλακίαν, ὅτι ἀπέστραπται τὸ πρόσωπον αὐτοῦ, ἠτιμάσθη καὶ οὐκ ἐλογίσθη.

3. But his form was ignoble, and inferior to that of the children of men; he was a man in suffering, and acquainted with the bearing of sickness, for his face is turned from us: he was dishonoured, and not esteemed.

29

KJV: 3. He is despised and rejected of men; a man of sorrows, and acquainted with grief: and we hid as it were our faces from him; he was despised, and we esteemed him not.

NIV: 3. He was despised and rejected by mankind, a man of suffering, and familiar with pain. Like one from whom people hide their faces he was despised, and we held him in low esteem.

JfJ: 3. He was despised and rejected by men, a man of sorrows and acquainted with grief; and as one from whom men hide their faces he was despised, and we esteemed him not.

In Isaiah 7:1, we find that Ahaz was terrified when the kings to his north, Pekah, the king of Israel, and Rezin, the king of Aram, formed a confederacy. While Ahaz was inspecting his defenses and water supply, Hashem sent Isaiah to meet him. The king had rejected the G-d of Israel and turned to idolatry. Isaiah greeted him: "Keep calm, and be quiet; fear not, neither let thy heart be faint, because of these two tails of smoking firebrands, for the fierce anger of Rezin and Aram, and the son of Remaliah." Since Ahaz refused to ask a sign of Hashem that Judah would not be conquered, Isaiah informs him:

יד לָכֵן יִתֵּן אֲדֹנָי הוּא, לָכֶם--אוֹת: הִנֵּה הָעַלְמָה, הָרָה
וְיֹלֶדֶת בֵּן, וְקָרָאת שְׁמוֹ, עִמָּנוּ אֵל.

טז כִּי בְּטֶרֶם יֵדַע הַנַּעַר, מָאֹס בָּרָע--וּבָחֹר בַּטּוֹב: תֵּעָזֵב הָאֲדָמָה אֲשֶׁר אַתָּה קָץ, מִפְּנֵי שְׁנֵי מְלָכֶיהָ.

14. Therefore the Lord Himself shall give you a sign: behold, the young woman [Ahaz's new wife, Abijah] has conceived and has borne a son, and (she) shall call his name *Immanuel* ("G-d is with us")... 16. Yea, before the child shall know to refuse the evil, and choose the good, the land whose two kings thou hast a horror of shall be forsaken. (Isaiah 7:14,16)

and

ה כִּי-יֶלֶד יֻלַּד-לָנוּ, בֵּן נִתַּן-לָנוּ, וַתְּהִי הַמִּשְׂרָה, עַל-שִׁכְמוֹ;

For a child was born unto us, a son was given unto us; and the government is upon his shoulder. (*ibid* 9:5)

Ahaz scoffed at Isaiah's prophecy regarding Ḥezekiah, as his son, Maaseiah, was his heir. However, when Ahaz fought Pekah, he lost "a hundred and twenty thousand in one day, all of them valiant men; because they had forsaken the LORD, the G-d of their fathers." Maaseiah was among the dead. Thus, the prophet was right, and Ḥezekiah became the new heir. Still, his father refused to look upon him as his son and heir. The boy was too weak and his defects caused him to be susceptible to frequent illness.

The JfJ, of course, believe that these passages refer to their god, yet they fail to clarify an important point. When their Yeshu was touring the land, teaching the people, where do we find that he was rejected and despised? Some disagreed with what he said, but they did not turn their faces from him because he was physically ugly or deformed.

I-4.4 Verse 4

ד   אָכֵן חֳלָיֵנוּ הוּא נָשָׂא, וּמַכְאֹבֵינוּ סְבָלָם; וַאֲנַחְנוּ חֲשַׁבְנֻהוּ נָגוּעַ מֻכֵּה אֱלֹהִים וּמְעֻנֶּה.

EDH: 4. <u>Surely/Truly/Indeed/But</u> our illnesses he <u>lifted-up/bore</u>, our suffering he carried; <u>and/but</u> we <u>thought/regarded</u> him stricken by G-d's touch and afflicted.

JPS: 4. Surely, our diseases he did bear, and our pains he carried; whereas we did esteem him stricken, smitten of G-d, and afflicted.

ASV: 4. But in truth, it was our ills that he bore, and our pains that he carried – but we had regarded him diseased, stricken by G-d, and afflicted!

LXX: 4. οὗτος τὰς ἁμαρτίας ἡμῶν φέρει καὶ *περὶ ἡμῶν ὀδυνᾶται*, καὶ ἡμεῖς ἐλογισάμεθα αὐτὸν εἶναι ἐν πόνῳ καὶ ἐν πληγῇ ὑπὸ Θεοῦ καὶ ἐν κακώσει.

4. He bears *our sins*, and is pained for us: yet we accounted him *to be* in trouble, and in suffering, and in affliction.

32

KJV: 4. Surely, he hath borne our griefs, and carried our sorrows: yet we did esteem him stricken, smitten of G-d, and afflicted.

NIV: 4. Surely, he took up our pain and bore our suffering, yet we considered him punished by God, stricken by him, and afflicted.

JfJ: 4. Surely, he has borne our griefs and carried our sorrows; yet we esteemed him stricken, smitten by God, and afflicted.

Isaiah loved Ḥezekiah because he was a gentle, kind, devout man and king. Ḥezekiah suffered his entire life from poor health and a deformed appearance, he was especially sensitive to the suffering of his people. Just like his father, the aristocrats – as well as the people in general – believed that his deformities were a divine affliction and shunned him. Likewise, the nations and their people have harbored this same sentiment regarding the Jewish people.

I-4.5 Verse 5

ה וְהוּא מְחֹלָל מִפְּשָׁעֵנוּ, *מְדֻכָּא* מֵעֲוֹנֹתֵינוּ; מוּסַר שְׁלוֹמֵנוּ עָלָיו, וּבַחֲבֻרָתוֹ נִרְפָּא-לָנוּ.

EDH: 5. And he was lost/profaned/defiled/pierced/wounded/slain for our rebellion/transgression/guilt, oppressed/depressed for our iniquities; the binding/fettering of our peace/benefit is upon him, and with his bondage we will be healed.

JPS: 5. But he was wounded because of our transgressions, he was crushed because of our iniquities: the chastisement of our welfare was upon him, and with his stripes we were healed.

ASV: 5. He was pained because of our rebellious sins and oppressed through our iniquities; the chastisement upon him was for our benefit, and through his wounds, we were healed.

LXX: 5. αὐτὸς δὲ ἐτραυματίσθη διὰ τὰς ἁμαρτίας ἡμῶν καὶ μεμαλάκισται διὰ τὰς ἀνομίας ἡμῶν· παιδεία εἰρήνης ἡμῶν ἐπ᾽ αὐτόν. τῷ μώλωπι αὐτοῦ ἡμεῖς ἰάθημεν.
5. But he was wounded on account of our sins, and was bruised because of our iniquities: the chastisement of our peace was upon him; and by his bruises we were healed.

KJV: 5. But he was wounded for our transgressions, he was bruised for our iniquities: the chastisement of our peace was upon him; and with his *stripes* we are healed.

NIV: 5. But he was pierced for our transgressions, he was crushed for our iniquities; the punishment that brought us peace was on him, and by his wounds we are healed.

34

JfJ: 5. But he was pierced for our transgressions; he was crushed for our iniquities; upon him was the chastisement that brought us peace, and with his wounds we are healed.

Instead of listening to Isaiah, Ahaz foolishly paid the Assyrian king, Tiglath-pileser III, to assist him against his enemies. The Assyrians were a cruel, ruthless nation. Throughout Hezekiah's lifetime, his people endured one devastating war after another. Samaria was besieged and destroyed (724-720 BCE) by the forces of Tiglath-pileser III's son, Shalmaneser V. His grandson, Sargon II, deported the ten northern tribes (719 BCE) to the region north of Nineveh, Assyria's capital. Sargon's son, Sennacherib, attacked Judah twice.

On the first (706-704 BCE), Hezekiah capitulated to the Assyrian co-regent. Judah became their vassal and paid a hefty tribute that included the king's daughter. Hezekiah knew that the Assyrians would return, so he fortified his cities and had a tunnel dug bringing Jerusalem's water source within its walls. In -691, he conducted his second attack on Judah (Is. 36 & 37). The Assyrians wanted a quick victory, tribute, and booty; but were met with more resistance this time. Sennacherib sent his servant, Rab-shakeh, to the walls of the city to taunt and dispirit the Jews with insults in Hebrew, so all the people could understand. The prophet informed Hezekiah, "Behold, I will put a spirit in him, and he shall hear a rumor, and shall return unto his land; and I will cause him to fall by the sword in his land." (Is. 37:7) He continues that Hashem would place a "hook" in Sennacherib's mouth (Is. 37:29) – an opportunity to avenge the murder of his son, Aššur-nadin-šumni, presented itself – and the Assyrian jumped at it. They withdrew overnight.

After the Assyrians withdrew in -691, we are informed that Ḥezekiah was ill and even Isaiah thought he would die. After a revelation, Isaiah told the king's attendants to place a plaster of figs דְּבֶלֶת תְּאֵנִים on the abscess עַל-הַשְּׁחִין, and he recovered. (II Kings 20:7) Since the cause of his illness was an abscess, we can deduce that, during the heated exchange with Rab-shakeh, Ḥezekiah was wounded by an enemy arrow. Isaiah chides the people that their righteous king suffered because, by following Ahaz, they brought the Assyrians to the land. The JfJ also agrees with us that the body of the Suffering Servant was pierced or punctured with a sharp instrument. However, they are referring to when a Roman soldier pierced their Yeshu in his side to hasten his death. We consider it when Ḥezekiah was pierced by an arrow and would have died, except he was saved by Divine intervention. Why do the righteous suffer while the evil ones prosper? King David answers us. "How great are Your deeds, Hashem; exceedingly profound are Your thoughts. A boor cannot know, nor can a fool understand this: when the wicked bloom like grass and

36

all the doers of iniquity blossom – it is to destroy them till eternity." (Psalms 92:6-8)

As we move to the next perspective, ASV informs us that the nations will ultimately realize that they are responsible for the suffering of the nation of Israel and will acknowledge: "We brought suffering upon Israel for our selfish purposes; it was not, as we had claimed, that God was punishing Israel for its evil behavior."

I-4.6 Verse 6

ו כֻּלָּנוּ כַּצֹּאן תָּעִינוּ, אִישׁ לְדַרְכּוֹ פָּנִינוּ; וַה' הִפְגִּיעַ בּוֹ אֵת עֲוֹן כֻּלָּנוּ.

EDH: 6. All of us as a flock will go astray, [like] a man to his own path we turn our face; and Hashem caused him to met/encountered/entreat/beseech (for) the iniquity/guilt of us all.

JPS: 6. All we like sheep did go astray, we turned everyone to his own way; and the LORD hath **made to light on him** the iniquity of us all.

ASV: 6. We have all strayed like sheep, each of us turning his own way, and Hashem **inflicted upon** him the iniquity of us all.

LXX: 6. πάντες ὡς πρόβατα ἐπλανήθημεν, ἄνθρωπος τῇ ὁδῷ αὐτοῦ ἐπλανήθη· καὶ Κύριος *παρέδωκεν* αὐτὸν ταῖς ἁμαρτίαις ἡμῶν.

6. All we as sheep have gone astray; everyone has gone astray in his way; and the Lord **gave him up** for our sins.

KJV: 6. All we like sheep have gone astray; we have turned every one to his own way; and the LORD hath **laid on** him the iniquity of us all.

NIV: 6. We all, like sheep, have gone astray, each of us has turned to our own way; and the LORD has **laid on** him the iniquity of us all.

JfJ: 6. All we like sheep have gone astray; we have turned—every one—to his own way; and the LORD has laid on him the iniquity of us all.

The JSV translations הִפְגִּיעַ as "made to light" on him *the iniquity of us all.*" ASV has "inflicted" upon him. Both the KJV and NIV have "laid" on him. The LXX translates it as *παρέδωκεν*, "gave him up *for our sins*". The CT has "handed him over" (Matt. 18:34) and "betrayed" him (Mark 3:19). The JfJ missionaries, like the other Christian translators, are determined to identify the suffered as much as their god, Yeshu. Thus, restricting the reader's understanding, they inflate the meaning of the words.

> The iniquity, which can also mean the punishment for iniquity, "hits," or "meets" the servant, with even an overtone of violence. Like sheep, the

people were vulnerable to attack (not by predators, such as wolves, but by the guilt of their sin), but the servant instead bears the brunt of sin's attack.

How do we sort through this variety of translations?

Ernest Klein illuminates the issue by informing us that in the Biblical Era הִפְגִּיעַ conveyed the meaning of "caused to meet, encounter, entreat, or beseech"; but in Post Biblical Hebrew – after the Babylonian destruction of Solomon's Temple – linguistic usage shifted to attack, hit, hurt, or harm. The ASV, LXX, KJV, NIV, and JfJ are using the PBH form.

Since this verb is in the *Hiph'il*, causative form, the meaning is that the subject, Hashem, causes him, the servant, to meet/encounter/entreaty/beseech Him for the iniquity/guilt of us all. Hence, when Ḥezekiah was near death, he prayed that Hashem would forgive His people's sins.

The ASV, presenting the rabbinic view that the other nations will repent of their mistreatment of Israel, states this verse. "We [the nations] sinned by inflicting punishment upon Israel. Such oppression is often described as "Hashem's punishment (see 10, Habakkuk 1:12) for He decreed that it should happen (Abarbanel).

I-4.7 Verse 7

ז נִגַּשׂ וְהוּא נַעֲנֶה, וְלֹא יִפְתַּח-פִּיו, כַּשֶּׂה לַטֶּבַח יוּבָל, וּכְרָחֵל לִפְנֵי גֹזְזֶיהָ
נֶאֱלָמָה; וְלֹא יִפְתַּח פִּיו.

EDH: 7. He <u>drew near/approached</u> and he was humbled, he would not open his mouth, as a fattened lamb/kid to the <u>slaughter/slaughtering place</u> is carried, and as an ewe before her shearer is dumb; and he did not open his mouth.

JPS: 7. He was oppressed, though he humbled himself and opened not his mouth; as a lamb that is led to the slaughter, and as a sheep that before her shearers is dumb; yea, he opened not his mouth.

ASV: 7. He was persecuted and afflicted, but he did not open his mouth; like a sheep being led to the slaughter or a ewe that is silent before her shearers, he did not open his mouth.

LXX: 7. καὶ αὐτὸς διὰ τὸ κεκακῶσθαι οὐκ ἀνοίγει τὸ στόμα αὐτοῦ· ὡς πρόβατον ἐπὶ σφαγὴν ἤχθη καὶ ὡς ἀμνὸς ἐναντίον τοῦ κείροντος αὐτὸν ἄφωνος, οὕτως οὐκ ἀνοίγει τὸ στόμα.

7. And he, because of his affliction, opens not his mouth: he was led as a sheep to the slaughter, and as a lamb before the shearer is dumb, so he opens not his mouth.

KJV: 7. He was oppressed, and he was afflicted, yet he opened not his mouth: he is brought as a lamb to the slaughter, and as a sheep, before her shearers is dumb, so he openeth not his mouth.

NIV: 7. He was oppressed and afflicted, yet he did not open his mouth; he was led like a lamb to the slaughter, and as a sheep before its shearers is silent, so he did not open his mouth.

JfJ: 7. He was oppressed, and he was afflicted, yet he opened not his mouth; like a lamb that is led to the slaughter, and like a sheep that before its shearers is silent, so he opened not his mouth.

Irrespective of which rabbinic perspective we are considering – the individual or national – the servant does not complain about his fate. Like a lamb/kid being carried to the slaughtering place or a ewe being sheared, these are simply poetic similes. Anti-Jewish missionaries, whose tradition views the death of the Suffering Servant as an act of human sacrifice, naturally envision sacrificial imagery. However, our Torah tells us that human sacrifice is an abomination.

I-4.8 Verse 8

ח מֵעֹצֶר וּמִמִּשְׁפָּט לֻקָּח, וְאֶת-דּוֹרוֹ מִי יְשׂוֹחֵחַ: כִּי נִגְזַר מֵאֶרֶץ חַיִּים,
מִפֶּשַׁע עַמִּי נֶגַע לָמוֹ.

EDH: 8. From <u>restraint/coercion</u> (m.n.) *or* From the <u>rule/throne</u> (m.n. *hapax legomenon*) and judgment he was taken away, and who will he <u>bow down to/be humbled by/converse with</u> his generation; because he was cut off from the land of the living, for a <u>rebellion/transgression/offense</u> of my people was touched to **them** [in rabbinic]/ **he was** [in CT] <u>death/stricken down</u>.

 JPS: 8. By oppression and judgment he was taken away, and with his generation who did reason? for he was cut off out of the land of the living, for the transgression of my people to **whom** the stroke was due.

ASV: 8. Now that he has been released from captivity and judgment, who could have imagined such a generation? For he had been removed from the land of the living, an affliction upon **them** that was my people's sin.

LXX: 8. ἐν τῇ ταπεινώσει ἡ κρίσις <u>αὐτοῦ</u> ἤρθη· τὴν δὲ γενεὰν αὐτοῦ τίς διηγήσεται; ὅτι αἴρεται ἀπὸ τῆς γῆς ἡ ζωὴ αὐτοῦ, ἀπὸ τῶν ἀνομιῶν τοῦ λαοῦ μου ἤχθη εἰς θάνατον.
8. In his humiliation his judgment was taken away: who shall declare his generation: for his life is taken away from the earth: because of the iniquities of my people, **he** was led to death.

KJV: 8. He was taken from prison and from judgment: and who shall declare his generation? for he was cut off out of the land of the living: for the transgression of my people was **he** stricken.

NIV: 8. By oppression and judgment he was taken away. Yet who of his generation protested? For he was cut off from the land of the living; for the transgression of my people, **he** was punished.

JfJ: 8. By oppression and judgment, he was taken away; and as for his generation, who considered that he was cut off out of the land of the living, (**he** was) stricken for the transgression of my people?

The most common meaning for the noun מֵעֹצֶר is "from restraint/coercion". During each of Sennacherib's attacks, he laid siege to Jerusalem, and Ḥezekiah was *restrained* within the city walls. The first siege ended when he was *coerced* into paying tribute and giving his beloved daughter to his enemy. The second time, he nearly lost his life. To translate the term as referring to the rule/throne would mean that Ḥezekiah was removed from ruling and judging his people. Yet, this usage has been deemed a *hapax legomenon* – meaning a word found only once in the Bible. (Judges 18:7) Thus, the preferred usage for מֵעֹצֶר is restraint/coercion. The probable gest of the verse is that, due to a harsh judgment, Ḥezekiah was restrained, coerced, and taken away; regarding his generation, to whom should he bow down, be humbled by, or converse with; because he was cut off from the land of the living and that the rebellion/transgression/offense of my (either Isaiah's or Hashem's) people caused his near-death experience during the second siege.

The JfJ website author writes:

> This verse presented an insurmountable difficulty to those who interpreted this passage as referring to Israel. It reads: "He was taken away from rule and from judgment; and his life who shall recount? for he was cut off out of the land of the living; through the transgressions of my people was he stricken."

In another location they translate it: "By oppression and judgment, he was taken away". Thus, they have presented both possible translations of מֵעֹצֶר. The editor above prefers the rarer one since it seems to refute the perspective of Israel as the Suffering Servant.

> **JfJ:** Were the Jewish people, forbid, ever cut off out of the land of the living? No! In Jeremiah 31:35-37, God promised that we will exist forever. We are proud that Am Yisrael Chai— "The people of Israel are much alive." Likewise, it is impossible to say that Israel suffered for the transgressions of "my people," which clearly means Isaiah's people. Surely Isaiah's people are not the Gentiles, but the Jews... Given the explicit mention of death in Isaiah 53:9 and the *fact that his life is a sacrificial offering* in Isaiah 53:10, we are not

speaking here of a metaphorical death but of a literal one.

Here the JfJ missionaries have further constricted the reader's autonomous thought. They are insisting that their interpretation is not an opinion but a fact! If they simply believed that their Yeshu was a mortal man, who was the Mashiaḥ ben Yosef, and that he went quietly to his death so that the Romans would not kill more Jews, then we would have no problem. Instead, they misguide our children by teaching the alien concept that human sacrifice is needed for Hashem to forgive us.

Concerning their mockery: "Were the Jewish people, God forbid, ever cut off out of the land of the living?" The answer is yes. By the Romans from 70-135 CE, by the Inquisition from 1480-1808, and under the Nazis from 1933-1945, the majority of the world's Jewish population was repeatedly exterminated for nothing more than to stroke their ego.

Regarding their statement that "surely Isaiah's people are not the Gentiles", we answer that in a spiritual sense they are. Just as the *cohenim* are the priestly family of the people of Israel, so is Israel the priestly family given by Hashem to the people of the world. The ASV explains: "When Israel's exile is finally ended, the nations will marvel that such a generation could have survived the expulsion from the land of the living, i.e., the Land of Israel."

The rabbis read מִפֶּשַׁע עַמִּי נֶגַע לָמוֹ as plural where it refers to the punishment of the people. The LXX and CT translations uses the singular, thus referring to a messianic figure. The plural is more consistent with the flow of the text and is the better translation. However, if the CT translators insist on reading it as singular, they have brushed aside the fact that the verbs are in the past tense, not the future. Since the subject suffered before the text was written, Ḥezekiah is a better fit than someone who would not even be born for another 700 years.

I-4.9 Verse 9

ט וַיִּתֵּן אֶת-רְשָׁעִים קִבְרוֹ וְאֶת-עָשִׁיר בְּמֹתָיו; עַל לֹא-חָמָס עָשָׂה, וְלֹא מִרְמָה בְּפִיו.

EDH: 9. And he gave/granted/permitted/put evil-ones his grave/tomb and a wealthy in/with his death; besides no violence had he made/done, and no deceit/fraud was in his mouth.

JPS: 9. And they made his grave with the wicked, and with the rich his tomb; although he had done no violence, neither was any deceit in his mouth.'

ASV: 9. He submitted himself to his grave like wicked men; and the wealthy [submitted] to his executions, for committing no crime and with no deceit in his mouth.

46

LXX: 9. καὶ δώσω τοὺς πονηροὺς ἀντὶ τῆς ταφῆς αὐτοῦ καὶ τοὺς πλουσίους ἀντὶ τοῦ θανάτου αὐτοῦ· ὅτι ἀνομίαν οὐκ ἐποίησεν, οὐδὲ εὑρέθη δόλος ἐν τῷ στόματι αὐτοῦ.

9. And I will give the wicked for his burial and the rich for his death; for he practiced no iniquity, nor craft with his mouth.

KJV: 9. And he made his grave with the wicked, and with the rich in his death; because he had done no violence, neither was any deceit in his mouth.

NIV: 9. He was assigned a grave with the wicked, and with the rich in his death, though he had done no violence, nor was any deceit in his mouth.

JfJ: 9. And they made his grave with the wicked and with a rich man in his death, although he had done no violence, and there was no deceit in his mouth.

Of the choices given above, it seems that the KJV is a more actuate translation. Except, it might be improved if we exchanged "even though" with "because". In support of identifying the Suffering Servant as Ḥezekiah, he was buried with his father, Ahaz, who was a wicked king.

The **ASV** supports their translation by noting: "Ordinary Jews chose to die like common criminals, rather than renounce their faith; and wealthy Jews were killed for no reason other than to enable their wicked conquerors to confiscate the riches of Israel, that the nations had sinfully inflicted upon it. (Radak)."

JfJ continues: "Likewise, how can Israel be the servant, the one who "had done no violence, nor was any deceit in his mouth" (Isaiah 53:9)? The implication is as always that Israel was a violent and deceitful nation. This is a mean-spirited statement.

All individuals make mistakes. (Kohelet 7:20) A person can strive for a lifetime to live righteously and still make very grave errors. Through recognizing of our errors and resolving not to repeat them, we make *teshuvah*, returning to the Torah, the righteous path. Hashem readily forgives all who do so. Nonetheless, if the individual is a Jew, it is very unusual for anti-Jewish missionaries to acknowledge any righteousness done by the person, instead, they jeer at us when we err. Likewise, the nations are slow to acknowledge the good Israel has done for the world, but quickly jump at any opportunity to condemn us. For instance, Hezekiah was a righteous Jew. However, to non-Jewish ears, this sounds like an oxymoron. How can a man be both a Jew and righteous?! Likewise, how can a nation be both Jewish and righteous? Due to the canonized slander recorded in their religious texts, anti-Jewish missionaries are, sadly, prejudiced against us.

The next statement on their website is central to Christology. After informing the reader that their Yeshu was "blameless", they add: "Israel is not now, nor ever has been *without sin*—the Scriptures are replete with examples of Israel's disobedience." We would ask in return: Where in the Tanach does it say that the Mashiaḥ must be totally blameless and without sin? To jump from one not being a violent or deceitful person to having never sinned is simply irresponsible. Besides, their Messiah, whom they worship as perfect, dishonored his mother (Matt. 12:46-50), which is most definitely a sin (Ex. 20:11, Lev. 19:3, and 5:16)

The CTs inform us that its Yeshu was in the comfort of a house with his closest followers. Outside in the heat, there was a multitude of enthusiasts who followed him where he went. His mother and brothers made their way through the crowd to the door. She only asked for a few minutes of his time; yet, he callously refused to even greet her. He publicly humiliated his mother! Perhaps it was due to this sin that his life was to be cut short.

Israel has suffered more at the hands of Christians than CT-Yeshu suffered at the hands of the Romans, or Moḥammed did from the Medeans. The slanderous utterances of Paul of Tarsus spread like wildfire over the world. Centuries later, Mohammed taught them to his followers. The cause of Israel's suffering stems from the malicious words included in the CTs and Qur'an. Their canonized slander has directly caused millions to be "cut off from the world of the living". In this respect, Israel is the Suffering Servant, who has mutely experienced horror and tragic death at every turn for 2000 years of history.

I-4.10 Verse 10

י וַיהוה חָפֵץ דַּכְּאוֹ הֶחֱלִי--אִם-תָּשִׂים אָשָׁם נַפְשׁוֹ, יִרְאֶה זֶרַע יַאֲרִיךְ יָמִים; וְחֵפֶץ ה' בְּיָדוֹ יִצְלָח.

EDH: 10. And/But Hashem desired to crush him by disease – if Y/you will appoint/make a guilt offering of **his** soul, he will see seed/offspring, he will lengthen days, and Hashem will desire in/with H/his hand that he will prosper.

JPS: 10. Yet it pleased the LORD to crush him by disease; to see if his soul would offer itself in restitution, that he might see his seed, prolong his days, and that the purpose of the LORD might prosper by his hand:

ASV: 10. Hashem desired to oppress him and he afflicted him; if his soul would acknowledge guilt, he would see offspring and live long days and the desire of Hashem would succeed in his hand.

LXX: 10. καὶ Κύριος βούλεται καθαρίσαι αὐτὸν ἀπὸ τῆς πληγῆς. ἐὰν δῶτε περὶ ἁμαρτίας, ἡ ψυχὴ ὑμῶν ὄψεται σπέρμα μακρόβιον·
10. The Lord also is pleased to purge him from his stroke. If ye can give an offering for sin, your soul shall see a long-lived seed:

KJV: 10. Yet it pleased the LORD to bruise him; he hath put him to grief: when thou shalt make his soul an offering for sin, he shall see his seed, he shall prolong his days, and the pleasure of the LORD shall prosper in his hand.

NIV: 10. Yet it was the LORD's will to crush him and cause him to suffer, and though the LORD_makes his life an offering for sin, he will see his offspring and prolong his days, and the will of the LORD will prosper in his hand.

JfJ: 10. Yet it was the will of the LORD to crush him; he has put him to grief; when his soul makes an offering for guilt, he shall see his offspring; he shall prolong his days; the will of the Lord shall prosper in his hand.

The ‎ו can be translated as "and" or "but". Here, it reiterates that the events of Ḥezekiah's life and/or Israel's history are the workings of the "hand" of G-d and not happenstance.

The phrase אִם-תָּשִׂים אָשָׁם נַפְשׁוֹ could be read several ways.

1. "If you" could refer to those (a) to whom Isaiah was speaking directly on the day of his eulogy of Ḥezekiah, (b) to all future generations of Israel, and/or (c) to the nations who would read his account in the future.

2. It could convey the meaning: "If Hashem will make the suffering of his (a) Ḥezekiah's, (b) the nation of Israel's, or (c) the Mashiaḥ ben Yosef's soul as a guilt-offering.

3. Another meaning of this form of the verb, תָּשִׂים, where the ‎ת could alternatively indicate the third person singular feminine "she". Since the word "soul" is a feminine noun, "his soul" would be the subject. Thus, we would have "If his soul will make a guilt-offering" (implying of itself).

Irrespective of how one translates this phrase, the remainder of the verse would be understood in mystical terms – then he will see his future offspring and be resurrected, because Hashem, our merciful G-d, desires that these efforts and suffering would not have been in vain.

Regardless, it is most important to note that this passage says that his soul was appointed as a *Korban asham*, guilt-offering; it does not say that his body was offered as a human sacrifice, which is ritual murder and a very serious sin incurring the death penalty. In addition, according to the CT, Yeshu did not have children; whereas Ḥezekiah did have children. Also, both the Mashiaḥ ben Yosef and the Mashiaḥ ben David will be fully capable of fathering children.

The ASV's perspective translates "he" as referring to Israel. "G-d replies to the nations that Israel's suffering was a punishment for its own [*i.e.* the nations'] sins; and when the people realize this and repent, they [the nations] will be redeemed and rewarded." In this sense אִם-תָּשִׂים אָשָׁם נַפְשׁוֹ would read: "if you [the nations collectively] will appoint his soul [Israel collectively] as a guilt offering", then, by acknowledging your sins, Hashem will lengthen his [Israel's] days. The fact that you [the nations collectively] were able to crush Israel for the last 2000 years is because Hashem desired to try both you and Israel. However, Hashem desired to lengthen Israel's existence because He desired that Israel would pray for you [the nations] and would repent so that Hashem also will bless you.

Regarding the second part of the verse, the JfJ author notes:

> Much ink has been spilled over whether **zera',** **"offspring" or "seed,"** here refers to literal descendants (hence, excluding Jesus from fulfilling

the passage) or spiritual descendants – and whether the latter can be a legitimate understanding of the word *zera'*. We get some insight from Psalm 22:30, where the psalmist says, "Posterity [literally, 'seed'] will serve him," indicating future generations, whether literally descended from the psalmist or not. Additional insight comes from the inter-testamental book *The Wisdom of Solomon*, which is usually dated to the second century BC.

They are referring to the following verses in *The Wisdom of Solomon, 3*.

> 12. Their wives are foolish and their children are wicked. Their descendants are cursed.
> 13. For the barren woman who is undefiled is happy, she who has not conceived in transgression. She will have fruit when G-d examines souls.

They continue with a very Jewish introduction to our concept that "rewards and punishment" are ascribed to right and wrong living. Hence, "the author[23] argues that 'the barren woman who is undefiled' and therefore has the *appearance* of transgression (Deuteronomy 28:4, 11, 18) is actually 'blessed' since 'she will have fruit when G-d examines souls' on judgment day (Wisdom 3:13).[17] This is beautiful. In Judaism, the reward of the righteous is *Olam haBa* "the World to Come", which is like this world, but perfected. There, the suffering righteous of this

---

23 The JfJ sight gives the name of the authors quoted. Anyone who is interested can find them there. However, I have omitted the names of all of their authors, the hope that they might repent and return to Hashem, I wish to avoid causing them embarrassment by recording their names.

world will enjoy everything that they lacked in this one. Equally beautiful is that the other rabbi thought that Hashem knows the heart of all.

There is good that appears good, and it is decisively good.
There is evil that appears evil, and it is decisively evil.
Then there is good that appears evil, and it is very good.
Yet there is evil that appears good, and it is very evil.

They felt the necessity of explaining this because, according to the CT, Yeshu never married nor procreated. However, in the past few decades, new textual discoveries have been brought to light that present Mary Magdalene as his wife and even suggest that they had a child. The very successful book and movie, *The Da Vinci Code*, were based on this prospect. Yet, most anti-Jewish missionaries cringe at the thought that their god experienced human pleasure. Be that as it may, we should point out that Ḥezekiah lived for another 15 years, during which time his son Menashe was born; so, he did see his seed. We believe that both Mashiaḥ ben Yosef and Mashiaḥ ben David will have children. In addition, even though the nations have tried repeatedly to annihilate the people of Israel, we live on through our children.

Also, the JfJ authors omitted an important point when they write about the Mashiaḥ ben Yosef. Joseph (Yosef) was a man of peace, who suffered so that a great many people could live and that his brothers could repent and be forgiven. Mashiaḥ ben David will be a man-of-war like King David. The titles of each signify from whom each messianic figure will be descended. In the CTs, the Books of Matthew and Luke indicate that the CT-Yeshu was a descendant of David; however, only once does he make a warlike statement. Throughout the CTs, he is the image of the peaceful, Suffering Servant.

I-4.11 Verse 11

יא מֵעֲמַל נַפְשׁוֹ, יִרְאֶה יִשְׂבָּע--בְּדַעְתּוֹ יַצְדִּיק, צַדִּיק עַבְדִּי, לָרַבִּים וַעֲוֹנֹתָם, הוּא יִסְבֹּל.

EDH: 11. From the travail of his soul, he will see, he will be satisfied – with his knowledge he will be <u>vindicated/justify</u>, my righteous servant, for the multitudes and their <u>iniquity/guilt/punishment</u> he will <u>carry/bear (סבלנות</u>).

JPS: 11. Of the travail of his soul he shall see to the full, even My servant, who by his knowledge did justify the Righteous One to the many, and their iniquities he did bear.

ASV: 11. He would see [the purpose] and be satisfied with his soul's distress. With his knowledge My servant will vindicate the Righteous One to multitudes; it is their iniquities that he will carry.

LXX: 11. βούλεται Κύριος ἀφελεῖν ἀπὸ τοῦ πόνου τῆς ψυχῆς αὐτοῦ, δεῖξαι αὐτῷ φῶς καὶ πλάσαι τῇ συνέσει, δικαιῶσαι δίκαιον εὖ δουλεύοντα πολλοῖς, καὶ τὰς ἁμαρτίας αὐτῶν αὐτὸς ἀνοίσει.

11. The Lord also is pleased to take away from the travail of his soul, to shew him light, and to form him with understanding; to justify the just one who serves many well; and he shall bear their sins.

KJV: 11. He shall see of the travail of his soul, and shall be satisfied: by his knowledge shall my righteous servant justify many; for he shall bear their iniquities.

NIV: 11. After he has suffered, he will see the light of life and be satisfied; by his knowledge my righteous servant will justify many, and he will bear their iniquities.

JfJ: 11. Out of the anguish of his soul he shall see and be satisfied; by his knowledge shall the righteous one, my servant, make many to be accounted righteous, and he shall bear their iniquities.

The ASV commentary is brief on this verse. It simply states that "Israel will teach the nations of G-d's righteousness."

We have no qualms with the JfJ comments on this verse.

As a result of his suffering, the servant will "see" – but see what? There is no grammatical direct object. Some Jewish commentators, therefore, suggest that what the servant sees is the "offspring" just mentioned. Among those who interpret it this way, we find Eliezer of Beaugency (twelfth-century French rabbinic commentator), Isaac Abravanel (fifteenth-century Portuguese rabbinic commentator), and Samuel Luzzatto (nineteenth-century Italian rabbinic commentator). Others add *tov*, "good," as the object: "he will see good": we find this interpretation in Ibn Ezra and Kimhi. The Septuagint and the documents among the Dead Sea Scrolls known as 1QIsaa,b have the word *or*, "light" – "he will see light." The Dead Sea Scrolls possibly preserve a more original text. Everyone wants to know just what the servant sees, and we cannot be sure!

"By his knowledge shall the righteous one, my servant, make many to be accounted righteous, and he shall bear their iniquities." The Hebrew words *avon* ("iniquity") and *sabal* ("bear") are picked up from earlier verses, reinforcing the message of the passage.

I-4.12 Verse 12

יב לָכֵן אֲחַלֶּק-לוֹ בָרַבִּים, וְאֶת-עֲצוּמִים יְחַלֵּק שָׁלָל; תַּחַת אֲשֶׁר הֶעֱרָה

לַמָּוֶת נַפְשׁוֹ, וְאֶת-פֹּשְׁעִים נִמְנָה; וְהוּא חֵטְא-רַבִּים נָשָׂא, וְלַפֹּשְׁעִים יַפְגִּיעַ.

EDH: 12. Therefore, I shall divide/determine/decree for him among/with the great/many, and the powerful/numerous he will divide/share/determine/decree a booty/plunder; because/on account of that he has laid bare/been shamed to death his soul, and the transgressors/rebels were reckoned with/assigned; and a great/many sins he up-lifted/bore and for the transgressors/rebels he will encounter/entreat/beseech/oppose.

JPS: 12. Therefore will I divide him a portion among the great, and he shall divide the spoil with the mighty; because he bared his soul unto death, and was numbered with the transgressors; yet he bore the sin of many, and made intercession for the transgressors.

ASV: 12. Therefore, I will assign him a portion from the multitudes and he will divide the mighty as spoils – in return for having poured out his soul for death and being counted among the wicked, for he bore the sin of the multitudes, and prayed for the wicked.

LXX: 12. διὰ τοῦτο αὐτὸς κληρονομήσει πολλοὺς καὶ τῶν ἰσχυρῶν μεριεῖ σκῦλα, ἀνθ' ὧν παρεδόθη εἰς θάνατον ἡ ψυχὴ αὐτοῦ, καὶ ἐν τοῖς ἀνόμοις ἐλογίσθη· καὶ αὐτὸς ἁμαρτίας πολλῶν ἀνήνεγκε καὶ διὰ τὰς ἁμαρτίας αὐτῶν παρεδόθη.

12. Therefore he shall inherit many, and he shall divide the spoils of the mighty; because his soul was delivered to death; and he was numbered among the transgressors; and he bore the sins of many, and was delivered because of their iniquities.

KJV: 12. Therefore will I divide him a portion with the great, and he shall divide the spoil with the strong; because he hath poured out his soul unto death: and he was numbered with the transgressors; and he bare the sin of many, and made intercession for the transgressors.

NIV: 12. Therefore I will give him a portion among the great, and he will divide the spoils with the strong, because he poured out his life unto death, and was numbered with the transgressors. For he bore the sin of many, and made intercession for the transgressors.

JfJ: 12. Therefore, I will divide him a portion with the many, and he shall divide the spoil with the strong, because he poured out his soul to death and was numbered with the transgressors; yet he bore the sin of many, and makes intercession for the transgressors.

"Therefore, I (Hashem) shall decree for him (Ḥezekiah) with the great-ones (the Mashiaḥ ben Yosef and Mashiaḥ ben David) and the powerful (of the nations) he

60

(Hashem) will divide as a booty; because that his soul (Ḥezekiah's) has been shamed unto death and the transgressors were dealt with; thus, a great many he uplifted and for the transgressors he will entreat (before Hashem on the day of Judgement)."

Again, the ASV is brief. "In exile, Jews prayed for the welfare of their host nations." However, the nation of Israel could be inserted above in the place of Ḥezekiah.

> The **JfJ** author states:
> "we are dealing here not with all of Israel but with an individual from *within* Israel who bears the sins of the nation through a sacrificial death that ends not in defeat but in victory. In this way, the individual servant prepares Israel the nation to continue and ultimately complete its designated role as a servant-nation."

If they were simply encouraging their followers to believe that their Yeshu was, in their opinion, the Mashiaḥ ben Yosef, then we would have not a problem with them. Judaism does not dictate to any individual who or what to believe regarding the prophecies of redemption. One is free to believe that they refer to the nation of Israel or an individual. However, if anyone, Jew or non-Jew, uses Scripture to justify foreign concepts, it is blasphemous heresy and that transgressor brings upon himself Divine retributions.

I-5 Misguiding the Reader

The next gate through which the JfJ missionaries herd their readers exhibits a blatant misuse of these verses in a deliberate attempt to misguide the reader. They disguise their ploy by claiming that the verses in 52:13-15 and 53:10-12 form a *chiasm*. They explain that they fashion "a concentric unit". Actually, a *chiasm* is a rhetorical device, often found in the Bible, in which the second part of a sentence is a mirror image (*i.e.* opposite meaning) of the first. For their comparison to be a true chiasm, the two tracts must have four points that cross each other with balancing *opposite* ideas and without the repetition of any of the words. This crisscrossing creates the Greek letter X (*chi*), hence the name. Yet, the JfJ site's sophistic, specious reasoning is that these two sets of verse form a circular unit joining complimentary statements. In reality, the author's sole intent is to connect certain words from the first phrase in 52:15 and 53:10, then to insert part of 52:13 to herd the reader into another stifling corridor toward Christianity.

I-5.1 Will he "Startle" or "Sprinkle"?

We begin with the translations of 52:15.

נב:טו כֵּן יַזֶּה גּוֹיִם רַבִּים, עָלָיו יִקְפְּצוּ מְלָכִים פִּיהֶם: כִּי אֲשֶׁר לֹא-סֻפַּר לָהֶם, רָאוּ, וַאֲשֶׁר לֹא-שָׁמְעוּ, הִתְבּוֹנָנוּ.

JPS: Is. 52:15 So **shall he startle** many nations, kings shall shut their mouths because of him; for that which had not been told them shall they see, and that which they had not heard shall they perceive. {S}

ASV: So **will** many nations **exclaim** about him, and kings will shut their mouths [in amazement], for they will see that which had never been told to them, and will perceive things they had never heard.

LXX: 52:15 οὕτω **θαυμάσονται** ἔθνη πολλὰ ἐπ᾿ αὐτῷ, καὶ συνέξουσι βασιλεῖς τὸ στόμα αὐτῶν· ὅτι οἷς οὐκ ἀνηγγέλη περὶ αὐτοῦ, ὄψονται, καὶ οἳ οὐκ ἀκηκόασι, συνήσουσι.

LXX: 52:15 Thus **shall** many nations **wonder** at him; and kings shall keep their mouths shut: for they to whom no report was brought concerning him, shall see; and they who have not heard, shall consider.

KJV: Is. 52:15 So shall he **sprinkle** many nations; the kings shall shut their mouths at him: for *that* which had not been told them shall they see; and *that* which they had not heard shall they consider.

NIV: Is. 52:15 So he will **sprinkle** many nations, and kings will shut their mouths because of him. For what they were not told, they will see, and what they have not heard, they will understand.

> **JfJ:** What exactly is the servant doing with the "many nations" (non-Israelites) in this verse? The English Standard Version (ESV) **has "sprinkle,"** but other translations say **"startle" or "spatter"** or something similar. There are two possibilities here. The first is that the nations are startled. The Septuagint (LXX) Old Testament into Greek originally made a few centuries before Jesus – has 'This would match the remainder of the verse describing how the kings shut their mouths. **The servant will startle the non-Jewish nations**, and the kings of those nations will be left speechless.'

In the EDH, we find that יַזֶּה is the future tense of the Qal intransitive verb נָזָה, meaning "it/he will spurt/spatter". Also, in the very ancient Semitic language of Akkadian, *nizu*, meant "to spatter". It takes on the meaning of "to sprinkle" in the Post Biblical Hebrew. Since the difference between "spatter" and "sprinkle" is only a matter of the quantity of the liquid tossed, there is no sense in arguing against using the latter form.

However, the JfJ author is playing a sleight-of-hand with LXX's translation by implying to their reader that it is similar to theirs. Their focus and that of the KJV and the NIV is on "spatter/sprinkle". Their comment that "other translations say 'startle' or 'spatter' or something similar", is disingenuous.

In the MT, the phrase read:
JPS: So, **shall he startle** many nations,
ASV: So, **will** many nations **exclaim about** him,
LXX: Thus, **shall** many nations **wonder at** him,

In the CT, the phrase read:
KJV: So, shall he **sprinkle** many nations,
NIV: So, he will **sprinkle** many nations,
JfJ: So, he will **sprinkle** many nations,

Thus, they side-stepped the LXX's actual wording in the quote above, and then they quickly insert the JPS's wording. Very well, let's take a closer look at the LXX's translation of οὕτω **θαυμάσονται** ἔθνη πολλὰ ἐπ' αὐτῷ.

One would expect that the LXX would use the PBH term "sprinkle" but it does not. Instead, it follows the MT translations. Why should the LXX use "wonder at" or perhaps better, "be astonished by" instead of "will be sprinkled by"? We would expect that it would be closer to the CT translations when actually it has more affinity with the MT translations.

θαυμάσονται is the future tense of the intransitive verb, θαυμάζω, meaning "they will wonder at, be astonished by, or to marvel at" him.[24] The JPS has that he "will startle" them, while the ASV gives that they "will exclaim about" him. The ASV probably

---

24 Danker, Frederick William, ed., A Greek-English Lexicon of the New Testament and other Early Christian Literature, 3rd Edition. (Chicago: University of Chicago Press, 2000), p. 444.

is using the derivative root, הזה, that appears in Isaiah 56:10 as the hapax legomenon הֹזִים meaning "raving". All of these terms convey a sense of surprise. Therefore, יַזֶּה was an idiomatic expression of surprise, reflecting that experienced when one was suddenly spurted by blood during a sacrifice.

I-5.2 Were many appalled or astonished?

יד כַּאֲשֶׁר שָׁמְמוּ עָלֶיךָ רַבִּים, כֵּן-מִשְׁחַת מֵאִישׁ מַרְאֵהוּ; וְתֹאֲרוֹ, מִבְּנֵי אָדָם. נב:

JfJ translate Is. 52:14 "As many were astonished at you – his appearance was so marred, beyond human semblance, and his form beyond that of the children of mankind. The JPS and NIV have "were appalled at you". The LXX has "ἐκστήσονται ἐπὶ σὲ", meaning "shall be amazed at you". The KJV agrees with the JfJ and give "were astonished at you." Thus, all essentially agree on the meaning of the verse. However, the JfJ add this opinion.

> The Hebrew literally reads "astonished at *you.*" Some translations try to smooth over this abrupt change in the same verse from "you" to "his." In biblical Hebrew, though, we sometimes find unexpected changes from the third person to the second person and vice versa. This is unnerving to a modern reader but apparently did not pose much of a problem to an ancient Israelite reader.

Actually, it is the JfJ author who is attempting to smooth over the change because they would prefer to replace "you" with "at him". We see this as a shift in Isaiah's attention from his audience at eulogy to address Ḥezekiah and then back again. Nevertheless, in a prophetic sense, it can also indicate the nation of Israel or the Mashiaḥ ben Yosef.

JfJ adds: "In the end, the point is clear: the servant will have the kind of appearance that invites a reaction of astonishment." This statement leads to an unavoidable question. Where in the CT does it say that its Yeshu suffered from a server disease, or that his appearance was so marred people were appalled/astonished when they saw him? On the contrary, he strolls confidently from village to village, a picture of health and with an intense determination to fulfill an all-consuming mission. No one carries him from one place to another. There are no mentions of scars or disfigurement. No one sneers at his appearance nor mocks him as deformed.

I-5.3 Who has become "exalted", "lifted-up", and "very high"?

נב:יג הִנֵּה יַשְׂכִּיל עַבְדִּי; יָרוּם וְנִשָּׂא וְגָבַהּ מְאֹד.

JPS: 52:13 Behold, My servant shall prosper, he shall be exalted and lifted up, and shall be very high.

ASV: 52:13 Behold My servant will succeed; he will be exalted and become high and exceedingly lofty.

LXX: 52:13 Ἰδοὺ συνήσει ὁ παῖς μου καὶ ὑψωθήσεται καὶ δοξασθήσεται καὶ μετεωρισθήσεται σφόδρα.
13 Behold, my servant shall understand, and be exalted, and glorified exceedingly.

KJV: 52:13 Behold, my servant shall deal prudently, he shall be exalted and extolled, and be very high.

NIV: 52:13 See, my servant will act wisely; he will be raised and lifted up and highly exalted.

Here the JfJ author starts with a lovely statement but in the next ruins it.

> The three terms in 52:13 contrast with three different terms in 53:2, which describe the servant as having no "form" or "beauty" or "majesty." They are also in contrast with three words in 53:4, which describe how we counted the servant "stricken," "smitten," and "afflicted." This puts the exaltation of the servant in the greatest possible contrast with his suffering. This is going to be some exaltation!

Ḥezekiah's appearance was marred and malformed. His father, Ahaz, rejected him as heir to the throne. The Assyrians repeatedly attacked them. The last time, Ḥezekiah was seriously wounded during the siege and was on the verge of dying. He prayed, made *teshuva*, and was healed. Also, Hashem added fifteen more years to his life. Thus, he was "stricken," "afflicted" and "marred". Of course, this is not the reply that the JfJ wants to hear.

> **JfJ:** So, this verse (1) is a "spoiler" that looks ahead to the end of the passage when the servant is vindicated; (2) implies that God's hand is at work in the life of this servant, both in the servant's wisely lived life and in his vindication; and (3) suggests that *the exaltation the servant undergoes is of the highest kind, usually reserved for God Himself.* (emphasis added)

The first two conclusions are good, and we have no problem with them. However, the third is a foreign interpolation. They have just nudged the reader through another gate towards the despotic missionaries' cage. Then they deceptively ask the simple question: "Who could this servant be?" The answer a Jew would naturally give would be "anyone who Hashem desires to exalt, lift up, and elevate."

In a delusional attempt to convince Jews to become Christians, the Messianic missionaries present the following argument.

> **JfJ:** The servant's vindication in this verse is described by three terms: Two of these terms were previously used together in Isaiah 6:1 in reference to God on His throne ("high and lifted up"), and both

are also used in Isaiah 33:10 and Isaiah 57:15 of God. On the other hand, in Isaiah 2:12, Proverbs 30:13, and Daniel 11:12, they are used to describe the arrogance of nations or people. The image is therefore positive when applied to God but negative when applied to human beings. In Isaiah 52:13, the positive vindication of the servant is unusual, spoken of in terms usually reserved for God Himself. This, at the very least, gives us a clue that this servant may be more than meets the eye.

We will examine these and similar verses, using the online JPS Tanach. We are especially interested in verses that contain forms of the terms used in 52:13 – "he shall be exalted (יָרוּם) and lifted up (וְנִשָּׂא), and shall be very high (וְגָבַהּ מְאֹד)".

Yes, we do find that the terms used indicate that Sennacherib was arrogant and proud in II Kings 19:22. "Yea, thou hast lifted up thine eyes on high, even against the Holy One of Israel!" And in **Isaiah 2:12, we find:** For the LORD of hosts hath a day upon all that is **proud and lofty (כָּל-גֵּאֶה—וָרָם)** and upon all that is **lifted up (כָּל-נִשָּׂא)** and it shall **be brought low (וְעַל וְשָׁפֵל). In Proverbs 30, we find** 12. There is a generation that is pure in their own eyes, and yet are not washed from their filthiness. 13. There is a generation, Oh, how **lofty are their eyes (עֵינָיו מָה-רָמוּ)**! and their eyelids are lifted up. Also, Daniel 11:12 states: "and the multitude shall be carried away, and **his heart shall be lifted up** [(וָרָם) ירום לְבָבוֹ]; and he shall cast down tens of thousands; but he shall not prevail." So, yes, these terms have been used to describe evil individuals. No, problem – they do exist, and they have inflicted suffering on their victims. Proverbs 16:18 warns us that "Pride goeth before destruction, and a **haughty spirit** (גֹּבַהּ רוּחַ) before a fall. Psalms 10:4 adds that "The wicked, in the **pride of his countenance** (כְּגֹבַהּ אַפּוֹ) [, saith]: 'He will not require'; all his thoughts are: 'There is no God.'" However, to the credit of Ḥezekiah, my candidate for the Suffering Servant, we find in 2Chr.32:26 Notwithstanding Ḥezekiah humbled himself for the **pride of his heart** (בְּגֹבַהּ לִבּוֹ) *both he and the inhabitants of Jerusalem*, so that the wrath of the LORD came not upon them in the days of Hezekiah." Note that the people of Jerusalem joined their righteous king in making *teshuvah*, returning to Hashem's Torah. Thus, in these verses, we are given the dark side of the terms יָרוּם וְנִשָּׂא וְגָבַהּ.

Regarding Hashem, the most common term is a form of high/exalted (רָם), as is found in Ps. 57:12, 46:11, and Is.30:18. We find forms of **exalted and lifted up** (רָם וְנִשָּׂא) in Is. 6:1 and 33:10, but the term **high/haughty** (גָבַהּ) is not included.

However, we are not without a counterargument to the JfJ's claim that the terms are only used in the positive when applied to G-d, and are only in the negative when applied to human beings. For instance, in the prophecy of Balaam concerning the nation of Israel (Num. 24:5-7), we find: "How goodly are thy tents, O Jacob, thy dwellings, O Israel! As valleys stretched out, as gardens by the river-side; as aloes planted of the LORD, as cedars beside the waters; Water shall flow from his branches, and his seed shall be in many waters; and his **king shall be higher** (וְיָרֹם) than Agag, and his kingdom **shall be exalted** (וְתִנַּשֵּׂא). Hmmm, let's see. He is prophesying about the descendants of Jacob - Israel *and* their king. The people of Jacob and the nation of Israel will be beautiful as well-watered valleys, gardens, aloes, and cedars trees. Their *king* will be higher than the king of Amalek, (perhaps Agag was a regal title instead of a name.) and his *kingdom* will be exalted. These sound very human to me.

Then in Psalms 27:6, we find: "And now shall my head **be lifted up** (יָרוּם) above mine enemies round about me." Psalms 131:1 reads: "A Song of Ascents; of David. LORD, **my heart is not haughty, nor mine eyes lofty** (לֹא-גָבַהּ לִבִּי--וְלֹא-רָמוּ עֵינַי)." To uplift one's self is arrogance, but our very human David was uplifted and exalted by Hashem, as will be his very human descendant, the future Mashiaḥ. This is promised in Psalms 89, the most pertinent verses of which are given here.

Ps.89:16 Happy is the people that know the joyful shout; they walk, O LORD, in the light of Thy countenance.
17 In Thy name do they rejoice all the day; and **through Thy righteousness are they** (the nation of Israel) **exalted** (וּבְצִדְקָתְךָ יָרוּמוּ).
18 For Thou art the glory of their strength; and in Thy favour **our** (the nation of Israel's) **horn is exalted** (תָּרוּם).

19 For of the LORD is our shield; and the Holy One of Israel is our king.

20 Then Thou spokest in vision to Thy G-dly ones, and saidst: 'I have laid help upon one that is mighty; **I have exalted (הֲרִימוֹתִי) one chosen out of the people.**

21 I have found *David My servant*; **with My** *holy oil* **have I** *anointed him* (בְּשֶׁמֶן קָדְשִׁי מְשַׁחְתִּיו);

22 With whom My hand shall he be established; Mine arm also shall strengthen him.

23 The enemy shall not exact from him, nor the son of wickedness afflict him.

24 And I will beat to pieces his adversaries before him, and smite them that hate him.

25 But My faithfulness and My mercy shall be with him; and through My name shall **his horn be exalted (רוּם).**

26 I will set his hand also on the sea, and his right hand on the rivers.

27 He shall call unto Me: **"Thou art my Father, my G-d, and the rock of my salvation."**

28 I also will appoint him first-born, **the highest (עֶלְיוֹן)** of the kings of the earth.

29 For ever will I keep for him My mercy, and My covenant shall stand fast with him.

30 His *seed* also will I make to endure for ever, and his throne as the days of heaven.

36 Once have I sworn by My holiness: Surely, I will not be false unto **David**;

We find here that like Hashem, who is exalted, the people of Israel (v. 17) are exalted, David (v. 20) is exalted, and his (v. 25) "horn" **and** the "horn" of the people (v. 18) is exalted. In addition, David is referred to here as **"the highest (עֶלְיוֹן)** of the kings of the earth." The term "**the highest (עֶלְיוֹן)"** is often used to refer to Hashem as "the G-d Most High (אֵל עֶלְיוֹן)"

If the JfJs are using these terms to argue that their Yeshu is a god, then shouldn't they have the same meaning for David and the people of Israel in general? Unless the JfJ authors are suggesting that all of the descendants of Jacob are deities. But, of course not. Also, if the JfJ folks are teaching Jews "true" Torah, then why don't we find any clear mention of David's or any other's divinity in any Jewish texts over the past 3000 years? This leaves us to conclude that if David was not a god, then neither was their Yeshu.

In addition, David was a true Mashiaḥ, since he was anointed with the holy anointing oil. Many years ago, a missionary was trying to convert me. I pointed to the fact that the Hebrew (מָשִׁיחַ) and Greek (Χριστος) terms for Messiah, derive, respectively, from משׁח and χρισις, both mean "anointing or smearing with **oil**" (שֶׁמֶן, χρισμα). Since, unlike David, CT-Yeshu was not anointed with the sacred oil, then he cannot be called the mashiaḥ. The missionary replied angrily, "Well perhaps David was a *little* Messiah."

It's just sad. Even when the truth is directly in front of their eyes, still they cannot acknowledge it. Now let's see how these missionaries combine Isaiah 53:10-12 and 52:13-15 to position the reader before the next two gates.

I-5.4 How have they connected the *asham* with sprinkling?

The CT of the KJV and NIV agree with the JfJ's translation of Is. 52:15 and have יַזֶּה as "will sprinkle", thus, creating a mental connection to the initiation ritual of sprinkling a newly "saved" individual, as practiced by many Christian denominations.

The JfJ authors open the next gate with this statement.

> The other possibility is to translate the word as "sprinkle," a term from Leviticus that refers to splashing blood, water, or oil over people or things to dedicate or cleanse them. In addition, the second set of verses contains the word *asham* which refers to a "guilt offering," one of the prescribed offerings in Leviticus. *Before the asham can be offered, the individual making the offering needs to be sprinkled.* Therefore, says scholar Richard Averbeck, "The reference to the 'guilt offering,' in Isaiah 43:10 echoes the reference to 'sprinkle' in 52:15a. *The Servant not only offers himself as a guilt offering but also cleanses the nations.* " (emphasis added)

The laws concerning sacrifices are found in Leviticus Chapters 4 thru 8 and 14, and also in Numbers Chapter 6. The verb יַזֶּה appears in only Lev. 6:20-21, where instructions are given on how to clean garments if sacrificial blood "will splatter" (יִזֶּה) on them. In Lev. (Lev. 8:30-36), Aharon, his sons, and their sacred garments are splattered (וַיַּז עַל) with a mixture of anointing-oil and blood from the sin-offerings (not the guilt-offering=*asham*) during their consecration-ritual. Again, in Lev. 5:9, this verb is used in

75

which the blood of a sin-offering is splattered/sprinkled (וְהִזָּה) on the side of the altar. The only other person who was splattered/sprinkled (וְהִזָּה) was the leper. A priest splattered/sprinkled the person cured of leprosy seven times with a mixture of spring water, the blood of a sacrificial bird, cedar wood, hyssop, and a scarlet thread. (Lev. 14:3-7) These purification rituals affected a status change for each. The leper's period of isolation ended, and he regained his former status within the community. Aharon and his sons ascended to the lofty status of anointed priests.

The sin-offering (אֶת-הַחַטָּאת) was given for the conscious sins that the devotee knew he committed; whereas, the *asham* (אָשָׁם), guilt-offering, was for those sins that he had committed without realizing it. "And the priest shall offer the *sin-offering,* and make atonement for him that is to be cleansed because of his uncleanness (מִטֻּמְאָתוֹ = pollution, defilement); and afterward he shall kill the burnt-offering." (Lev. 14:19) On the other hand, the guilt-offering, is for the unintentional, unconscious sins that were committed thoughtlessly (Lev. 5:2-5, 15) or impulsively (Lev. 14:20).

The JfJ statement that the individual making the guilt-offering needed to be sprinkled *before* he could make his sacrifice and obtain atonement is *completely false*. The next statement – *"The Servant not only offers himself as a guilt offering but also*

76

cleanses the nations." – is an obfuscation of the Torah. Ancient Israel's sacrificial system was given specifically to save mankind from the sinister ritual of human sacrifice that was implanted in society during a dark, primordial era. This is evident in the *akedah*. Hashem commands Abraham to sacrifice his son; but, when he is just about to strike, He stops him. This object lesson taught him and all of his descendants that Hashem does not sanction human sacrifice.

But, let's return to the JfJ's website where the sixth gate is being opened for us.

> "The exile from the Promised Land amounted to a desecration of sancta – the specific sancta being Israel itself as the Lord's 'kingdom of priests and… holy nation' (Exodus 19:6). In this way, the sacrificial suffering of the Servant as an *asham* makes perfectly good sense in the context of Isaiah 40-66." Moreover, just as the *asham* restored the status of the person defiling God's holy things, "the Servant in Isaiah 53 offered himself as a 'guilt offering' (Isaiah 53:10b) to make reparation and atonement on behalf of Israel for its sin and corruption so that they could come out of exile to be restored to their Holy Land and to their holy 'servant' status. This is what the term when rendered 'guilt offering' brings to the interpretation of the passage; not just redemptive atonement and reparation, but actual *restoration*."

All I can say is Wow! Now, that Hashem has begun the process of our national restoration and redemption, the anti-Jewish missionaries want to step in and claim credit in the name of their god! Newsflash – that person died 2000 years ago! If the restoration of Israel was due to him, then wouldn't it have occurred immediately after their purported "atonement/reparation"?

I-6. Where are we now?

If the reader reaches this point, then they, more often than not, have at least accepted the possibility that the CT-Yeshu was the Mashiaḥ. Many would have even come to consider themselves as a "Jew for Jesus". The others craftily praise them for having discovered the "truth" on their own. But the truth is that their thoughts have been guided and now caged. They have been herded about to the extent that they are confused and cannot freely think outside of this box. Understandably, family and friends are anxious to bring their loved one home again to Torah. They rarely understand the seriousness of this mindset, which is complicated by several factors.

Some Messianic followers have complained that they were angered to find serious character flaws in this or that rabbi. Due to their intense disappointment, they come to view all rabbis as charlatans. Such situations are extremely disturbing on many levels. However, are they really that naïve as to think that there are no charlatans or injustices among the Christians? What will they do when they come to realize that people in every country and every religion, including Christianity, suffer from the evil or thoughtless deed of the arrogant few?

Then there is the fact that anti-Jewish missionaries treat them as celebrities. The CT specifically commands their followers to work tirelessly to convert any and all Jews they encounter. They are suddenly special and important. Even if their knowledge of Judaism is very shallow, they are listened to as if they are a great scholar. Among other Jews, they were overlooked or perhaps pushed aside, but the anti-Jewish missionaries are so eager and happy to see them. What they do not understand are the alterative motives behind those smiles. If they succeed at capturing a Jew soul, they will acquire a grand reward in Heaven.

In addition to these influences, the victim often has become romantically involved with a Christian. This wound causes unrelenting sorrow to the apostate's parents. From that point, they view every *pasuk* in the Tanach as if it refers to the Christian god. They have not stopped at this, but have gone even further. In their delusional state of mind, they twist the words of our sages, until they are satisfied that those great minds agree with them.

It is our prayer that, *b'etzrah Hashem*, we will be able to address this mindset and guild our lost sheep back to Hashem's pasture. This journey begins with a sound understanding of how we, the people of Israel, came to be in this situation.

To recap, the JfJ authors have herded the reader through several misleading gates as they direct them towards Christianity.

1. They are informed that the rabbis, having lost sight of true meaning of the scriptures, are confused, intransigent, and obstinate.

2. They repeatedly identify the servant's suffering is as a _korban_ (_i.e._ a human sacrifice), because this is an essential tenant of Christianity.

3. They employ pseudo-sophisticated terminology, such as referring to the verses in Isaiah 52:13-15 and 53:10-12 as forming a _chiasm_. It would be better to describe this as circular logic – this is what it means, because our religion teaches us that this is what it means.

4. The blatantly state that when "to be exalted" and "to lifted up" are used in a positive manner, they can only be designating "G-d Himself". But, if they describe a person, they always carry negative connotations. Since in Isaiah 52:13 they are used in a positive sense, then they are a clue that the Suffering Servant is divine.

5. Next, they make the totally misleading assertion that before the _asham_ (guilt-offering) could be offered, the individual making the offering needed to be sprinkled. This is a reference to CT-Yeshu's encounter with John the Baptist, before he was arrested and executed.

6. The reader is assured that the Servant "offered himself as a 'guilt offering' to make reparation and atonement on behalf of Israel for its sin and corruption so that they could come out of exile to be restored to their Holy Land and to their holy 'servant' status."

Having been prepared in this manner, the reader is set to enter the seventh gate. As they state: "Next, we'll look at what the New Testament has to say about Isaiah 53." The reader is then directed to download the Book of Matthew. And it's true – all was orchestrated to deliver the reader to precisely this point. But where exactly are we? How can anyone say that they have reached an informed judgment of the content of the Christian Texts if they are not well informed of the socio-political dynamics that produced its context? Thought they would protest otherwise; I doubt that the authors of JfJ website understand the historical context that produced the Christian Texts. They may have taken a course on the subject history. Yet remember that each course was developed with a particular goal in mind. Grant me your tolerance and listen to what I have gleamed over many years of research.

Part II: How we got where we are

II-1 Ἱστορία – History: An Inquiry into the Past

Two people were walking home and began to quarrel – "a" entered the house and after thinking a few minutes "b" entered. Two others, "c" and "d", were out for a walk and observed this. They heard a scream. Then "c" rushed into the house and, seeing "b" standing over the body of "a", ran out yelling: "b" murdered "a" – so, "d" called the police and "b" was arrested. The trial resulted in the conviction of "b" for the murder of "a". Everyone watching the newscasts, podcasts, and social media postings believed that justice was done. Except, only Hashem knows "The Truth" – "e" was hiding in the house and, out of envy and a personal vendetta, murdered "a", just as "b" entered the front door. Therefore, even though everyone in the world may be totally, sincerely convinced that "b" murdered "a", this does not alter "The Truth" that the crime was actually committed by "e". Therefore, a belief can influence our understanding of an event, but it cannot alter its concrete reality.

II-1.1 Primordial Spiritualism

Among the earliest known artifacts are small statues of rather obese females, the most famous of which is known as the "Venus of Willendorf". They are believed to have been a fertility fetish. Early tribes hunted herds of wild bison, horses, and bulls. They recorded the sacred rites of the chase in the cave paintings of France and Spain. From the perspective of secular archaeologists these mystical Paleolithic art forms dated between 10,000 and 8,000 BCE and express the hunters' deep awe and respect for the courageous spirit of their prey, and perhaps, gratitude to the Great Spirit, who created them with the capacity to overpower them and, thus, survive.

Early hunters brought home the orphaned young of their prey and predator alike, probably for a future meal. Eventually, they domesticated them. They provided them with flocks of sheep and goats, herds of cattle, and dogs to protect them and their livestock. Consequentially, the family units morphed into migrant herdsmen. The hunter's reverence crystalized into recognizable symbols and later into images of the sacred animal spirits. The Great Spirit, who sustained their lives, also morphed. He and his retinue required sacrifices for the bounty they provided them. Usually, these were from their flocks or herd. However, at times they required the death of one of them. This was reasonable, since often during a chase the lives of one or more hunters would be surrendered so that the entire tribe might survive.

At some point, they discovered that the seeds of certain plants could be easily collected, crushed, and cooked into a quick, nutritious meal. Since they could be easily stored and transported, they could provide food year-round. This was the gift of the vegetation spirit, who surrendered his body to be crushed so that they might be nourished and survive.

Extended families banded together to claim the richer pastures, resulting in permanent settlements. The need to defend their territory resulted in walled encampments. Perhaps the earliest of these formed the Natufian culture (12,500 to 9,500 BCE) in the Levant, the southeastern coastal region of the Mediterranean, and Anatolia, modern Turkey. At Jericho (*Yeriḥo*) several human skulls were discovered on which the features had been "reconstructed" in plaster. The eyes were inlaid sea shells and even the hair was painted. They present a strikingly lifelike appearance. Since the skulls were detached from the bodies before burial and displayed above ground, they may have been regarded as 'spirit traps'.[25] They might also indicate cultic, ritual murder.

In about 9,000 BCE, the cultivation of rye, wheat, and barley became widespread through the grassy plains of the Near East. Neolithic culture begins with the establishment of cities between 8,000 and 6000 BCE. They flourished at Jericho, on the Anatolian plateau (Turkey) at Hacilar and Çatal Höyük, and in Mesopotamia at Qal'at Jarmo. At these ancient cult centers, shrines were decorated with wall paintings, plaster reliefs, skulls and horns of the fierce wild bulls, and cult statuettes representing

---

25 Horst de la Croix and Richard G. Tansey, Gardner's Art Through the Ages, Fifth Edition (New York: Harcourt, Brace World, Inc., 1970), p.13

their gods, both male and female. Magic and fertility symbolism were the dominant subject matter. Another gift of the vegetation spirit was the sweet clusters of grapes in the vines. Once squeezed and left to ferment, the blood-colored drink brought joy to men and visions to shamans.

Yet, it was in the thick, fertile soil of the Nile River that the deep-rooted, traditional animal spirits were expressed as hybrid animal/human forms. Throughout its 5000-year history, Egypt held fast to its primordial, prehistoric gods.

II-1.2 In Egypt

At the dawn of time, Osiris and his sister/wife Isis ruled Egypt in harmony and peace. But their brother Seth became discontent. Desiring that he and his sister/wife, Nephthys would replace them, he brought an ornate sarcophagus as a gift and lured Osiris to lie down in it. Entrapped, Osiris soon died. To ensure that Isis, the mistress of incantations and magical spells, could not resurrect her husband, Seth cut him into pieces and scattered his parts throughout the Nile Valley. Temples were established claiming to house the relics. Isis, with the aid of Nephthys, mournfully sought out each relic but could not find his reproductive organ. She returned them to his coffin and, reassembled the body. Thus, Osiris was the first ruler to be mummified. According to Egyptian sources, Isis transforms herself into a bird and by fanning Osiris with her wings, she brings him back to life long enough to be impregnated by him. Afterward, Osiris ruled the distant land of *Duat*, the realm of the dead

According to Plutarch, Isis was so preoccupied with her sorrow that she did not notice that the coffin had floated down the Nile and out to sea. It landed on the shore of Byblos where the people, enthralled by its beauty, took it to the palace. No sooner had they set it down than a great tree grew and encased it. Noticing that it was gone, Isis searched all lands until she found the tree. Disguising herself as a nursemaid, she obtained a trusted position in the palace. At midnight, the virgin-goddess transformed herself into a bird and, fluttering over the tree, she conceived a son, the divine Horus.

In both versions, Horus ultimately triumphed over his uncle, the evil Seth, and secured his father's throne. From that time onward, each new king became the embodiment of *maat,* (cosmic and social order = "truth"), and was identified as Horus, just as the recently deceased king was now identified with his father, Osiris.

In addition, every king of Egypt had been proclaimed the Son of Amon-Ra. The god Ra was the personification of the sun at its noonday zenith. Horus was the falcon-god, another manifestation of the sun. The root word *amen* meant 'what is hidden,' 'what is not seen,' and 'what cannot be seen'.[26] Hence Amon was the unseen god of secret knowledge. As the incarnation of Amon-Ra, every word uttered by the Egyptian king was the divine melody of the goddess *Maat* – "Truth."

The queens played a central role in the king/god cult of ancient Egypt and enjoyed a powerful position in society. The "King's Daughter" and "Great God's Wife" was married to the god Amon-Ra:

> The queen was the repository of that (divine) power which, when bestowed at birth upon her offspring, distinguishing him from all other quasi-royal progeny as the rightful heir to the throne. Other royal relatives, even the king himself, did not really figure in determining the succession: The queen was the heiress, and the right to the throne passed through her. In order to better ensure the purity of the line, the doctrine had it that on the night of the conception the god Amon had become incarnate in the person of the reigning king and had impregnated the queen with divine seed. By virtue of this fact the queen could call herself "God's wife", and her offspring could justifiably maintain that in a mystical sense he was truly the "son of Amon."[27]

---

26 John A. Wilson, The Culture of Ancient Egypt (Chicago: University of Chicago Press, 1963) p. 130.
27 Donald B. Redford, The History and Chronology of the Eighteenth Dynasty of Egypt (Toronto: Toronto UP, 1967). 65-71.

II-1.3 In Greece and Crete

Linear B tablets (ca. 1450 BCE) from Pylos and Crete mention Dionysos, testifying to the antiquity of the vegetation deity of grain and wine. A Dionysos sanctuary at Ayia Irini on Keos, Crete (1470-1200 BCE), displays his earliest votive inscriptions and Minoan sculptures.

According to his myths, Zeus, (the patron god of sex offenders), transformed himself into a horned serpent to seduce Persephone, who then gave birth to Dionysos Zagreus. His wife, Hera (the patron goddess of the envious and malicious), perceived that he was contemplating declaring Dionysos his successor, instead of their children. She, therefore, incited the Titans to kill him. These brutal giants seize Dionysos and, tore him to pieces, boiled and then roasted the parts, after which they sit down to eat the young god. Only Ἀθήνα ἡ Παρθέος (*Parthenos*), Athena the Virgin (the patron goddess of all technical skills), is wise enough to save the heart of Dionysos. Meanwhile, Zeus had moved on to another conquest, Semele, the daughter of Kadmos, king of Thebes. When she conceived through the still beating heart of Dionysos – sort of an early form of cloning. However, Semele dared to look directly at Zeus and immediately was consumed by his thunderbolt. Unable to save the maiden, Zeus retrieved the divine embryo from the flames, and, cutting open his thigh, created a womb for the child.

Upon his second birth, Dionysos was carried by Hermes (the patron god of thieves) to the *maenads* (μαινας – "raving women") of Nysa. In his myths, he wanders the world demanding acknowledgment, honor, and worship; and, woe to those who refuse. When Dionysos reentered his native city of Thebes, his cousin, Pentheus, who was then king, forbade his worship and attempted to imprison him. Through his *mania* (from μαινω – "to make mad, insane"), frenzied mental power, he caused the chains to drop from his wrists and ankles. The doors opened on their own. As he walked the streets of the city, the women and sometimes men dressed as women, abandoned their homes and work, dancing after him in a frenzied, intoxicated state.[28] Pentheus, seeing his mother among them dressed as a maenad, followed them. When he was discovered, his mother and aunts rip off his arms and legs, reveling in his blood. Thus, the dismemberment of Dionysos Zagreus parallels that of Osiris, but the frenzied state was uniquely Dionysian.

> Frenzy is described as a pathological outburst by the anger of a god. As well as the pathological frenzy of the individual, there is also ritual and institutionalized, collective frenzy, especially the frenzy of the women of a city as they break out at the festival of license. The aim, nonetheless, in reality

---

28 Walter Burkert, Greek Religion, John Rafin, trans. (Cambridge: Harvard University Press, 1985), p. 162.

and in myth is to bring madness back to sense, a process which requires purification and the purifying priest.[29]

Common characteristics of the Dionysos/Bacchus mysteries included wine-drinking, women uprisings, madness, human sacrificial and cannibalistic fantasies, goat or bull sacrifices, phallos processions, and orgies. Most of these elements suggest Paleolithic origins, where periodic food sparsity resulted in cannibalism and the fear of starvation and enslavement by rival tribes resulted in primitive piety expressed through ritual murder.

In another myth, the daughters of Minyas are so absorbed with weaving for Athena Ergane that they refused to set aside their work to dance in the Agrionia festival of Dionysos. The infuriated god caused ivy and grape vines to grow around their looms. The eldest, Leukippe, vows to make a sacrifice to the god, and with her sisters' help, tore her own infant son to pieces. They then rushed off to join the other *maenads* in the mountain rituals.[30] Hence, we could refer to Dionysos as the "patron god of the mentally ill" and consider his myths as a window to primitive attitudes toward the mentally ill among early European people.

Instead of reading these gory myths literally, let's consider them metaphorically. Perhaps then they will become more comprehensible. As noted above, during the hunter/gatherer people

---

29 Burkert, p. 110.
30 Burkert, p. 164.

often faced starvation. The insistent cries of the children and their hunger were enough to drive any mother mad. In a frenzy, they scoured the mountainsides for any game they could catch, net, or trap, while their husbands were away for days hunting larger game. The *maenads* were usually pictured with fawnskin draped over their shoulders. It is a sad thought that women would tear apart a little Bambi or Thumper, but the urgency of feeding their own young would demand such cruelty. This was their reality until the discovery of grain.

Before the women of the tribe (symbolized by Hera) gave the new grain, (the infant Dionysos) to their husbands (the Titans), they would crush them and remove the outer husks (tore him to pieces). They first boiled the grain and then placed it on a hot surface to roast it, after which the family sat down to eat the new food source (the young god). The tribe was continually, painfully aware that any slack in vigilantes could cause them to lose the favor of the life-giving grain and revert again to the horrors of starvation.

Likewise, we find that the daughters of Minyas had become so obsessed with their ambition to produce the most beautiful robes imaginable for the honor of Athena that they neglected to honor Dionysos. When they realized their error, they rushed to take a loaf of bread that Leukippe had baked fresh that morning and ripped it into pieces to appease the god.

There are varying opinions regarding the etymology of the name Dionysos Διόνῡσος.[31] The first element is easy Dio-Διο is "God/Zeus". The most obvious meaning of the second -nysos from the verb νύσσω ("to pierce/stab")[32], which gives us "God pierced", referring to when "Zeus stabbed" himself in the thigh. As the god of grain, the crushed body of Dionysos nourished life. From this came the Greco-Roman custom where the devotee, before eating the bread of life, would break off a small piece, thank the god and toss it into the fire on the household hearth. As the god of wine, the blood of the crushed body Dionysos gave joy, comfort and consoled the brokenhearted.[33] Each morning the head of the household would pour a libation of wine (his blood) on the family altar and pray for his blessing.

However, the myths presented above were part of "sacred history". For instance, the term *mythos,* μυθος, originally conveyed the meaning of "the true words, story of the gods". In the minds of the Greeks and Romans, these were true and accurate accounts.

Dismemberment and cannibalism have a long, dark history. Essentially, there are two forms of cannibalism described. As described above, there were incidences when people resorted to consuming human flesh during times of famine. There were also occasions of ritual cannibalism, which consisted of eating a small

---

31 Burkert, p.162.
32 Danker, p. 682.
33 Burkert, p.163-164.

part of a victim, often a warrior. This was usually a part associated with a specific skill of the deceased or the deity he epitomizes. With both types of cannibalism, those participating in the action believed that eating a person's flesh or drinking his blood endowed the cannibal with some of the characteristics of the deceased or the deity.

Besides being disgusting and barbaric, cannibalism resulted in the spread of the prion disease *kuru*, which is a rare, incurable, and fatal neurodegenerative disorder. It is a form of transmissible spongiform encephalopathy (TSE). The symptoms are tremors, loss of coordination, and pathologic bursts of laughter, which remind of us the characteristics of the *maenads*. According to research published in *Science* magazine in 2003, genetic markers have been found in many sectors of modern humans worldwide suggesting that their ancestors once suffered from TSE.

II-1.4 Asia Minor and the Levant

Scholars are divided on the role of *Molek* among the ancient כְּנַעֲנִים Canaanites. The noun *melek* refers to a ruler, a king. As a verb, *mlk* is thought to have originally meant "to counsel or consult". In the much later Punic language, it actually meant a "sacrifice". In Biblical Hebrew, it usually has the article הַ or לַ attached, meaning "the" *Molek* or "to the" *Molek*.

Such scholars as Wm. F. Albright, G. C. Heider, and John Day have connected the Akkadian term *maliku* (referring to the shades of the dead) with the Ugaritic deity *Mlk* and the Mesopotamian *Malik,* (who is also connected with Nergal – the god of the underworld), and included with these Isaiah's association of the Hebrew *Moleḳ* with *Sheol* (defined as a subterranean underworld where the souls of the dead went after the body died). Thus, we find that passing the children through the fire of *Moleḳ* transported them to the realm of death. The concept of animal sacrifice in the ancient Levant pivoted on the belief that due to personal or national sins blood atonement was required in restitution. Hence, a child was offered on the funeral pyre as a vicarious atonement for the guilty by the priests. To this Hashem emphatically states, that He did not instruct the people to sacrifice their children and that to do so is to defile His sanctuary, and to profane His holy name.

> And thou shalt not give any of thy seed to set them apart to Molech, neither shalt thou profane the name of thy G-d: I am the LORD. (Lev. 18:21)
> Moreover, thou shalt say to the children of Israel: Whosoever he be of the children of Israel, or of the strangers that sojourn in Israel, that giveth of his seed unto Molech; he shall surely be put to death; the people of the land shall stone him with stones. I also will set My face against that man, and will cut him off from among his people, because he hath given of his seed unto Molech, to defile My sanctuary, and to profane My holy name. And if the people of the land do at all hide their eyes from that man, when he

giveth of his seed unto Molech, and put him not to death; then I will set My face against that man, and against his family, and will cut him off, and all that go astray after him, to go astray after Molech, from among their people. And the soul that turneth unto the ghosts, and unto the familiar spirits, to go astray after them, I will even set My face against that soul, and will cut him off from among his people. Sanctify yourselves therefore, and be ye holy; for I am the LORD your G-d. (Lev. 20:2-7)

Albright points out that the Canaanite gods Ba'al and Horon and their goddesses Anath and Astarte were identified with the native Egyptian deities Seth and Horus, Nephthys, and Isis. In the Levant, worship was similar to that of Egyptian temples and cults but combined with local forms of worship.

Among the Canaanites extremely depraved practices were inextricably bound up with religion. Ritual prostitution of both sexes was rampant, and the variety of evil practices is attested by the multiplicity of names employed to designate those "professions". The _cinaedus_ (homosexual) formed a recognized guild in Canaanite temples, and there were other groups which combined dancing and singing with divination in a peculiarly unholy union. Snake worship and human sacrifice were rife. The "Creatress of the Gods" (Asherah) was represented as a beautiful naked prostitute, called "Holiness" in both Canaan and Egypt. The two other principal Canaanite goddesses, Anath and Astarte (Heb. Ashtaroth), are called "the Great Goddesses which conceive but do not bear", and the rape of Anath by

97

> Ba'al formed a standing theme in Canaanite mythology, in spite of the fact that she was at the same time regularly called "the Virgin". Anath is represented as a naked woman astride a stallion, brandishing her lance, in Canaanite literature, she figures in scenes of incredible ferocity."[34]

The Canaanites maintained a belief in El as the head of the pantheon, but his authority was challenged by advance of the worship of Ba'al (lit: "Master"). The Israelites would naturally be enraged by the depraved forms of worship within the cult of Ba'al. To add insult to injury, Ugaritic mythology paints El as a weak, inept personality. An example of this is the scene where Anath, an eastern version of Artemis/Diana confronts her father, El, with the demand that her "brother", Ba'al, be allowed to build his house in defiance of El's wishes.

ANAT:
> Rejoice not, rejoice not!...
> I shall wound the crown of thy scalp
> I shall make thy gray hair flow with blood,
> Thy grey beard with gore! 5AB E:27-33; 3D6: 7-12

EL:
> While a daughter's demand flatters the heart.
> Thou mayst (then) take whatever is in thy mind,
> Accomplish whatever is in thy heart
> Thy heel shall surely crush
> Any adversary of the Virgin Anat. 5AB 2:35-37

---

34 Albright, William F. The Biblical Period: From Abraham to Ezra (Baltimore: John Hopkins Press, 1949) p.10.

The Ugaritic poetry reflects an acute crisis, in which the supreme authority over the pantheon shifts from the aged El to the younger Baʿal. The Canaanites believed that El, a fertility-god who assured men of an heir, was the head of their gods, but he was now old and weak. The goddesses began to undermine El's authority in favor of advancing the younger, stronger Baʿal, the god of rain and thunderstorms.

The transfer of power from the Semitic El to Baʿal/Zeus is finalized after Anath coerced their father into allowing Baʿal to build his house on Mount Saphar. Just as, the transfer of power from the aged Chronus to Zeus, whose thunderbolts were feared by gods and men, was accomplished due to the guile of Zeus' mother Rhea, in Greek mythology. The storm/rain-god, Baʿal's coup was actualized by the volatile Virgin-Anath.

Baʿal gained the support of all the gods and goddesses except for Mot, the god of Death. Mot then sends a dinner invitation to Baʿal, who, unaware that he is not only the guest of honor but also the main course, accepts. Mot consumes Baʿal, just as he does all living. The goddesses Anath, Shamesh, and Astarte descend to the Underworld and violently punish Mot. The poem ends with the return of the morning light, the spring rains, and the sprouting of crops. Baʿal, with a little help from his friends, has triumphed over Death and with his return, resurrected life on earth. It is interesting

to think that Ahab and Jezebel once believed that they were
assured eternal life through the death and resurrection of Baʿal.

Some sources identify Baʿal as the son or manifestation of
Dagon (grain-god). In Hebrew, *dagan* means gain. The worship of
Dagon was brought to the Levant by the Philistines (Judges 16:23)
, Greek related European invaders. Thus, this metaphysical
conflict might well reflect the culture-social conflicts caused by the
conquest of the region by the "Sea-Peoples". I Samuel 5 relates
the misfortunes that befell the Philistines who had captured the Ark
of the Covenant. They set it as a trophy in the temple of Dagon.
The next morning, they found that the idol had fallen to the ground
be the Holy Ark. The restored it to its place. The next morning, not
only had the idol fallen again but its head and hands were severed
from it body and were outside the temple. Chapter six describes
how the Philistines returned the Ark to the Israelites.

The name of Dionysos' mother, Semele, is associated with
Phrygia[35] (region of Central Turkey), where the 'Mother of the
Gods', Kybele, placed an almond to her breast and conceived the
divine Attis. In a frenzied state, he castrated himself under a pine
tree. The Phrygians would tie an effigy of the god to a pine tree
and place it in a tomb on the vernal equinox. Upon finding it empty
at sunrise on the third morning, his devotees shouted that Attis had
risen and triumphed over death.

---

35 Burkert, p.163.

The alternate name for Dionysos, Bacchus, seems to be of a Semitic root, meaning 'to cry or wail' and is probably related to Jeremiah's description of the women of Jerusalem crying for Tammuz. Thus, pushing the connection back to the ancient Sumerian goddess Ianna, the Queen of Heaven, who was not content to mourn the death of her young lover, Tammuz. She descended into the netherworld and retrieved him from the jaws of death.

This descent into the underworld theme was common throughout Western Asia and the Mediterranean region. Adonis, the young shepherd lover of Aphrodites, was gored to death by a wild boar. His blood stained the white roses red. Aphrodites ensured his resurrection. Throughout the eastern Mediterranean, women joined Aphrodites in mourning for Adonis (*adon* = lord), who was gored to death by a wild boar. Several such stories were popular during the Classical Period (600-350 BCE)

Apollo assisted King Admetus in the contest that enabled him to marry the beautiful princess Alcestis. However, he forgot to make the required offering to the huntress, Artemis, the goddess of virgins and childbirth. She determined that he should suffer an early death. Apollo again helped Admetus by assuring him that, if he could find someone who would die in his place, he would be allowed to live. This was easier said than done. No one came forward. His family and friends backed away. Even his parents seemed too busy to discuss the issue. Only his bride loved him

101

enough to step forward and died so that he might live. Hearing of his friend's loss, Heracles descended to the underworld and retrieved Alcestis.

Orpheus, whose music and voice could charm wild beasts, trees, and even rocks, was not as lucky. When his beloved bride died on their wedding day, he resolved to use the miraculous power of his lyre to charm Hades, the god of the Underworld. Because he lacked the courage of Alcestis, he was only shown a phantasm of his lost wife and was told to take her but not to look back until they had left the dark realm. Holding her hand, he led her out, but, exiting first, he forgot and turned to look at her. Unfortunately, she was still on the other side and vanished before his eyes. Mourning her for the remainder of his life, he refused to worship any god except for Apollo, the sun-god. When he was worshipping at dawn on Mount Pangaion, he was ripped apart by Thracian *Maenads* because he had not honored Dionysos. It is said that nightingales still sing over his grave.

II-2 A Spiritual Revolutionary

Certainly, Abraham was not the first to contemplate the metaphysical realm. Long before he was born, priests had formulated a reasonable explanation for the dynamics that directed their lives. Their existence was ruled by several overwhelmingly persuasive and devastatingly forceful powers – the gods, who were embodied in the stars. Enlivening every beam of joy and lurking at each dark turn were lesser spirits – some benevolent, some demonic. To navigate the swift currents of existence, one sought the expert direction of the star-gazers and clutched tightly his talismans. Evil was diverted and prosperity assured by frequent, feverish prayers to images of one's patron deity; but, since the gods were jealous and capricious, only a fool would neglect his duties to the others. This, of course, kept the priest very busy and very wealthy.

It is said that young Abram's father was a master craftsman and merchant of household gods. Abram had been taught that the gods knew and saw all things. They controlled each person's destiny – bestowing blessings or inflicting curses at their whim. Yet, he had watched his father knead the clay, mold it, fire it in the kiln, and paint it with either a compassionate or malefic expression. He must discover the truth even if it destroyed his life. He was alone in the workshop when he challenged the gods. With a slug-hammer in hand, he declared war; and, when the dust settled, he stood victorious over the shattered shards. Terah trembled not only with anger but also with fear as he rebuked his son. The family kept the deed a secret and waited for a response, but none came. Surprisingly, his family prospered. Abram had proved that the idols were powerless. Renouncing the conventional gods, he set his heart to deciphering the metaphysical – the source that is above or beyond nature.

Abram sought the counsel of his elders, who explained that in ancient times their ancestors had worshipped only El, the Creator. Displeased by the behavior of mankind, El destroyed them in a great deluge. Later, they attempted to build a tower that would place them on a level with the Creator. So, El confused their language. Instead of speaking one, they each spoke a different language. Their confusion spread. They began to see every manifestation of El as a separate power and gave each of these forces personal names. At the head of these gods was Anu (Sumerian - An; Greek - Uranus), the head of the pantheon of Ur. But they grew tired of Anu and advanced his son over him. Enlil was the storm and wind god, breath and the 'word' of Anu. They sang hymns of praise to him. "The spirit of the word is Enlil, the spirit of the heart is Anu, that which stilleth the heaven above, but he is also a rushing deluge that troubles the faces of men, a torrent which destroys the bulwarks."[36]

II-2.1 Abraham the Monotheist

Now that Abram knew the truth that the multitude of gods, אֱלֹהִים *elohim* ('powers'), were actually manifestations of one force, the One G-d. he would never again worship the false gods created by foolish men. He would bow only before the most revered, אֵל־שַׁדַּי, El-Shaddai. As a member of a traditional merchant family, he knew that it was a fitting name, reflecting the Creator's multifaceted nature.

In Akkadian, *shadū* meant 'mountain' and in Ugarit, שָׂדֶה *sadeh* meant 'field'. Thus, his power extended over all land, both high and low. In Aramaic there is a related word שְׁדָא, 'he hurled, threw', thus, His anger manifests in 'arrows of lightning and thunder. In his tongue, he saw two meanings. In שַׁד *shad*, breast, he saw the characteristic of 'Provider, Sustainer'. Then the root שָׁדַד, which means to 'overpower, devastate, or ruin', indicates that El-Shaddai is the All-Almighty.[37] But, the inner meaning of *Shaddai* is derived from דַּי *dai*, 'enough'; as one would say 'for the

---

36 N. K. Saunders, The Epic of Gilgamesh (London: Penguin Books, 1960) p. 24.
37 Ernest Klein, pg. 641.

stuff they had was sufficient' (Ex. 36:7). The שׁ *shin* adds *asher*,

'which' as in *sh'cavar*, 'which already' (Eccl. 2:16). The name

Shaddai, therefore, signifies 'he who is sufficient'[38] The name *El*

designates power. Therefore, *El-Shaddai* means the *G-d Who is*

Sufficient for all of our needs and who alone is worthy of

worship.[39] If Abram's G-d was contained in all forces and was

sufficient for all His devotee's needs, then his faith was

monotheistic – the belief in one and only one deity.

Professor Albright expressed his view of El-monotheism

rather emphatically.

> There is no solid basis for the idea which is
> sometimes expressed that there was a kind of "El"
> monotheism among the early Western Semitics and
> in particular among the early Hebrews. It is true that
> very few specific names of gods appear among them
> during the nomadic or semi-nomadic stage and that
> the use of different appellations of gods in personal
> names seems to increase rapidly under sedentary
> conditions. However, there are too many divine
> names known to have been common to the ancestors
> of the various Semitic peoples and there is too much
> evidence for polytheistic beliefs among the earliest
> South Arabians after the 8th century B.C. to warrant
> any such hypothesis."[40]

---

38 Michael Friedländer, trans., Guide of the Perplexed of Maimonides (New
York; Hebrew Publishing Co. 1881), Part I, Chap..LXIII, p. 240.
39 Ibid, Part I, Chap. LXI – LXV. pp. 226-246.
40 William F. Albright, From the Stone Age to Christianity (Baltimore: John
Hopkins University Press, 1957), p. 246.

This statement seems too broad. The Torah does not imply that the beliefs in *El-Shaddai* were widespread. Quite the contrary, Abram and his wife, Sarai, left Ḥaran only with the young family of his nephew, Lot, and "the souls that they had made" there. Albright uses the two extremes – "the ancestors of various Semitic peoples" (2500-1950 BCE) and the population of the southern Arabian Peninsula of 800-700 BCE – as his evidence. This argument does not negate the conviction that Abram promoted the belief in an *El-Shaddai* monotheism sometime between those dates.

Abram followed *El-Shaddai* from Ur to Ḥaran and then to Canaan, where He blessed him and changed his name to Abraham. Wherever he traveled, Abraham readily taught his beliefs to anyone interested in learning. Maleḳi-Tzedeq, the high priest of El-ʿElyon (G-d Most High) in Shalem (Jerusalem), was most likely a convert of Avraham. (Gen. 14:18) His efforts – or those of his descendants – could account for the appearance of the Semitic god, El, in a similar position in the Ugaritic pantheon as the Sumerian god An. Also, there are various "el" group names found among the early *Habiru* (*Apiru* in Egyptian) tribes of the Amarna papyri (1360–1332 BC). Even though many of Abraham's converts were sincere worshippers during their lifetime, their descendants did not remain true to his teachings. They allowed the teachings to degenerate into the corrupted practices of the Canaanites.

Regardless, presently it is true that Abraham left no tangible, hard archaeological evidence of his *El*-monotheism.

El-Shaddai blessed Abram and changed his name to Abraham (Avraham). He in turn blessed his children. The significance of the parental blessing that Abraham bestowed on his son, Isaac (Itzḥak) was much more than the transfer of material possessions and clan title to an heir. It indicated the person responsible for carrying on the covenant between Abraham and the Almighty. An example of this is the difference in the blessings of Jacob and Esau. Both men are blessed with material possessions, but it was Jacob who succeeds his father as the spiritual leader in the worship of *El-Shaddai*.

II-2.2 עֲקֵידַת יִצְחָק – The Binding of Isaac

In Genesis 22, we are informed that G-d tested Abraham. And He said: 'Take now thy son, thine only son, whom thou lovest, even Isaac, and get thee into the land of Moriah; and offer him there for a burnt-offering upon one of the mountains which I will tell thee of.'

This was an extremely strange command. First of all, Isaac was his long-awaited, promised child of his beloved Sarah. For G-d to ask him to butcher him was an inconceivably cruel request of the aged parent. Additionally, Abraham had lived among the

Canaanites for many years. He was aware of their barbaric cults and deprived customs. It would not have surprised the Canaanites that he was taking his son to *Molek*, they would only have been confused that he had waited so long to do it. For Abraham, this request is in stark contrast to everything he understood about *El-Shaddai*. It contradicted everything that he had been teaching the Canaanites regarding the nature of his G-d. Still, he has been commanded, so he called his son and two other youths and traveled three days to Mount Moriah.

When they arrived at the place, he and Isaac are walking alone to the final destination. Isaac asks, "'My father." And Abraham answers, "Here am I, my son." And Isaac continues, "Behold the fire and the wood; but where is the lamb for a burnt-offering?" Abraham replies, "G-d will provide Himself the lamb for a burnt-offering, my son." This is pure faith. Abraham is completely confident that his son will not be harmed. Regardless, he arranges the wood, ties his son's hands and ankles, and lays him on the pyre. Then as he raises the knife, he is again called and instructed, "Lay not thy hand upon the lad, neither do thou anything unto him; for now I know that thou art a G-d fearing man, seeing thou hast not withheld thy son, thine only son, from Me." Then Abraham saw a ram, whose horns are caught in the brush, and knew that the comforting words he spoke to his son had been realized. Hashem did provide the required sacrifice.

This is a very beautiful and inspiring story. But we must not become so entranced by its dramatic prose that we lose sight of its true significance. From that point in time forward, even until this very day, we have not only been verbally commanded not to sacrifice our children but we have been provided with an object lesson that demonstrates to us just how abominable the deed was.

The Age of the Hebrew Patriarchs was a highly sophisticated period. Evidence for this can be found in the development of legal codes, concepts of human rights, and the practice of medicine. By the beginning of the Second Intermediate Period in Egypt, learning began to be replaced by superstition and sound medical knowledge by magical incantations. Religious philosophies continued to show signs of progress toward monotheism, but immoral, religious rituals and practices increased at a remarkable rate. Most of the other descendants of Abraham joined their Canaanite neighbors and added to the belief in a host of minor gods called *ba'alim* ('masters'). As an example, even though Ishmael was a loyal son to his father Abraham, his descendants did not long remain true to his teachings. Not for 2,400 years after the death of Ishmael would his descendant, Mohammed, re-establish monotheism among his descendants.

By the time hunger drove Jacob and his family down to Egypt, there were probably few outside his family who were exclusively monotheistic followers of *El-Shaddai*. Joseph, Jacob's eldest son by his beloved wife, Rachel, suffered enslavement and

110

false imprisonment. He was not only miraculously free from the dungeon; but, due to his prediction of the approach of a great natural disaster, he was elevated to the vizier of Egypt. Neither degradation nor adulations moved him to abandon his faith in *El-Shaddai*. Thus, Joseph is the archetypical Suffering Servant and the traditional ancestor of the Mashiaḥ ben Yosef. As long as Joseph lived, the Children of Israel were safe; but, then a new Pharoah, (*i.e.* new dynasty) gained control of Egypt.

II-2.3 A Spiritual Exodus

The descendants of Jacob were enslaved in Egypt until Moses led them to freedom. He revealed another secret name to the Children of Israel, in the name *yod, heh, vav, heh* that scholars express as *Yahweh*. Religious Jews refrain from pronouncing or writing this name of

G-d since it is very impolite to call the Almighty by his proper name. Hence, we refer to it simply as Hashem, "The Name". According to the Rambam, it is a form of the verb "to be" or "to exist." The credo of the Hebrew/Israelites/Jews has ever since been "Hear (also meaning understand) Israel (literally: 'He will wrestle with/for *El*') *Hashem* (the Existing) [is] *Elokinu* (the source of "all Powers for us" – *k* is substituted for *h* here, again to show respect) *Hashem* (the Existing) is One (an Indivisible single Unit)."

111

Scholars point to Exodus 15:11, מִי־כָמֹכָה בָּאֵלִם ה', "Who is like You among the powers Hashem" and interpret אֵלִם as "gods". This they claim is evidence that originally the Israelites were originally monolatrists. Another perspective is that during those long sorrowful years, the people were influenced by their environment. Perhaps this is the reason that part of the Song at the Sea seems to echo monolatry, meaning the worship of one major G-d while accepting the existence of other lesser deities. However, it is clear that Moses, like his forefather Abraham, taught a strictly monotheistic form of worship. (Deut. 4:11-24, 33-39)

Likewise, the Torah cautions us

> Moreover, thou shalt say to the children of Israel: Whosoever he be of the children of Israel, or of the strangers that sojourn in Israel, that giveth of his seed unto Molech מִזַּרְעוֹ לַמֹּלֶךְ; he shall surely be put to death; the people of the land shall stone him with stones... And the soul that turneth unto the ghosts, and unto the familiar spirits הָאֹבֹת וְאֶל־הַיִּדְּעֹנִים, to go astray after them, I will even set My face against that soul, and will cut him off from among his people... A man also or a woman that divineth by a ghost or a familiar spirit, shall surely be put to death; they shall stone them with stones; their blood shall be upon them. (Lev. 20:2, 6, 27)

> When thou art come into the land which the LORD thy G-d giveth thee, thou shalt not learn to do after the abominations of those nations. There shall not be found among you any one that maketh his son or his daughter to pass through the fire, one that useth

divination, a soothsayer, or an enchanter, or a sorcerer, or a charmer, or one that consulteth a ghost or a familiar spirit, or a necromancer וְשֹׁאֵל אוֹב וְיִדְּעֹנִי. For whosoever doeth these things is an abomination unto the LORD; and because of these abominations the LORD thy G-d is driving them out from before thee. (Deut. 18:9-12)

According to the JPS translation, the term אבת or אוֹב refers to necromancy. Its root is אב father, origin or progenitor. In Genesis 15:15 Abraham is reassured: "As for you: you shall come to your ancestors (אֲבֹתֶיךָ) in peace." We are forbidden from seeking communion with the spirits of the deceased. Such activities are a source of ritual contamination. In the Canaanite inscriptions of the Ugaritic Texts, *ib* was a gemstone and *ib-nkl* referred to a lunar goddess. Thus, it could also refer to a stone that was associated with or used to communicate with a lunar goddess. In Hebrew *ib-nkl* אָב־נָכֵל would instead mean a "source of deception"[41] The root for the term יִדְּעֹנִים, a soothsayer or magician, is ידע which means "knowing, wise; to be familiar or intimate". A soothsayer or magician is one who presents himself as an expert in secret powers often related to those who attempt to contact the spirits of the dead or who use their natural powers to seduce the naïve either financially or intimately.

---

41 Gordon, Cyrus H. Ugaritic Textbook (Rome, Pontifical Biblical Institute, 1965), p. 348, 9-10.

There are individuals who, like Moses (but to a much lesser degree) naturally have premonitions, persuasive talents, or charisma; but, as with any gift, one must be especially careful how it is used. Such an individual would experience a strong, sometimes overpowering impulse to take advantage of the naïve, weak, or emotionally injured person for their selfish desires or gain. Moses is our model of one who resisted such impulses. As an example, a man once said to the Vilna Gaon, "If I had your evil-inclination, I would also be a great saint." The Vilna Gaon replied, "If you had my evil-inclination, you would not last one day." Focusing one's intellectual and spiritual powers on the greater good is the characteristic that distinguishes the greatest.

From these verses, we arrive at an understanding of the Jewish prohibition as a means of protecting a person from the deception that would have an adverse effect, since their cognitive abilities are clouded through a corruption of the imagination. Through association with these negative forces, one is pulled down into the gloomy world of spirits and demons and becomes obsessed with unnatural acts. The people had descended to Egypt. They were existing in a land steeped in the dark arts. This exodus was not only physical but also spiritual. Therefore, they are cautioned not to turn to these negative obsessions, which had come to dominate the Land of Canaan. Thus, Torah reaches deep into our psyche and stops us from engaging in even symbolic rituals through which individuals attempt to rule over G-d.

For a few years, Egypt was ruled by a pharaoh, who was known as the "heretic king. Earlier scholars considered his religious reforms to be a monotheistic movement. Since Akhenaton (1350–1330 BC) never denied the existence of Egypt's other gods, today most consider him a monolatrist. According to the hymns of Akhenaton, he was the "life" and "one true son" of the Sun-disc, Aton. Thus, only he and his immediate family could worship his divine father, while all others approached the deity through worshipping Akhenaton, the Aton incarnate. Throughout its long history, all forms of Egyptian religion were rank with grotesque iconography, dominated by superstitions and magic, and obsessed with procurement of a materialistic, self-aggrandizing, hedonistic afterlife.[42]

Scholars such as William F, Albright endorsed the position that Israel's religion evolved from polytheism to monotheism. According to his proposition, the religious movement of Moses must have been influenced by that of Akhenaton.[43] If this were true, then wouldn't Moses have insisted that the people worship him and his family, while only they could worship Hashem? On the contrary, Hashem demanded that no one should know the site of Moses' grave. In all of this talk about Egypt, the more important point has been brushed aside. Monotheism began with Abraham,

---

42 William F. Albright, *From the Stone Age to Christianity*, p. 206.
43 Mark S. Smith, The Early History of G-d: Yahweh and the Other Deities in Ancient Israel, 2nd ed. (Grand Rapids: Eerdmans; Dearborn, Dove, 2002), pp. xlvi, 243.

not with Moses. Joshua, Gideon, Samson, and David fought for it, while the prophets invigorated it. It was and remains today a radical concept that has had a profound effect on aristocrats and plebians alike.

II-2.4 Ḥezekiah, the Righteous King

In Part I, we presented arguments supporting Ḥezekiah as the Suffering Servant. We find further support for this position in relevant historical passages. In Isaiah 7:1, we find that Ahaz was terrified when the kings to his north, Pekah, the king of Israel, and Rezin, the king of Aram, formed a confederacy. While Ahaz was inspecting his defenses and water supply, Hashem sent Isaiah to meet him. The king had rejected the G-d of Israel and turned to idolatry. Isaiah greeted him: "Keep calm, and be quiet; fear not, neither let thy heart be faint, because of these two tails of smoking firebrands, for the fierce anger of Rezin and Aram, and of the son of Remaliah." Since Ahaz refused to ask a sign of Hashem that Judah would not be conquered, Isaiah informs him:

יד לָכֵן יִתֵּן אֲדֹנָי הוּא, לָכֶם--אוֹת: הִנֵּה הָעַלְמָה, הָרָה וְיֹלֶדֶת בֵּן, וְקָרָאת שְׁמוֹ, עִמָּנוּ אֵל.

טז כִּי בְּטֶרֶם יֵדַע הַנַּעַר, מָאֹס בָּרָע--וּבָחֹר בַּטּוֹב: תֵּעָזֵב הָאֲדָמָה אֲשֶׁר אַתָּה קָץ, מִפְּנֵי שְׁנֵי מְלָכֶיהָ.

14. Therefore the Lord Himself shall give you a sign: behold, the young woman [Ahaz's new wife, Abijah] has conceived and has borne a son, and (she) shall call his name *Immanuel* ("G-d is with us")... 16. Yea, before the child shall know to refuse the evil, and choose the good, the land whose two kings thou hast a horror of shall be forsaken. (Isaiah 7:14,16)

and

ה כִּי-יֶלֶד יֻלַּד-לָנוּ, בֵּן נִתַּן-לָנוּ, וַתְּהִי הַמִּשְׂרָה, עַל-שִׁכְמוֹ;

For a child was born unto us, a son was given unto us; and the government is upon his shoulder. (*ibid* 9:5)

At this Ahaz scoffed for his son, Maaseiah, was his heir, not Ḥezekiah. However, when Ahaz fought Pekah, he lost "a hundred and twenty thousand in one day, all of them valiant men; because they had forsaken the LORD, the G-d of their fathers." Maaseiah was among the dead. Thus, the prophet was right, Ḥezekiah became the new heir. Still, his father refused to look upon him as his son and heir. The boy was too weak and his defects caused him to be susceptible to frequent illness.

Instead of listening to Isaiah, Ahaz foolishly paid the Assyrian king, Tiglath-pileser III, to assist him against his enemies. The Assyrians were a cruel, ruthless nation. Throughout Ḥezekiah's lifetime, his people endured one devastating war after another. The Assyrian aggression against Israel and Judah is best understood by widening our scope to include their drama with the Babylonians.

Samaria was besieged and destroyed (724-720 BCE) by the forces of Tiglath-pileser III's son, Shalmaneser V, and his grandson, Sargon II, who deported the ten northern tribes (719 BCE). During the siege, Shalmaneser V died in 722 BCE. The Babylonian, Marduk-Baladan, took advantage of Sargon II's absence and sieged the throne. When Sargon returned in -720, he recognized Marduk-Baladan's rule and gave him the Assyrian name Marduk-apla-iddina. However, he later drove him from the province in -710. Sargon held the thrones of Assyria and Babylon until his death in 704 BCE. For two years, no king sat on the Babylonian throne. Marduk-apla-iddina II returned for a short time in -700 but was again forced to flee.

Sargon's son, Sennacherib, attacked Judah twice. On the first (706-704 BCE), Ḥezekiah capitulated to the Assyrian co-regent. Judah became their vassal and paid a hefty tribute that included the king's own daughter. Ḥezekiah knew that the Assyrians would return, so he fortified his cities and had a tunnel dug bringing Jerusalem's water source within its walls.

In 699 BCE, Sennacherib placed his son, Aššur-nadin-šumni, on the Babylonian throne. In -693, he was betrayed and handed him over to the Elamites, who killed him. Sennacherib ached for revenge; but, to punish his enemies, he needed more funds. Hence, his army again marched to collect tribute and/or booty.

In -691, he conducted his second attack on Judah (Is. 36 & 37). The Assyrians wanted a quick victory but were met with more resistance this time. He sent his servant, Rab-shakeh, to the walls of the city to taunt and dispirit the Jews with insults in Hebrew, so all the people could understand. The prophet informed Ḥezekiah, "Behold, I will put a spirit in him, and he shall hear a rumor, and shall return unto his own land; and I will cause him to fall by the sword in his own land." (Is. 37:7) He continues that Hashem would place a "hook" in Sennacherib's mouth (Is. 37:29) – an opportunity to avenge his son's death presented itself – and the Assyrian king jumped at it.

To reassure his king, Isaiah stated, "And this shall be the sign unto thee: ye shall eat this year [691 BCE] that which groweth of itself," – since the planting season had already passed; "and in the second year [690 BCE] that which springeth of the same," – since this was a Sabbatical year; "and in the third-year [689 BCE] sow ye, and reap, and plant vineyards, and eat the fruit thereof." (Is. 37:30) To put this in context, a Babylonian, whom the Assyrians called Mušezib-Marduk, had made himself king in 693 BCE and ruled for six years, until -689.

After the Assyrians withdrew in -691, we are informed that Ḥezekiah was ill and even Isaiah thought that he would die. After a revelation, Isaiah told the king's attendants to place a plaster of figs דְּבֶלֶת תְּאֵנִים on the abscess עַל-הַשְּׁחִין, and he recovered. (II Kings 20:7) Since the cause of his illness was an abscess, we can deduce that, during the heated exchange with Rab-shakeh, Ḥezekiah was wounded by his enemy's arrow. Isaiah chides the people that their righteous king suffered because, by following Ahaz, they brought the Assyrians to the land.

II Kings 20:12 informs us that "Berodach-baladan, the son of Baladan, king of Babylon, sent a letter and a present unto Ḥezekiah; for he had heard that Hezekiah had been sick." Considering the historical context, we suggest that this king should be identified as Mušezib-Marduk (693-689 BCE) and that he was the son of Marduk-Baladan/Marduk-apla-iddina II. The Assyrians with their Median allies subdued the Elamites and Babylonians between 691 and 689 BCE. Then, Sennacherib pillaged, burned and tore down the walls of Babylon. To wash out its remains, he had his forces divert the flow of the Euphrates River through the ruined city. Isaiah had predicted this destruction years earlier.

15 Every one that is found shall be thrust through;
and every one that is caught shall fall by the sword.

120

16 Their babes also shall be dashed in pieces before their eyes; their houses shall be spoiled, and their wives ravished. **17** Behold, I will stir up the Medes against them, who shall not regard silver, and as for gold, they shall not delight in it. **18** And their bows shall dash the young men in pieces; and they shall have no pity on the fruit of the womb; their eye shall not spare children. **19** And Babylon, the glory of kingdoms, the beauty of the Chaldeans' pride, shall be as when G-d overthrew Sodom and Gomorrah. **20** It shall never be inhabited, neither shall it be dwelt in from generation to generation; neither shall the Arabian pitch tent there; neither shall the shepherds make their fold there. **21** But wild-cats shall lie there; and their houses shall be full of ferrets; and ostriches shall dwell there, and satyrs shall dance there. **22** And jackals shall howl in their castles, and wild-dogs in the pleasant palaces; and her time is near to come, and her days shall not be prolonged. (Isaiah 13:15-22)

When Ḥezekiah was born in 744 BCE, Isaiah told his father that within 65 years Ephraim would be broken and it would no longer be a people. (Is. 7:8; 744-65 yrs.=679 BCE). For 65 years, the Assyrians oppressed Israel and Judah. In 691, Isaiah foresaw that Sennacherib would die a violent death in his homeland. Actually, he was murdered by his sons in 680 BCE. The 65 years ended the year following the death of the murderous Sennacherib, when his son, Esarhaddon, assumed the throne.

Likewise, years before it occurred the prophet foresaw the complete destruction of Babylon in 689-688 BCE. Ptolemy's

Canon informs us that after a hiatus of eight years without a king, Esarhaddon took the throne from his rebellious brothers. He then rebuilt Babylon. Over the years, it even surpassed its former splendor. When Cyrus took the city, there was neither destruction nor mass slaughter. Later, Alexander the Great also entered the city peacefully and ruled his extensive empire from Babylon. Yet upon his death, the center of power shifted from Mesopotamia to the Mediterranean and Babylon was ultimately abandoned and fell into ruin. Thus, Isaiah saw in the flash the future of this ancient city, from its brutal conquest by the Assyrians and Medes to its final desolation.

II-2.5 From Unity to Exile

The twelve tribes of Israel were united when the prophet Samuel anointed Saul as its first king. United Monarch of Israel continued through the reigns of Saul, David, and Solomon. However, Solomon and his son, Rehoboam did not keep the laws as they should have. According to the Torah, a king could have eighteen wives, but Solomon is said to have had a thousand.

> For it came to pass, when Solomon was old, that his wives turned away his heart after other gods; and his heart was not whole with the LORD his G-d, as was the heart of David his father. For Solomon went after

Ashtoreth עַשְׁתֹּרֶת the goddess of the Zidonians, and after Milcom מִלְכֹּם the detestation of the Ammonites. And Solomon did that which was evil in the sight of the LORD, and went not fully after the LORD, as did David his father. Then did Solomon build a high place for Chemosh לִכְמוֹשׁ the detestation of Moab, in the mount that is before Jerusalem, and for Molech וּלְמֹלֶךְ the detestation of the children of Ammon. And so did he for all his foreign wives, who offered and sacrificed unto their gods. (1 Kings 11:4-8)

He permitted the people to make sacrifices on the "high places" and in groves, to perform forbidden activities. Hence, the prophet Aḥiya was sent to Jeroboam and informed him that Hashem had given him ten of the twelve tribes to rule. (I Kings 11:31) Solomon's son, Rehoboam, when he was the king, also engaged in such behavior himself. When Solomon died, the northern tribes rejected Rehoboam as their king in a dispute over taxation. The tribes of Reuben, Issachar, Zebulun, Dan, Naphtali, Gad, Asher, Ephraim, Manasseh, and Benjamin formed the Kingdom of Israel with Jeroboam as their king. Rehoboam was left with only two landed tribes, those of Judah and Simeon, who formed the Kingdom of Judah. Nevertheless, Jeroboam's rule was far more offensive than Rehoboam's. He permitted all of the offenses of Judah, plus he instituted the worship of golden calves, ordained non-Levite priests, and altered the festivals. After Jeroboam's death, hostilities erupted between Baasa, king of Israel, and Asa, king of Judah, resulting in Judah gaining the territory of Benjamin. (I King 15:22) Asa instituted religious reforms that inspired devout members of the tribes of Ephraim, Manasseh, Benjamin, and Simeon, who still lived in the Kingdom of Israel, to flee to Judah.

Many also fled south to Jerusalem, which appears to have expanded in size fivefold during this period, requiring a new wall to be built, and a new source of water (Siloam) to be provided by King Ḥezekiah Furthermore, 2 Chronicles 30:1-11 explicitly mentions northern Israelites who had been spared by the Assyrians—in particular, members of Dan, Ephraim, Manasseh, Asher, and Zebulun—and how members of the latter three returned to worship at the Temple in Jerusalem at that time.

In II Kings 17:6, we find: "In the ninth year of Hoshea, the king of Assyria took Samaria, and carried Israel away unto Assyria, and placed them in Halah, and in Habor, on the river of Gozan, and in the cities of the Medes." The Gozan River is the upper part of the Khabur system in the region now known as Kizzel-Ozan. At this time the "cities of the Medes" would have been in an area south of the Caspian Sea. (see also I Chron. 5:26; II Kings 18:11, 19:12; Isaiah 37:12).

Yḥezqiyahu (Ḥezekiah) was a true son of Abraham and David. As noted, he turned many of the survivors from paganism back to their ancestral worship of Hashem. Unfortunately, his only son, Menasha, was weak. As a child, the Assyrian campaigns had left him traumatized. He had found comfort in the illusion that the Babylonians were his allies and friends. Therefore, it was fear of the Mesopotamian empire builders' war machine that pulled him into idolatry immediately after his father's death. "He built again the high places which Ḥezekiah his father had broken down; and he reared up altars for the Ba'alim, and made Asheroth, and worshipped all the host of heaven, and served them." II Chron. 33:3) He also discontinued the daily sacrifices to Hashem in the Jerusalem Temple. In 665 BCE, the king of Assyria, Asshur-bani-pal destroyed Sidon, during his campaign against Egypt. At this time, he took Manasseh as a captive to Babylon (II Chron. 33:11-12), in his thirtieth year, when he was 42 years old. This captivity opened his eyes, and he made a sincerely teshuvah. Unfortunately, the damage was done – the people were steeped in idolatry. (II Chron. 33:13-17) Manasseh's son, Amon, was anointed king in his father's last year, when he was 22 years old, but preferred the worship of idols and was an abusive ruler. After only two years, he was murdered in his own house.

Yoshyahu יֹאשִׁיָּהוּ, better known as Josiah, was only eight-years old when he became king. When he was only sixteen years old, he began learning Torah. For years later, he began a campaign to cleanse the Jewish nation of idolatry. For his first eighteen years, the nation continued to follow the pagan practices of his father Amon. Then in his eighteenth year, when he was 26 years old, he sent his servants to repair and cleanse the Temple in

Jerusalem. Hilkiah, the High Priest, discovered an ancient Torah scroll, written in Moses' hand, hidden in a secret room of the Temple. Shaphan, the scribe, read the scroll to Josiah, and the king began to tremble and tore his clothes.

He sent his servants to find a prophet who could interpret it for him. They found only a woman, the prophetess Huldah. She informed them, "Thus saith the LORD: Behold, I will bring evil upon this place, and upon the inhabitants thereof, even all the curses that are written in the book which they have read before the king of Judah; because they have forsaken Me, and have offered unto other gods, that they might provoke Me with all the works of their hands; therefore, is My wrath poured out upon this place, and it shall not be quenched." (2 Chron., 34:21-30)

Josiah was a strong and righteous king, who like his great-grandfather, Hezekiah, turned whole-heartedly to the worship of Hashem. May Hashem soon send us one like him, who will return those of you who have been lured away by this New Age idolatry.

In 586 BCE, The Babylonians subjugated the Kingdom of Judah and destroyed Solomon's Temple. The ruling classes of Judahite society were exiled to Mesopotamia ("the land between two rivers"). Over the centuries most of the "lost ten tribes" were reunited with the exiled tribes of Judah and became part of Babylonian Jewry.

Such was the sad ending of the first Jewish Commonwealth. It is a testimonial of the powerful pull of pagan religions and hedonism.

> And they have turned unto Me the back, and not the face; and though I taught them, teaching them betimes and often, yet they have not hearkened to receive instruction. But they set their abominations in the house whereupon My name is called, to defile it. And they built the high places of Baal, which are in the valley of the son of Hinnom, to set apart their sons and their daughters unto Molech; which I commanded them not, neither came it into My mind, that they should do this abomination; to cause Judah to sin. And now therefore thus saith the LORD, the G-d of Israel, concerning this city, whereof ye say: It is given into the hand of the king of Babylon by the sword, and by the famine, and by the pestilence. (Jer. 32:33-36)

Fortunately, the chastisement was effective. During those harsh years of exile in Babylon, the wayward descendants of Abraham corrected their path. They returned not only to the Land of Israel but also to the G-d of Israel. They restructured every aspect of their lives basing all on the Torah. From that time until today, our lives have been unshakably rooted in the Torah of Judaism.

> Behold, I will gather them out of all the countries, whither I have driven them in Mine anger, and in My fury, and in great wrath; and I will bring them back

127

unto this place, and I will cause them to dwell safely; and they shall be My people, and I will be their G-d; and I will give them one heart and one way, that they may fear Me forever; for the good of them, and of their children after them; and I will make an everlasting covenant with them, that I will not turn away from them, to do them good; and I will put My fear in their hearts, that they shall not depart from Me. Yea, I will rejoice over them to do them good, and I will plant them in this land in truth with My whole heart and with My whole soul. For thus saith the LORD: Like as I have brought all this great evil upon this people, so will I bring upon them all the good that I have promised them. (Jer. 32:37-42)

It is my personal opinion that, due to the sincere spiritual return (*teshuvah*) of our people to Hashem while in Babylon, we were mercifully permitted a temporary physical return to the Land of Israel, during the Second Temple Era. This is only because we rebuilt our lives based on both the Written and Oral Law. However, we remained under the prophecy of exile (*galut*) until modern times when the prophecy of Jeremiah 32:37-42 of the great ingathering began.

II-3 The Spiritual Revolution Spreads

Following the exile of the kingdoms and Israel and Judah, which resulted in the destruction of Solomon's Temple in the sixth century before the Common Era, dynamic new ideologies that either broke with or greatly modified venerated socio-religious traditions sprang up. To suggest that these changes were the direct result of Israelite or Jewish intervention would make us guilty of unforgivable hyperboles. Yet, it is awe-inspiring that the metaphysical realm on a global scale was shaken as it were by inaudible shock waves after the desecration of that holy site.

Zarathushtra or Zoroaster (650–600 BC or 559–522 BCE) in Persia, Mahavira (599–527 BCE) and Siddhārtha Gautama (558–491 BCE) in India, Lao-Tze (580–500) and Confucius (551–479 BCE) in China, and Socrates (470–399 BC), Plato 428– 348 BCE) and Aristotle (384–322 BCE) in Greece, all exercised a profound influence on the world as we know it. However, we must remain focused on those who directly impacted the conflict between Judaism and Christianity.

II-3.1 Spiritual Revolution of Zarathushtra

From 743 through 705 BCE, the majority of the northern tribes of Israel were deported to the region southwest of Lake Van, northwest of Nineveh (the modern city of Mosul), and to cities south of the Caspian Sea.[44] At the same time, the Median tribes were establishing their empire. Since friends are those with the same enemies, it stands to reason that they supported and perhaps even fought alongside the Medes in the war that destroyed the Assyrians. By the time Cyrus of Persia had taken sole control of this empire in 550 BCE, it extended to central Bactria. Israelite merchants of Lake Van and the Caspian Sea came in contact with Bactrians. Thus, tangency was created with the cultures of the Israelites, Medians, Persians, and Bactrians.

The *Gathas* (songs) that were attributed to Zarathushtra contain elements of archaic language. According to comparative linguistics, his origin can be assigned to the northeastern regions near the Oxus River of ancient Bactria, where it forms the northern border of modern Iran and Afghanistan.[45] Zarathushtra's family name, Spitama, meant "who was brilliant (aggressive) in strength." Through his religious zeal, visionary intellect, and drive to proselytize, Zarathushtra lifted himself from anonymity to a place in history. He became the prophet of one of the most influential religions of the ancient world, Zoroastrianism.[46]

---

44 https://en.wikipedia.org/wiki/Ten_Lost_Tribes
45 William W. Malandra, An Introduction to Ancient Iranian Religion: Readings from the Avesta and Achaemenid Inscriptions (Minneapolis: University of Minnesota Press, 1983), pp. 16-17.
46 Malandra, p. 18.

The Neo-Persian Sassanids (224 to 651 CE) preserved the tradition that the Persian prophet lived 258 years before Alexander. If we understand this to mean Alexander's defeat of Darius III in 331 BCE, then he taught in about -589.[47] This was the year in which the Babylonians began their final siege of Jerusalem, approximately the time in which the Homeric and Hesiodic poems were fixed and preserved in written form, and roughly twenty years before Cyrus of Persia seized the Median throne and began the conquests that would establish the Persian Empire.

Ahuramazda (Wise Lord) was a creator-god and head of the Indo-Iranian pantheon. Then a young priest, Zarathushtra,[48] elevated him to a more exclusive status of primary deity. Zarathushtra taught that it was Ahuramazda who had created twin brothers, *Spenta Mainyu* and *Angra Mainyu.* They embodied the contrasting principles of 'good' and 'evil'. Yasna (30.5) states that regarding the two "Spirits," the followers of the "Lie" (*Druj*) chose the worst actions, and the most beneficent "Spirit" chose "Truth" (*Asha*). Zarathushtra advanced the teaching that through an exercise of free-will one could become an *ashawan,* "righteous man" (lit. 'Truth-possessor'). The righteous were those who followed his trilogy of "good thought, good speech, and good

---

47 This date is, of course, debated, but space does not permit a lengthy discussion of the issue. Most Zoroastrian scholars accept a date around 1200 B.C.E.
48 Zoroaster is the Greek pronunciation.

action." Those who chose not to live by his tenants were the *drugwant* (lit. 'Lie-possessor').[49]

The Achaemenid kings adopted the reforms of Zarathushtra as the guiding principles of the state religion. In his inscriptions, Darius gives this account of his rise to power.

Inscriptions of Darius I (521-486 BCE)

Darius the king says: Ahuramazda, who is the greatest of the gods, created me. He made me king. He delivered the empire to me which is great with good horses and men. By the will of Ahuramazda, Wishtaspa my father and Arshama my grandfather both were living when Ahuramazda made me king over this earth. Such was Ahruamazda's pleasure that of the entire earth he chose me, a man. He made me king over the entire earth. I worshipped Ahuramazda, (and) Ahuramazda bore me aid. He made successful for me what I commanded to be done. All that I did was by the will of Ahuramazda. (DSf8-22)[50]

Since Darius describes Ahuramazda as 'the greatest of the gods', we probably should classify the belief systems as monolatry at this stage. Later, *Ahuramazda* seems to have absorbed the characteristics of *Spenta Mainyu,* becoming the supreme force of good, while *Angra Mainyu* formed his perfect counterbalance as

---

49 Malandra, pp. 19-20.
50 Malandra, p. 50.

the supreme force of evil. In this dualistic perception, mankind was trapped in the middle of an eternal battle between the forces of good and evil. As Zoroastrianism diffused through the Mediterranean world, Ahuramazda was identified with Amon-Re, Zeus, Jupiter, and even Hashem, and *Angra Mainyu* became known as the Devil, which has an interesting etymology. The term "evil" is a Middle English word derived from the Old English *yfel,* meaning morally reprehensible.[51] The term "devil" is from the Middle English word *devel* derived from the Old English *deofol,* which is related to the Late Latin *Diabolus* which in turn is derived from the Greek διαβαλλοσ (*dia + ballein*), meaning "he [who] throws across or through", *i.e.* the slander.[52] Since *yfel* means "evil" then *deofol* would be de-evil – "The Evil One". Thus, this name evokes a mental image in which the "Evil-One", taking lies in his hands, throws them at Truth in an attempt to discredit good and ultimately destroy it.

Nevertheless, the Jewish people never accepted the Persian belief in a dualistic division of G-d. There is no Devil in Judaism. The Satan is simply an angel. Each *malak* מַלְאָךְ is an entity created by Hashem for a specific purpose or mission. Unlike humans, they lack free-will and are capable of only responding to Hashem's

---

51 Merrian Webster's Collegiate Dictionary 10th edition (Spring, MA: Werriam-Webster, Inc.) 1996, p. 402.

52 Ibid, p. 317.

commands. In the Christian Text, the Hebrew term, Satan, was misappropriated to be synonymous with the Devil, which it is not. The term *satan* סטן is from סטה *satah*, 'to turn away'. [53] He is a combination of a tempter, who encourages a person to turn away from Torah, and a prosecuting attorney, who brings the evidence against him before Hashem. Of course, this is a very simplistic analogy. We find a more comprehensive explanation in the *Kabalah*, Jewish mysticism, where Rabbi Moses Cordovero states, "For a destroying angel is created whenever a man sins, as we have been taught: 'He who commits a sin acquires a prosecuting angel who stands before the Holy One. Blessed be He, saying: 'So and so made me'".[54] In this sense, we create the evil that afflicts us by our own free-will sin (*het* lit. "missing the mark").

II-3.2 Spiritual Revolution of Buddha

To relate the story of the Buddha, the Bodhisattva or Enlightened One, we will combine traditional accounts with those recorded in the *Lalitavistara*.[55] While enjoying the pleasures of the heavenly realm, the Bodhisattva was reminded of his aspiration to

---

53 The Guide of the Perplexed, Part II.30 plus footnotes.
54 Cordovero, Moses, The Palm Tree of Deborah, Louis Jacobs translator (New York: Sepher-Hermon Press, 1974) pp. 48-49.
55 https://en.wikipedia.org/wiki/Lalitavistara_S%C5%ABtra

134

attain awakening and teach the path to humans. (Chapter 3) Hence, he entered the human world via the womb of Queen Māyā. (Chapter 6) Tradition has it that Siddhārtha Gautama was the son of King Suddhodana and Queen **Ma**hamayadevi. The adoring parents were informed by an ascetic that their tiny prince would grow to be either a great ruler or the Buddha. His parents preferred the former, so they surrounded him with beauty and happiness. Nothing was denied him. They moved to their palace in Kapilavastu, on the Ganges Plain. When the first day of his schooling arrived, they were dismayed that he had by far surpassed even the most learned of his teachers. (Chapter 10) When he became a young man, they arranged a marriage for him to the most beautiful princess in of all India. Soon Gautama was a proud father. His life was perfect, perhaps too perfect. Haunted by a sense that this was not his true purpose, he became distracted and dissatisfaction.

While traveling outside the palace to visit a royal park, he encountered three people who shocked him – a man suffering from a chronic disease, a corpse, and a religious beggar. Deeply disturbed by these unhappy sights, Gautama began to question his life. Why did he have everything while others had nothing? Even worse, many were afflicted with horrible sufferings, and others were not given a proper burial. (Chapter 14) Renouncing his royal pleasures, Gautama transferred his position and possessions to his son and began his spiritual journey, but his path was not to be an easy one. (Chapter 15)

Māra, the most powerful demon of the realm of desire, was determined to prevent him from obtaining enlightenment. He sent to Gautama his most seductive daughters, but Gautama was not to be deterred. Māra withdrew in defeat. (Chapter 21) He then entered into a strict fasting regime, but abandoned it, stating that one cannot become enlightened when all he can think of is his empty stomach. His goal was to end suffering, so he focused on its cause and discovered the Four Noble Truths. (Chapter 26) People grasp at and cling to impermanent states of being and things. Since we cannot be satisfied and this brings us to evil behavior, we are caught in an endless cycle of repeated rebirths. Each life is painful and unsatisfying. Suffering will only end when one is no longer reincarnated. To accomplish this end of karma, one must cease grasping at and clinging by following the Noble Eightfold Path. In choosing a righteous life guided by a high standard of ethics, Buddhism and Judaism share many similarities. In contrast, we embrace life as the means to reach our spiritual goals, and, since there is too much to learn and to improve in this life, we are thankful for all additional opportunities to further refine ourselves.

3.3 Aristotle and the Jew

136

Between the Assyrian and Babylonian exiles and the conquests of Alexander the Great, the Jews were active in international trade, not only of goods but also in philosophies. I have often wondered if this encounter between Aristotle and an unnamed Jew could have influenced the great thinker's theory of the "Immoveable Mover". Aristotle's disciple, Clearchus, recorded in his first book on *Sleep* (*i.e.* Hypnosis) that he was present when Aristotle related the following story during a dialogue with his students.

> "It would take too long to repeat the whole story, but there were features in that man's character, at once strangely marvelous and philosophical, which merit description. I warn you, Hyperochides,' he (Aristotle) said, 'that what I am about to say will seem to you as wonderful as a dream."
>
> Hyperochides respectfully replied, "That is the very reason why we are all anxious to hear it.'
>
> "Well," said Aristotle, "in accordance with the precepts of rhetoric, let us begin by describing his race, in order to keep to the rules of our masters in the art of narration."
>
> "Tell the story as you please," said Hyperochides.
>
> "Well," he replied, 'the man was a Jew of Coele-Syria. These people are descended from the Indian philosophers.[56] The philosophers, they say, are in

---

56 The footnote for this text reads: "Clearchus in his work On Education traced the descent of the Indian gymnosophists from the Magi, and Diogenes Laertius (proem. 9), who is our authority, adds, "Some assert that the Jews also are descended from the Magi." Jews and Brahmans are also associated by Megasthenes (Clem. Strom. i. 15). I owe this note to Th. Reinach."

India called *Calani*, in Syria by the territorial name of Jews; for the district which they inhabit is known as Judaea. Their city has a remarkably odd name: they call it Hierusaleme (Jerusalem). Now this man, who was entertained by a large circle of friends and was on his way down from the interior to the coast, not only spoke Greek, but had the soul of a Greek.

"During my stay in Asia (347-344 BCE), he visited the same places as I did, and came to converse with me and some other scholars, to test our learning. But, as one who had been intimate with many cultivated persons, it was rather he who imparted to us something of his own." (Flavius Josephus, *Against Apion* I, 176-182. Quoted also by Eusebius. *P.E.* ix. 5.)

When scholars discuss cultural diffusion, they think in scientific terms of moving from a greater to a lesser concentration. Ancient Greece produced a unique, dynamic culture. It dominated large sections of territory over an extensive period of time. By the laws of osmosis, Jewish culture, whose people controlled much less territory and for a much shorter period of time, would have been the receiver of cultural influence and not the provider. However, a paradigm change is like a spark that ignites a forest fire. It comes suddenly and often from the most unexpected source. We cannot say to what extent Torah concepts influenced classical Greek philosophers, but the similarities are tantalizing. Josephus also comments that the essential teachings of Greek philosophers were in perfect harmony with those of the great law-giver, Moses.

Not wishing to step on the toes of devout Grecophiles, it is probably best not to pursue this line of inquiry any further.

II-4 A Spiritual Reactionary

The understanding of Alexander of Macedon is clouded by more than 2300 years of shifting social standards. Though our vision of him is hazed by the mist of legend, his accomplishments still awe us today. Not even the horrors of his atrocities distract from his persona. What drove Alexander to "the ends of the earth?" Was he a genius, a madman, or both? Did he consider himself a god? Somewhere, between the dazzling radiance of Tarn's saint and the nefarious gloom of Badian's monster, existed a man who possessed both the *sophia* of a strategist and the *mania* of a fanatic. In our pursuit of answers, let us examine not only the events of his remarkable life but how reverence for his genius inspired the preservation of the essence of the world into which he was born.

From the evidence in surviving manuscripts, the single most consistent characteristic of Alexander's personality was his intense religiosity.[57] However, his biographers differ widely concerning his claims of divinity. For Worthington, it was Alexander's desire "to outdo his father's achievements" that obsessed him and ultimately drove him to megalomania.[58]

---

57 Ernst Fredricksmeyer, "Alexander's Religion and Divinity," Joseph Roisman, ed., Brill's Companion to Alexander the Great (Boston: Leiden, 2003), p. 253.
58 Ian Worthington, Alexander the Great: A Reader (New York: Routledge Taylor & Francis Group, 2003), p. 236.

According to Milns, the priests of Amon at Siwah profoundly affected Alexander's self-image. He took seriously their declaration that he was indeed the "son of Zeus", and therefore divine. Milns seems to propose that the priests influenced Alexander to the extent that any mockery of his descent from the god would "provoke a violent outburst of rage."[59] Fredricksmeyer blames his mother, Olympia, who, according to Plutarch, claimed that not Philip, but a god, had been his father.[60] Hamilton asserts that his use of the title "son of Zeus-Amon" was nothing more than politically motivated propaganda.[61] Tarns viewed his request for deification by the Greek poleis as a clever political maneuver to circumscribe the Covenant of the League of Corinth that might bound Alexander of Macedon, but could not bind Alexander, the god.[62] At the other extreme, Badian's Alexander, void of noble characteristics, was a psychopathic "master plotter."[63]

Our inquiry will begin with Arrian's simple statement that he was "most conscientious in his devotion to the gods." (Arr. 7.28.1) Alexander was especially careful to honor the cults of the gods and heroes with generous sacrifices, games, and precessions.

---

59 R. D. Milns, Alexander the Great (New York: Pegasus, 1965), p. 107.
60 Fredricksmeyer, p. 255.
61 Joel R. Hamilton, Alexander the Great (Pittsburgh: University of Pittsburgh Press, 1982), p. 77.
62 W.W. Tarn, Alexander the Great: Narrative (New York: Cambridge University Press, 1947), p. 113.
63 E. Badian, "Conspiracies," Boswoth and Baynham, eds., Alexander the Great in Fact and Fiction (Oxford: Oxford University Press, 2000), p. 88.

He officiated at these functions in the capacity of a priest. Not only did he express reverence towards the Greek gods, but also towards the gods of Asia Minor, Egypt, and Babylon. Alexander, like his father Philip before him, was a devout polytheist.[64]

II-4.1 Alexander III of Macedon

The cry to free the cities of the Ionian coast from Persian dominion had echoed in Greek ears for more than 200 years. The greatest propagandist for a Pan-Hellenic offensive against the Persian "barbarians" was Isocrates. (Phil. 104) Philip II had accepted the challenge and was preparing for the invasion of Asia when he was treacherously murdered by his bodyguard, Pausanias. Was Alexander party to his father's murder? Each side of the debate has its supporters. A full exposition of this thorny issue is beyond the scope of this paper. However, since it touches on an essential part of Alexander's religious makeup, we should address it.

Patricide was a heinous crime to the ancient Greeks. Consider the story of Orestes. His mother, Clytemnestra, inspired her lover, Aegisthus, to murder her husband, King Agamemnon.

---

64 The argument presented here is a deliberate polarization of Polytheism and monotheism. Space does not permit an in-depth study of tangents, such as the Persian cult of Anahita and the Greek fire-temple in Bactria. The terms pagan and paganism will be avoided due to the negative connotations associated with them.

Clytemnestra did not take Agamemnon's life with her own hands, yet she shared Aegisthus' guilt for the crime. Orestes avenged his father's murder by also killing his mother. Even though his actions were justifiable, Orestes still experienced pollution, *agos*. Consequently, he was driven from the city until he later found a protector who would take charge of his ritual "purification by blood."[65] Until this point, Orestes remained defiled, and no one could eat with him.

Both Alexander and Olympia were known to have been religious to a degree that we would consider superstitious. To have been party to the death of Philip would have set them at odds with the gods that they worshipped. As far as we know, Alexander was not haunted by anguish of remorse or fear of retribution. Nor was he tormented by his own psychological Furies (evil spirits), as was Orestes in the tragedy of *Aeschylus*.[66] Scholars who implicate Olympia and Alexander in the death of Philip ask us to assume that they were not only unscrupulous hypocrites, but also capable of deceiving the entire population of Macedonia.

Life is usually difficult for the son of famous men. It would be natural for Alexander to compete with his father's military legacy. However, Worthington may have overstated the antagonism between Alexander and his father. The young king,

---

65 Burkert, p. 81.
66 Prof. Dora Pozzi, e-mail message to author, November 26, 2004.

having proven himself on the battlefield, was worthy of the title of Hegemon, supreme military ruler of Greece, before he turned his attention to the Persians.

II-4.2 The Punishment of Thebes

In 335 BCE, Alexander stood before the walls of the ancient city of Thebes. At the age of twenty-one, he was a seasoned warrior, having killed in combat from the age of thirteen. Now that his strategy had won this prize, what should he do with it? Thebes' new crimes were as well-known as its ancient sacrilege. A simple fine would be too lenient for they had arrogantly refused to bow in homage before him. Thebes must be destroyed as a warning to all Greek city-states who refused to join his coalition against the barbaric Persians.

His mother, Olympia, was a devout follower of Dionysos, and Alexander had worshipped him from childhood. Euripides' play, *Bacchae*, expressed dramatically the hubris and blasphemy of Pentheus and the Thebans. They rejected and abused their divine kinsman. The Thebans and their current leaders likewise had rejected him, Alexander, son of Philip, their rightful *hegemon*, supreme military ruler. They had oppressed their neighboring kingdoms, who stood with him and supported his Pan-Hellenistic invasion of Persia. The verdict was clear, the Thebans must pay for their crimes both ancient and present. With that Alexander commanded that the city be leveled to the ground, with all males put to the swords and all females sold into slavery. Only the house and descendants of the poet Pindar were to be spared.

Before moving on, let me just add a thought on Euripides' (480 c.-406 BCE) work. His classic tragedy, the *Trojan Women* (Τρῳάδες, *Troiade* – 415 BCE) was written as a protest against the Athenians' slaughter and enslavement of the people of the island of Melos, during the Peloponnesian War. In 405 BCE, Euripides' play *Bacchae* debuted in Athens. In it, the master play-write created the perfect counterbalance between the primitive, irrational, and blood-thirsty Dionysos in contrast with the industrious, civic-minded Pentheus. I would suggest that via this play Euripides protested the crimes of the brutal Thirty Tyrants of Athens, represented here by Dionysos. Pentheus possibly represents the senseless execution of Leon of Salamis, "a man of high and well-deserved reputation" who "had not committed the shadow of a crime". (Xenophon's *Hellenica* Book II). Socrates (470 c.–399 BCE) had been ordered to arrest Leon, but he refused. Euripides and Socrates were both accused of being leaders of decadent intellectualism. (Plato's *Apology*) Euripides died as an exile in Macedonia five years before Socrates was tried, sentenced to death, and forced to drink hemlock. It is also worth noting that Aesop (620 c.–564 BCE), the famous fabulist, is also said to have been put to death for insulting the gods. Thus, we find that the

Greeks, more so than the Jews, seemed to jump at opportunities to execute troublesome individuals.

II-4.3 The Hellenistic-Persian Conflict

Crossing the Hellespont, Alexander (Ἀλέξανδρος lit. "defender of men")[67] embarked on a heroic struggle to free Asia from Persian oppression. For the young Macedonian monarch, the opportunity to participate in *agônes* of such epic proportions would have been as irresistible as the promise of fabulous wealth in the booty. Alexander rallied Macedonian and Greek troops to avenge the loss of life and the desecration of Greek holy sites during the invasions of Darius and Xerxes. The destruction of the Acropolis in Athens was an affront to the gods which had never been avenged. Religion and politics share a very intimate relationship. In this instance, it is difficult to determine where one ends and the other begins.

Why had the Persians attacked the Acropolis? The obvious answer is to bring the Greeks under Persian rule. For the supporters of this line of argument, the war against the Greeks was simply a military maneuver carrying with it a strong political message. The burning of the Acropolis, the cultural center of the Athenians, which was venerated by all the Greeks, was symbolic

---

[67]
http://www.etymonline.com/index.php?search=Alexander&searchmode=none.

of their destruction. This is, of course, a valid argument yet perhaps too simplistic. Have we possibly missed the wider picture?

The foundation for the conflict between the Greeks and Persians was laid in the Middle Bronze Age (2000-1500 BCE). As pastoral tribes moved southward into Asia Minor some went westward into the Balkans and on into Greece, while others went eastward in the region of Iran and on into northern India. This division created a linguistic and cultural schism, which separated them into the Indo-Europeans (Greeks and Latin based) and Indo-Iranians (Medes/Persians). Though they continued to share many common cultural elements, their religious expressions developed into mirror images of each other.[68] This schism can be illustrated by contrasting the significance of key religious terms.

The Greek word for "justice" is *dike,* and its opposite, "injustice," is *adikia.* Now notice the mirroring of concepts between the Old Iranian *arta* and Old Indian *rta;* both carry the basic meaning of 'truth' and 'cosmic order', albeit in the Vedic tradition it was early on replaced by *dharma,* as cosmic order.[69]

The *ahuras* were revered deities among the Indo-Iranians but were considered malefic forces among the early Indo-Europeans. The etymology of the word "hero" is unclear.[70] The terms *ahura* and *hero* may share such a mirrored relationship.

---

68 Malandra, p. 12.
69 Ibid.
70 Burkert, p. 204.

Also, the *daewas* were revered by the Indo-Europeans but were feared as malefic forces among the Indo-Iranians.[71] *Daimon* in Greek is found in some texts in the sense of 'a divinity' that existed between the gods, *theoi,* and heroes, *heroes* (Pla., Rep. 392a). The term sometimes carried also the meaning of 'destiny'. The epic Greek *daimon*, as a semi-divine being, spirit, or higher power, lacked the negative connotations found in later works.[72]

> Two groups of deities are encountered in the Vedas (Indo-European) and in the Avesta (Indo-Iranian). They are the asuras (Old Indian and Old Iranian *ahura*) and the *devas* and *daiwas*. The earliest parts of the Rgveda indicate that the asuras are the older generation, while the devas are upstarts. Although they may show some signs of antagonism, the two groups coexist in a state of alliance against the common enemy, the anti-cosmic demons, variously called the *danavas, dasas,* and *dasyus*. In the latter parts of the Rgveda and especially in the Brahmanas, whomever, there is a curious development: the asuras as a group (which includes among others Mitra and Varuna!) become the demons, whereas the *devas* emerge as the true gods. The antagonism between *devas* and *asuras* is one of the most common themes of the later Vedic ritual literature, where the two groups frequently fight with one another over the sacrifice.[73]

---

71 It is a testimony to the influence of Zoroastrianism that our concept for an evil spirit is derived from the Iranian daewas, even though the word "demon" is Greek.
72 A passage from Herodotus (5.87.1) also illustrates the concept of daimonion.
73 Malandra, pp. 13, 14.

148

Compare this to Hesiod (*Works and Days*, 122 ff.) who told how the "deathless Gods, who dwelt on Olympus, made a "golden race of mortal men." After their death, they were called the "pure spirits", the *daimones.* Those who took their place, the "generation of silver," were inferior to them. Then the generation of heroes, who were worshipped by the common men, arose. The European Greeks and Indians came to revere *daimones/devas*, while the Iranian, Persians and Medes, revered the *ahuras/asura.*

Two irreconcilable beliefs separate the Persian Zoroastrians and Greek polytheists. The Persians were devoted to one god, Ahura Mazda, at the expense of others. This was a crime in Greek religious myth. The punishment was to be torn apart by those most beloved of the misguided devotee. Due to his exclusive worship of Artemis and rejection of Aphrodite, Hippolytos was torn apart by his beloved horses. When King Pentheus scorned Dionysos, he was torn limb from limb by the *maenads*, who included his mother and aunts. The second was the contrasting nature of the Persian *daewas* and Greek *daimon.*[74] By the time the Christian Texts were widely circulated a *daimon* had the connotation of a *daewas,* an evil spirit or demon.

---

74 Jamsheed K.Choksy, Triumph over Evil: Purity and Pollution in Zoroastrianism (Austin: University of Texas Press, 1989), p. 13.

II-4.4 Earlier Wars

The Greeks believed that Heracles, Athena, and Theseus aided them in the defeat of the forces of Darius at the battle of Marathon in 490 BCE. Darius raised taxes in the summer of 486, thus arousing suspicion that he was gathering resources to finance a new invasion of Greece. Darius' project had to be delayed, however, because of a rebellion in Egypt - sparked by the increase in taxes. In the fall of 486, he fell ill and died. Not until 481 did his son, Xerxes, resume the conflict. During his campaign, he burned the Acropolis in Athens and then returned to Persia. In the spring of 479 at Plataea near the border between Attica and Boeotia, Xerxes' general in Greece, Mardonius, was defeated by the largest Greek army ever to have taken the field. The Theban leaders who had gone over to the Persians (had "medized") were subsequently executed without trial.[75] Xerxes' inscriptions explain his motive for the invasion.

Xerxes' *Daiwadana inscription*
Xerxes the king says: When I became king there was (one country), among these which are written above, (which) revolted. Then Ahuramazda bore me aid. By the will of Ahuramazda I smote that country and set it in its (proper) place. And among these countries was (one) where formerly the *daiwas* were worshipped. Then by the will of Ahuramazda I

---

75 Sarah B Pomeroy, Stanley M. Burstein, Walter Donlan, and Jennifer Tolbert Roberts, Ancient Greece: A Political, Social, and Cultural History (New York: Oxford UP, 1999), pp. 188, 191,192, 196.

destroyed that *daiwa*-temple. And I decreed, "Let the *daiwas* not be worshipped!" There where formerly the *diawas* were worshipped, I worshipped Ahuramazda at the baresman (?) in accordance with Truth (?). And there was another (matter) which had been done badly. I made it good. All that I did I did by the will of Ahuramazda. Ahuramazda bore me aid until I had done what was to be done. You, whoever you are who (shall live) afterwards, if you think, "May I be happy while living and may I be blessed when dead," behave according to that law which Ahuramazda established, worship Ahuramazda at the baresman in accordance with Truth(?). The man who behaves according to that law which Ahuramazda established and worships Ahuramazda at the baresman in accordance with Truth (?), he becomes happy while living and (is) blessed when dead. (XPh 28-56)

For the Persians, the attack on the Acropolis, therefore, was a strike against the "Lie" of the Greeks. This was a confrontation not only between two great political powers competing for territorial control but also, between two religiously polarized cultures. Each side was convinced that they possessed the "Truth" and viewed their opponent as the infidel. Into this "holy war" stepped the young, idealistic Alexander.

The *Iliad* was Alexander's sacred text, and he was careful to follow its precepts throughout his career. He sincerely believed that Achilles was his ancestor through his mother's family and

Hercules from his father's. The exploits of these heroes carried for Alexander the force of orthodoxy. He was a religious absolutist who perceived the Homeric epics to be historic and resisted the trends of his time to rationalize the gods.

II-4.5 His Friends & Foes

As a general, even Alexander's detractors concede that he was bold and brilliant. He easily overcame the Persian forces in his march through the territory of modern Turkey. The only battle of consequence was at the Granicus River, which was remarkable. Victory led to victory and the cities of the Ionian coast were at last "liberated" from the rule of Persians to the rule of Macedonians. In the eyes of Greek intellectuals, the Persians were "barbarians," and true wisdom was the province of Greeks, Egyptians, and Babylonians. If any had doubts about the legitimacy of Alexander's mission, the battle of Issus ended them. The cities of coastal Syria hurried to welcome him.

The harbor cities of the Levantine had surrendered and suffered no harm, yet the Tyrians resisted. They refused to allow Alexander to enter the city to sacrifice to his ancestor Hercules. (Arr.2.16) Tyre was willing to endure the horrors of the siege, possibly even destruction, and enslavement to remain *neutral!* This seems very strange. In contrast, Alexander's request to perform a religious ritual within their walls seemed simple enough.

Josephus tells the story of how, during Alexander's siege of Tyre, the king sent letters to the High Priest of the Jews in Jerusalem demanding assistance and the tribute that they had in the past sent to Darius. (*Jewish Antiquities* XI, 3-6; 317-345) The Priest replied that they had given their oath to Darius and that as long as he lived, they could not violate it. Alexander resolved to attack Jerusalem after conquering Tyre. This also is interesting; like the Tyrians, the Jews were willing to face death for the sake of neutrality!

The religion of the Jews and Persians shared the belief that there is one G-d who is the ruler of the Universe. Within the context of Jewish history, Zarathushtra taught roughly 132 years after the exile of the northern kingdom of Israel by the Assyrians, one year before the first Babylonian exile of the Jews, and twelve years before the destruction of Solomon's Temple (see the map for the distribution of these exiles). Let us entertain a hypothesis that the Tyrians, like the Jews and Persians, were monotheists and that it was the sacrifice to Hercules that offended them.

Josephus continues that when Alexander had taken Gaza, he turned back and marched against Jerusalem. The Greeks called this region Palestine, Παλαιστίωην, from the stem *palaio παλαίω,* which like the Hebrew root of ישראל (Israel), שרה, means 'to fight, strive, wrestle' with someone. The High Priest, who had been warned in a dream by G-d not to fear, went out to meet him on

Mount Scopus. When he saw the "multitude in white garments
and the priests at their head clothed in linen, and high priest in a
robe of hyacinth-blue and gold, wearing on his head the *miter* with
the golden plate on it on which was inscribed the name of G-d, he
(Alexander) approached alone and prostrated himself before the
Name (προσεκύζησε τό όνομὰ) and first greeted the high priest."
(*Antq.* 11. 8. 3-5, Loeb 313-339). The account preserved in the
Babylonian Talmud differs from Josephus on several points (only
one is of importance here). The High Priest and his supporters
walk all night to meet Alexander near a coastal village (Kephar
Saba) northeast of the modern city of Tel Aviv. Yoma 69a
continues: "When he (Alexander) saw Simeon the Just,[76] he
descended from his carriage and bowed down before him והשתחוה
לפניו. They said to him: A great king like yourself should bow
down before this Jew? He answered: His image it is which wins for
me in all my battles."

Since there are no corroborating accounts that Alexander
went to Jerusalem, the Talmudic source seems more acceptable
than Josephus'. The comment that Alexander performed
proskynesis before the priest or his G-d is emphatically rejected by
scholars. It should be pointed out that while the Hebrew root שחה
(without a *vav*) means to "bow down," as when Jacob prostrated
himself before Esau (Gen. 33:3), this variant root שחוה (with a *vav*)

---

[76] Josephus gives Jaddus as the name for the High Priest.

is used in the sense of to "worship." Had Alexander made any motion that the Jews might have interpreted as ritualistic, they later could have applied this term.

Both Josephus and the Talmud agree that the reason for his worship was that something about the priest resembled an image that Alexander had seen in a dream. Arrian also mentions a dream that Alexander had during the siege of Tyre: "That night he had a dream that he was approaching the wall of Tyre and that Hercules was welcoming and escorting him into the city." (Arr. 2.18) These three sources, though differing on the details, concur on an essential element – Alexander had been impressed by the image in a dream.

The Samaritans, who shared not only the land of Palestine but also the religious tenants of the Jews, killed Andromachus, who was left as commander of the region by Alexander when he entered Egypt. Later, as he marched in search of Darius, he ordered the deaths of those guilty of this crime. (Curtius 4.8.9-10) Among Darius' ethnically mixed forces at Gaugamela were men from this region: "On the right wing were drawn up the forces from Hollow Syria and Mesopotamia." (Arrian 3.4) "The right was composed of people from greater Armenia, Cadusia, Cappadocia, Syria, and Media, and these also had fifty scythed chariots." (Curtius 4.12.12) Josephus (Ap. 1. 22 or Loeb 169-171; *Antq*. 8. 262) quotes Herodotus (2. 104) in identifying the Palestinian Syrians with the

Jews. The Israelites captive of the Assyrian campaigns were scattered through the regions of northern Iraq and Iran (II Kings 16:6). The Babylonian captives were concentrated in the cities of Babylon (II Kings 25:28) and Susa (Esther 1:2). From this we can surmise that while Alexander was resting his troops in Egypt, the monotheists of the region were using a plea of neutrality to disguise their active support for Darius.

II-4.6 As God/King of Egypt

From Archaic times the Greeks had held the Egyptians in high esteem. While in Egypt, Alexander journeyed to the oasis of Siwah to inquire of the oracle of Amon. This long trek through the desert seemed strange since the traditional temple/oracle of Amon-Ra was at Karnak beside the Nile in Upper (southern) Egypt. The Egyptians had welcomed Alexander as a deliverer because the Persians had persecuted their traditional polytheistic faith. The Egyptian priests may have moved their center of worship to this remote site to save it from destruction by the monotheistic Persians. At the oracle, the priests declared Alexander the son of Zeus-Amon-Ra. Milns has asserted that this experience had a profound effect on the young king, but Hamilton maintains that he used the title as propaganda.

Plutarch recounts Olympias' declaration that Zeus, not Philip was Alexander's father. Perhaps this was the secrets that the priests of Siwah communicated to Alexander, which he promised to relate to his mother alone. It was not that Philip was any less his father, but that in a mystical sense he had acted as a proxy for the god when Olympias had conceived their son. Alexander was divine in the same sense as the kings of Egypt had always been. He was Horus just as the last king, Nectanebo his royal Egyptian "father," was now Osiris. Since we lack a primary source written either by Alexander or a companion of his, we cannot say how this revelation affected him. However, we do not see a dramatic change in personality. It is doubtful that Olympias was aware of these stories until years later, or perhaps she never heard of them at all.

II-4.7 Alexander the Bacchant

After his victory at Gaugamela, Alexander entered Babylon and ordered "its inhabitants to rebuild the temples that Xerxes has torn down, especially the temple of Bel, the god the Babylonians honour most of all… In Babylon, too, Alexander met the Chaldaeans. He followed all their advice regarding religious offerings in Babylon, and in particular sacrificed to Bel following the prescription they gave him." (Arrian 2.16.4) As in Egypt, Alexander reestablished the polytheistic religions that the Persian monotheists had suppressed.

The heart of Persian power, both political and religious, was the beautiful city built by Darius I that the Greeks called Persepolis, "Persia's city".[77] During a drunken, orgiastic victory celebration, the courtesan Thais and his *hetairoi* (champions) incited their king to inflict the ultimate blow of defeat on their ancestral foe. Wearing a Dionysian wreath and robes, Alexander led them as they torched the palace. According to Zoroastrian tradition, they found the sacred text of Zarathushtra written in gold letters on cowhide and destroyed them along with the palace.[78] For the following 500 years, his religious teachings survived only in oral tradition. A few days later, Darius III met a miserable death at the hands of his nearest friends and relatives. With his death and the destruction of their capitol and sacred texts, the Persians' insults to the Greek gods had been avenged, and proper polytheistic practices were reinstated in Babylon. There now remained only one final stronghold of the teaching of Zarathushtra, his home territory of Bactria.

Alexander spent more time conquering Bactria than any other region. The Bactrians' resistance was relentless guerilla warfare. Plots against his life and unrest among his troops were symptoms of the severe stress of battle fatigue. Now more than ever, Alexander turned to drinking parties. As he became

---

77 George Rawlinson, Seven Great Monarchies of the Ancient Eastern World (New York: John B. Alden, Publisher, 1885), Vol. 2. p. 270.
78 Malandra, p. 30.

increasingly infatuated with the "Frenzied One,"[79] his behavior became more bizarre.

> In the Dionysos cult, ecstasy plays quite a unique role, with the result that Dionysos almost acquires a monopoly over enthusiasm and ecstasy, but this ecstasy is ambivalent. In theology the frenzy may appear once again as a catastrophe sent by the implacable Hera, but since the god himself is the Frenzied One, the madness is at the same time divine experience, fulfillment, and an end in itself; the madness is then admittedly almost inseparably fused with alcoholic intoxication.[80]

He remained in the rough country of Bactria until all military resistance, and probably teachers of Zoroastrianism, had been crushed. His most brilliant adversary, Spitamenes, was beheaded by his own troops and the trophy sent to Alexander (Arrian 4.17.7). However, Curtius says (8.3.1-16) this act was done by his own wife! Dismemberment by those nearest to the victim is Bacchic in nature. With Spitamenes' death, Macedonian military supremacy was assured.

The Alexander who entered India was not the Alexander who had entered Egypt. Since Persepolis, Alexander increasingly identified with Dionysos. The frenzied massacre of virtually

---

79 The state of ecstasy is a common tangent between the worship of Dionysus in ancient Greeks with the "Hari-Krishna" of Hindus and the "Speaking in Tongue" of the Christians.
80 Burkert, p. 110.

defensive villages north of the Indus resembled more the actions of Dionysos. We appear to have lost Alexander somewhere in the rugged mountains of Bactria. Δαιμοωάω is to be possessed or mad due to a divine visitation. Was Alexander a bacchant *daimonaon* and completely under the control of Dionysos?

Such frenzied worship sounds remarkably like the Hindi worshipper of Krishna. Could we be dealing with deities from a common Indo-European concept? Krishna, like his Greek counterpart Dionysos, led his devotees into states of religious ecstasy.

> It was on the basis of such stories that people designated certain individuals by the tribal name "Nysaeans", and also called a city amongst them "Nysa" (as being founded by Dionysos) and the mountain overlooking the city "Meron". They adduced as their reason the ivy growing in the region, along with the vine, which did not, in fact, reach the fruit-bearing stage (the grapes falling off before they darkened because of the excessive rainfall) They also identified the Sudracae as descendants of Dionysos because of the existence of the vine in their culture and the extravagance of their parades; their kings made military expeditions in bacchic fashion, and conducted their other official marches to the sound of drums and wearing flowery robes (a custom amongst the other Indians, as well). (Strabo, 15.8)

The major competitor of Hinduism in Indian was Buddhism. The Buddha, Siddhartha Gautama, began preaching in

160

India roughly 26 years after Zarathushtra. His father, a chief of the *kshatriya* clan. was of the warrior/king caste, *Shakyas,* in the northeastern region of the Ganges valley. For 237 years before Alexander, his followers were spreading his doctrine. This system of *dharma*, "truth of reality," taught release from the "wheel of deaths and rebirths" and that there was no deity worthy of worship. *Nivanna* could be reached by understanding the "Four Noble Truths: Life inevitably involves suffering, is imperfect and unsatisfactory; suffering originates in our desires; suffering will cease if all desires cease; there is a way to realize this state: the Noble Eightfold Path."[81]

By the time Alexander's army engaged Porus with his war-elephants on the Hydaspes River, Buddhism had spread from the Ganges Valley over most of Northern India, and polytheistic Hinduism was restricted in the south and along the western coast. Alexander urged his men to press further southeastward into the Ganges Valley and deeper into Buddhist territory. But the men were homesick and tried of perpetual war. They mutinied and refused to continue.

---

81 Mary Pat Fisher, Living Religions, 5th edition (Upper Saddle River, NJ: Prentice-Hall, 2002), pp. 141-148.

II-4.8 Alexander, the Divine

What drove Alexander to the ends of the earth? We have here considered, Alexander, the "true believer", who led a polytheistic religious revitalization movement against the heresies of monotheism. His personal devotion provided the catalyst that began the process of Hellenism, which meshed the pantheons of the East and West into one polytheistic system. Our Alexander did not believe in the "brotherhood" of *all men*, but he did seem to strive for the brotherhood of all polytheists.

Was he a genius, a madman, or both? From the perspective of his military allies the Greeks, Egyptians, and Babylonians, he was the embodiment of Tarn's saint. However, from the perspective of his military adversaries the Zoroastrians, Jews, and Buddhists, he was Badian's bloody monster. Seneca (*On Tranquility of Mind*, xvii. 10-12) expressed it best: "For whether we believe with the Greek poet that 'sometimes it is a pleasure also to rave,' or with Plato that 'the sane mind knocks in vain at the door of poetry,' or with Aristotle that 'no great genius has ever existed without some touch of madness' - be that as it may, the lofty utterance that rises above the attempts of others is impossible unless the mind is excited. Perhaps Aristotle was thinking of Alexander when he made this observation.

Did Alexander consider himself a god or was this propaganda? When he leveled Thebes, he acted with the fury (*mênis*) of Achilles. When he took Tyre, he entered into the *mythos* of a Herculean *hero*. In Egypt, he ascended the throne as Pharaoh, the immortal king/god. At Gaugamela, he personified Ares. In the flames of Persepolis, he was the incarnate of Dionysos. In the monsoon down-pour at Hydaspes, Alexander, emerged supreme, "stealing Zeus's thunder."[82] He stamped a memorial that clearly stated he was indeed ὁ Διὸς υἱὸς - the "Son of God/Zeus", and for centuries his devotees prayed and anticipated his divine return.

II-4.9 To the Victors go the Spoils

The true beneficiaries of Alexander's exploits were his generals, who fought each other to the death for supremacy of his over-extended empire. Two generals emerged as the triumphant power players—Ptolemy I Soter (Savior), so called because he saved Alexander's life during the siege of that fateful Indian city, and Seleucus I Nicator (Victor), so called because he retook Babylon from another general, Antigonus. Ptolemy ruled Egypt and its surrounding territory, while Seleucus held the eastern provinces. Ptolemy I, who was an ally of Seleucus I, met Demetrius, the son of Antigonus, in a decisive battle near Gaza. For the Jews this meant only one thing, they were now subservient to the Greeks. (*Antq.* XII, 1-3)

---

82 Frank L. Holt, Alexander the Great and the Mystery of the Elephant Medallions (Los Angeles: University of California Press, 2003), p. 153.

Later, Seleucus established his new capitol, Antioch on the Orontes River (in Modern Turkey), and, in -292, he made his son co-regent. Eleven years later, Seleucus died and Antiochus I became sole ruler. As a token of respect, the new king continued counting from the beginning of his father's regal power instead of starting a new one with his. His sons continued the custom and, thus, the Seleucid Era begins with his victory at Babylon in 312 BCE.

In -310, Ptolemy I defeated Demetrius at Gaza. He then marched to Jerusalem under the pretense of offering sacrifice. The Jews did not oppose him because until then he had not acted in a hostile manner. However, when the people were resting on the Shabbat, he attacked and gained control of the city. Ptolemy claimed the region and took many captives from Jerusalem as well as the surrounding region back to Egypt. He settled them mostly in Alexandria to work at building the new city. In turn, he transferred hundreds of Greeks and Egyptians to Judaea and Samaria. (*Antq.* XII, 4-8) In this way, he mimicked the Assyrian conquerors.

Ptolemy I's son, Ptolemy II Philadelphus, commanded his librarian, Demetrius Phalerius, to collect copies of all the wisdom written in the world. In Ptolemaic Egypt, the Egyptian tradition merged with Greek astronomy and Babylonian astronomy, with the city of Alexandria in Lower Egypt becoming the center of scientific activity across the Hellenistic world. They also desired to have the Hebrew Scriptures translated into Greek. To this end 72 scholars, "six from each tribe", were placed in separate rooms. Miraculously, all 72-versions matched exactly. This story, or versions or it, are found in the writings of Philo of Alexandria, Flavius Josephus, and St. Augustine, Letter of Aristeas to Philocrates, and in Babylonian Talmudic, Tractate Megillah 9a/b. This first translation of the Hebrew Scriptures, completed in 282 BCE, is known as the Septuagint (LXX). It was the ransom paid for the release of 120,000 Jewish slaves. (*Antq.* XII, 11-59) Most of the new freedmen, however, chose to remain in Alexandria.

One would think that Jews would find pride in that this translation has had a profound impact on World culture. Nonetheless, it is included among those many catastrophes that sadly befell the Jewish nation over the centuries, which include the Inquisition and Holocaust. Perhaps this is because so many of them can be traced back to that translation. For in it, Hashem often rebuked His people via the prophets for their sins. This was done as a loving Father would do to correct His beloved sons and daughters. However, until this day, millions of people have misinterpreted these passages as a total rejection of an irredeemable people. Nothing could be further from the truth for in each case they made *teshuvah* (lit. "return") or repentance. But our enemies prefer to ignore those sections in Scripture. Regardless, we must return to our story.

Part II. How we got where we are

II-5. Jewish Conflicts and Sectarianism

At about this time the distinct philosophical differences began to crystalize within the tiny Jewish nation. Most scholars concur that the four Jewish philosophies, as they are called by Josephus, actually represented the major political factions that had developed during the Second Temple Period, shortly after the conquests of Alexander of Macedonia. However, Josephus states clearly: Ἰουδαίοις φιλοσοφίαι τρεῖς ἦσαν **ἐκ τοῦ πάνυ ἀρχαίου τῶν πατρίων**, ἥ τε τῶν Ἐσσηνῶν καὶ ἡ τῶν Σαδδουκαίων, τρίτην δὲ ἐφιλοσόφουν οἱ Φαρισαῖοι λεγόμενοι. "The Jewish philosophies were three **from the absolute beginning of the traditions**: that of the Essenes and that of the Ṣadducees, and the ones being called Pharisees are expounding a third." (*Antq.* 18, 11) Was Josephus simply expressing national pride, and thus overstating the antiquity of these sects? Or, should we pause to reconsider their origins, interactions and fate?

During his adolescence, Josephus explored these three major sects (53-57 CE). He seems to have been especially attracted to the Essenes and was the disciple of an ascetic named Bannus for three years. However, he returned home and remained a devout Pharisee until he died in about 100 CE. (Life, 9-12)

II-5.1 The Ṣadducees

This sect took its name from the Zadok (צָדוֹק = Tzadoq = Ṣadōc), who was the High Priest in the days of David and Solomon. They were assured of holding the High Priesthood in the future Jerusalem Temple.

וְהַכֹּהֲנִים הַלְוִיִּם בְּנֵי צָדוֹק אֲשֶׁר שָׁמְרוּ אֶת־מִשְׁמֶרֶת מִקְדָּשִׁי בִּתְעוֹת בְּנֵי־יִשְׂרָאֵל מֵעָלַי
הֵמָּה יִקְרְבוּ אֵלַי לְשָׁרְתֵנִי וְעָמְדוּ לְפָנַי לְהַקְרִיב לִי חֵלֶב וָדָם נְאֻם אֲדֹנָי ה'...

"And the Cohens (Priests) - the Levites, the Sons of Zadok who guarded my holy charge at the time the Sons of Israel strayed from Me, let them draw near Me and they will minister and stand before Me to sacrifice to Me the fat and blood – the word of my Lord... (Ezekiel 44:15)

Josephus was less inspired by the Ṣadducees, whom he described as cut and dry. They were "boorish" towards each other and very argumentative. For them, G-d is too omnipotent to be associated with the evils of mundane life. They denounced any form of predestination and ascribed all good and evil to mankind's free-will choices. (*Wars* II, 164-166) They observed only the Written Law and scorned the Oral traditional Law with its rabbinic interpretations. They believed that the soul perished along with the body, and considered it a virtue to dispute with their teachers. Though they were the men of the highest standing, the masses would not follow them, and so they submitted to the decisions of the Pharisees." (*Antq.* XVIII, 16-17)

The Talmud relates that they broke with tradition: "The Mishna relates: At the conclusion of all blessings recited in the Temple, those reciting the blessing would say: Blessed are You Lord, G-d of Israel, until everlasting [*ha'Olam*], 'the world'. But when the Ṣadducees strayed and declared that there is but one world and there is no World-to-Come, the Sages instituted that at the conclusion of the blessing one recites: From everlasting [*ha'Olam*] to everlasting [*ha'Olam*]." (Mas. Berachoth 54a)

Beginning in *Antiquities* XX, 224, Josephus gives a detailed account of the high priests. We are only concerned here with those of the Maccabean and Hasmonean periods. Shimon haTzadeq ("the Righteous or Just") had three sons who all became high priests (*Antq.* XII, 238)., Jason (from the Greek accusative Ἰησοῦν for Yoshua), did not hold office for long before the Greeks deposed him. His brother, Onias Menelaus I, was put to death, and they installed Yohaḥim (Jacimus), who was from a different line of priests for three years. It was at this time that Onias III, the nephew of Onias Menelaus, built a Temple in Egypt like the one in Jerusalem. (*Antq.* XX, 224)

Josephus then reports that the office of the high priest was vacant for a period of seven years, which would have been from 158 to 152/1 BCE. (*Antq.* XX. 237) This hiatus must have been while the Maccabeans were engaged on the battlefield with the Syrio-Grecian armies. But, when it was stabilized, Jonathan Hasmonean returned. He then held the position of high priest for seven years, until he was murdered by Tryphon. (*Antq.* XIII 45-46) Jonathan's brother, Simon, became high priest for eight years but was then murdered by his son-in-law, Ptolemy. Simon was the last of the Maccabeans, who fought so valiantly to regain Jewish independence in their hereditary territory.

II-5.2 The Essenes

Josephus tells us that the Essenes cultivated peculiar sanctity. They shunned pleasures as a vice and perfected the control of passions as a special virtue. Except for one group, most of them refrained from marriage, but they all adopted the children of others. They despised riches and held all property in common. They resembled children in dress and deportment and took new garments only when those were worn out. They worked in crafts or agriculture all day, ate together, wore only linen, bathed in cold water for purification, said grace before and after eating, ate in silence, and did not speak until after the morning prayers, which had been handed down to them from their forefathers.

They settled in large numbers in every town, welcomed guests, and shared resources with members from other communities, but carried nothing with them except weapons for

self-protection. (Wars II, 120-161) They numbered about 4000.
They did nothing without orders from their superiors, except
helping the needy. They gave no presents to relatives, were
champions of fidelity, and ministers of peace. The only oath they
swore was to their sect. They concealed nothing from the members
of the sect, and would never tell their secrets. They were stricter
than all others regarding the Shabbat. Attributing all things to Fate
and regarding the soul as immortal, they left everything in the
hands of G-d. (*Antq.* XVIII, 18-22) Of all the praise that Josephus
lauds on the Essenes, the most constant one was their ability to
foretell the future.

From where did the Essenes derive their name? In Modern
Hebrew, they are called אִיסִי. Josephus seems to give a key in the
section where he describes the priestly apparel. τῷ δὲ διακένῳ τοῦ
ἐνδύματος σύνεισι περίτμημα σπιθαμῆς τὸ μέγεθος χρυσῷ τε καὶ
τοῖς αὐτοῖς τῷ ἐφώδη βάμμασι διηνθισμένον: **ἐσσὴν** μὲν καλεῖται,
σημαίνει δὲ τοῦτο κατὰ τὴν (Ἑλλήνων γλῶτταν λόγιον: "But into
the gap in this vestment is inserted a piece of the dimensions of a
span, variegated with gold and with the same colors as the ephod;
it is called *essen* a word signifying in Greek speech logion, the
"Word of God". (*Antq.* III, 163) The Mesoretic Text, that
corresponds to this selection, reads־אֶל־**חֹשֶׁן** הַמִּשְׁפָּט אֶת־הָאוּרִים וְאֶת
וְנָתַתָּ הַתֻּמִּים, "Into the **Breastplate** of Judgement shall you place
Urim and the Tumim, (Exodus 28:30)

The meanings of the terms, ἑσσῆν and חֹשֶׁן, are both obscure. A more precise transliteration of חֹשֶׁן into Greek would be χόσην. The sound in Greek nearest to the Hebrew ה is the χό, but χ phonetically corresponds to the Hebrew כ. A better transliteration of ἑσσῆν into Hebrew would probably be אֶסֶן. The *dagesh* gives the ס a "sse" sound.

What do these two terms have in common? They are both nouns and both end with a ן. The final נ can be an archaic form that transforms a verb into a noun. As an example, adding the second suffix ן to שִׁקֵּר (intense form), which means "to lie intentionally," gives us שַׁקְרָן, "a liar." Therefore, the possibility that these terms are both verbal nouns should be explored. Could חֹשֶׁן be derived from the verb חשה, which means "to be still or quiet?" By the same token, could הֶסֶן be derived from the verb הסה, which also means "to still or silent someone?"

הסה is a rare verb, occurring only twice in the biblical text. In Numbers 13:30 it is used alone, but in Nehemiah 8:11 is linked with חשה. וַיַּהַס כָּלֵב אֶת־הָעָם אֶל־מֹשֶׁה "Caleb silenced the people toward Moses..." (Numbers 13:30) וְהַלְוִיִּם **מַחְשִׁים** לְכָל־הָעָם לֵאמֹר **הַסּוּ** כִּי־הַיּוֹם קָדֹשׁ "And the Levites //**were**// **quieting/stilling** all the people saying: **Be silent** because the day is holy..."

It does seem that Josephus has provided us with the key in the passage describing the Essenes. οὔτε δὲ κραυγή ποτε τὸν οἶκον οὔτε θόρυβος μιαίνει, τὰς δὲ λαλιὰς ἐν τάξει παρα-χωρ-οῦσιν ἀλλήλοις. καὶ τοῖς ἔξωθεν ὡς μυστήριόν τι φρικτὸν ἡ τῶν ἔνδον σιωπὴ κατα-φαίν-εται. "Not at any time does screaming nor uproar defile the household. And they make way for each other in order of conversation. To those outside, their essential silence is viewed as some awesome, secret-rite." (*Wars* II, 132-133)

It is also interesting that in post-Biblical Hebrew, חשה takes the form of חֲשַׁאי, meaning "a secret." Then there could also be a connection between the "Breastplate of Judgment" חֹשֶׁן, the Essen הֶסֶן, and קוֹל דְּמָמָה דַקָּה "the small, still voice," through which prophecy was revealed to Elijah in the cave (I Kings 19:12). This becomes clear when we consider that the intransitive verb דְּמַם means "he was made silent" and דַקָה means "minute." Hence, we find a direct link between prophecy and silence.

Rabbi L. H. Schiffman, who assisted in the translation of the "Ḥalakhic Letter", identifies the authors as temple priests, who broke away from the Ṣadducees. The cause of the schism that created the so-called "Dead Sea Sect" was a series of disputations over the sacrificial rituals and purity laws.

> Because the Ṣadducees, in this and many other cases, share the same positions we find in the Halakhic Letter, we can convincingly show, using this and other Qumran texts, that the Qumran sect had a substratum of Ṣadducean halakhic views... we can conclude that the Ḥalakhic Letter was written by the collective leadership of the sect in those initial years.

This explains why the teacher does not appear in this text.[83]

These are some of our (legal) rulings [regarding Go]d's [Torah] which are [some of the] rulings of [the] laws which w[e hold, and a]ll of them are regarding [sacrifices] and the purity of... (Halakhic Letter B1-3)

[You know that] we have separated from the mainstream of the peo[ple and from all their impurities and] regarding these matters. But you k[now that there cannot be] found in our hands dishonesty, falsehood, or evil. (Halakhic Letter C7-9)[84]

The sectarians tell us when this schism occurred.

And in the period of wrath, three hundred ninety years after He had handed it (the Temple) over to Nebuchadnezzar king of Babylonia, He remembered them (Israel) and caused to grow from Israel and Aaron the root of a plant (i.e., the sect). (Zadokite Fragments 1:5-7)[85]

If we take 390 years from the date most accepted by historians for the destruction of Solomon's temple, 586 BCE, we arrive at the year 196 BCE when the Dead Sea Sect began.

Then they understood their transgression and knew that they were guilty. They were like blind (men) groping on the road for twenty years. Then G-d paid

---

83 Lawrence H. Schiffman, Reclaiming the Dead Sea Scrolls (Philadelphia: Jewish Publication Society, 1994), p. 87.
84 Schiffman, pp. 84-5.
85 Schiffman, p. 90.

attention to their deeds for they sought Him whole-heartedly, and He set up for them a Teacher of Righteousness to direct them in the ways of his (the teacher's) heart. (Zadokite Fragments 1:8-11 = D^{d}2 I 12-15)[86]

Hence, we find that the "Teacher of Righteousness" began his leadership in 176 BCE.[87] Rabbi Schiffman was of the opinion that, since the Teacher was not mentioned in the Letter, then it was written before he arrived. Yet, it could be that he is not mentioned because he wrote it in conjunction with the older leadership.

Let's return to Josephus' report that the office of the high priest was vacant for a period of seven years, which we identified as between 158 and 152/1 BCE. (*Antq.* XX. 237) This hiatus in the High Priesthood is curious. Are we to believe that there were no sacrificial services performed for seven years and that Yom Kippur was simply canceled during that time? It is reasonable, therefore, to suggest that the Ḥalakhic Letter was in response to news from Jerusalem of a military emergency. While the Maccabeans were engaged on the battlefield with the Syrio-Grecian armies, the sectarians assumed responsibility for the temple services. But,

---

86 Schiffman, p. 92.
87 Rabbi Schiffman identifies the usurpers of the Temple services, who cause the schism and self-imposed exile of the founders of the Dead Sea Sect, as Pharisees under the Hasmonaean high priests. I have simply demonstrated the dates according to sectarian accounts.

when it was stabilized, Jonathan Hasmonean returned and forced the sectarians to flee.

How then can we account for Josephus' claim of antiquity for the Essenes as a recognized sect? The priestly sect that broke away from mainstream worship may have been joined by another, much older mystical sect that was derived from the mysterious, חֶבֶל נְבִיאִים / προφήταις ἐκκλησιάζουσιν, "the Gathering of Prophets" (I Samuel 10:5 / *Antq.* VI, 56) Thus, the sect began its transition from a Ṣadducean sect to the Essenes after other fringe groups joined them in the desert.

The oldest scrolls of the Dead Sea sect are written in paleo-Hebrew (First Temple Era) characters and Aramaic on papyri. Aramaic was the *lingua franca* of the Late Babylonian and Persian Empires and was the common language of the Second Temple era Jews. Their dates are based on paleographic evidence; however, some have been carbon-dated to the third or even fourth centuries BCE but most are from the second century BCE through the first CE.[88]

II-5.3 The Pharisees

In Wars II, 162-163, Josephus gives only a brief description of the Pharisees. They were considered the most accurate

---

88 Schiffman, p. 32.

interpreters of the laws and were the leading sect. While accepting, on one hand, predestination, they still maintained that men have been granted free-will by G-d. The soul is imperishable, but only the souls of the good pass into another body, while the souls of the wicked suffer eternal punishment.

However, in *Antiquities* XVIII, 12-15, his tone takes to turn towards the superlative. The Pharisees follow the very highest standards. They simplify their mode of living, making no concession to luxury and following only the guidance considered good by their doctrine. Of the greatest importance to them is observing traditional commandments, showing respect to the elders, and never contradicting them. Due to their righteous lifestyle and doctrine, they were extremely influential among the people. Thus, all prayers and sacred rites of divine worship were performed according to their exposition.

The name, Pharisees (פְּרוּשִׁים), is derived from פָּרַשׁ, meaning "stretched, and extended." A פָּרוּשׁ is an "explanation, commentary, or interpretation," as well as, indicating one who is a "seceder, abstemious and saintly." Their antiquity and authority are assured in the Mishna, Mas. Avoth Chapter 1. "Moses received the Torah at Sinai and transmitted it to Joshua, Joshua to the Elders, the Elders to the Prophets, and the Prophets to the Men of the Great Sanhedrin (Jewish Senate)." In support of this, Josephus states: "The forefathers assigned the task of keeping their records to their chief priests and prophets... Seeing that with us it is not open to everybody to write the records and that there is no discrepancy in what is written; seeing that, on the contrary, the prophets alone had this privilege." (Ap. I. 29, 37) The rabbis are the heirs of the Pharisaic traditions. Anyone converting to Judaism today is converting to Pharisaic/Rabbinic Judaism, except those who follow either the Karaites or the Noahites.

II-5.4 Wars of the Maccabean

Ptolemy I and his sons ruled Egypt as the incarnate of Amon-Re. There are advantages to ruling as a demi-god. Awe-inspired subjects were less likely to plot the ruler's assassination. Perhaps this, coupled with human jealousy, prompted Seleucus' descendant, Antiochus IV, to take on the surname Epiphanes, and thus, became Ἀντίοχος Δίος ὁ Ἐπιφανής – "Antiochus, the God/Zeus Manifested".

Antiochus found it expensive to maintain such an extensive empire. Also, the cultural and religious diversity of its population proved bothersome. To solve the financial issues, he reasoned that as the manifestation of Zeus, the king of the gods, all of the wealth accumulated in all existing temples within his domain should by right be his. Therefore, whenever the empire was pressed for funds, he felt that he had the right to plunder them. To solve the thorny issue of diversity, he imposed an intensive cultural

178

unification policy on all his subject states. The Olympic Games were used to win the hearts of the youth and those who accepted Greek religion were rewarded. In 168 BCE, which was 143 SE, he attacked Jerusalem and looted the Temple. (*Antq.* XII. 246) He rewarded those Jews who assisted him and killed those who did not. Two years later in -166, which was 145 SE, he returned and reinstated his man, Menelaus, as High Priest and murdered many pious Jews.

> "[A]s it happened, in the *145th [SE] year*, on the 25th day of the month, which by us is called *Chasleu* and by the Macedonians *Apellaios*, in the [2nd year of the] *153rd Olympiad*, the king [Antiochus] went up to Jerusalem, and pretending to offer peace, overcame the city by treachery." (Flavius Josephus, *Antq.* XII. 248)

He then issued an edict prohibiting major Jewish festivals, Sabbath observance, traditional Temple sacrifices, and circumcision. He set up an idol of Zeus, which probably had a striking resemblance to himself, in the Temple, and sacrificed a pig, the sacred animal of the Aphrodites/Adonis[89] cult, on the holy altar of the Jews.

As can be imagined, his Jewish subjects did not appreciate these tyrannical policies. Antiochus demanded that the "sacred" pig be sacrificed by the Jewish priests throughout the country. In

---

89 The cult of Aphrodites/Adonis to that of Ishtar/Baal, during the time of Ahaz and Jezebel, and that of Inanna/Tammuz, during the time of Avraham.

the rural town of Modiin, the local priest, Mattathias Hasmoneus, refused to conduct the required sacrilegious sacrifice; so, another Jew stepped forward to accommodate them. In a fury, Mattathias and his sons rushed forward and killed him and the soldiers. He cried out, "Whoever is zealous for our country's laws and worship of G-d, let him come with me!" Thus, he began what was both a civil war against the Hellenized Jews and a "holy" war for religious freedom against the forces of the Greco-Syrian king.

After being in command for a year, Mattathias fell ill and died. He was succeeded by his son Judah, also known as Maccabaeus, in 146 SE, which was in the summer of 165 BCE. (*Antq.* XII. 265-286) There are three explanations for the name Maccabee מַכַּבִּי, *Makkabi*. The best know is from the Hebrew word for "hammer". They continued to hammer the Greeks until they won. The next two are acronyms. One is formed from the name and title of their patriarch, *Matityahu Kohen ben Yochanan"* – Mattathias, Priest, son of Jonathan. *The other is* for a battle cry from the Torah, "Who is like You our Master, Hashem!"

> But when they came to Jerusalem with the entire multitude and found the temple desolate, the gates burned down and plants growing up by themselves in the sanctuary because of the desolation, he (Judas) began to lament... And when he had carefully purified it... on the *twenty-fifth* of the month *Chasleu* (Kislev),.. on the same day on which, three years before, their holy service had been transformed into an impure and profane form of worship... And the

180

temple was renovated... in the 148th year (SE), in the 154th Olympiad." (*Antq.* XII, 317-321)

Thus, the Temple was rededicated on 12 December -163 CE. Unfortunately, this did not end the war with the Greeks. How could anyone expect that it would? The Seleucid and Ptolemaic Dynasties were the cultural heirs of Alexander III, whose life was defined by his love of war, conquest, and traditional beliefs.

Lured by stories of the fabulous treasure of the Temple of Artemis, Antiochus IV left his throne but never returned. His youthful son, Antiochus V Eupator, gathered a great army fully equipped with elephants and attacked Judea in -161, which was the year 150 SE and a sabbatical year. Judah's brother, Eleazar Auran, died during this battle. *(Antq. XII, 378)* News of a new threat to his rule forced Eupator to enter into a peace treaty with Judah and return home. However, the war continued to shadow the Maccabeans. In -151 Judah died and the control of the country was passed on to his brother Jonathan. His rule, like his brother's, was one of constant danger and war. Another brother, John Gaddis, died during one of those seemingly endless battles. The war for full independence raged on until after Jonathan's death in -141, when Simon, the last son of Mattathias, defeated the Seleucid forces. Finally, freedom for the tiny Jewish Commonwealth became a reality in the year 141 BCE / 170 SE. (*Antq.* XIII, 231; *Wars* I, 53; I *Maccabee* XIII, 41)

II-5.5 Ḥasmonean King-Priests

As stated above, Simon's son, Hyrcanus I, held the high-priesthood for 31 years and left the office to his son, Yehuda Aristobulus I, who died of an illness after one year. Hyrcanus I's brother, Alexander (Yannai), who was a man of intense energy and ambitions, took the throne and became a high priest for 27 years. He married Salome Alexandra, by whom he had two sons, Hyrcanus II and Aristobulus II. Yannai ruled the country (c. 103-76 BCE) with a harsh hand. It is known that he employed Roman mercenaries. They are conjectured to be the *Kittim* who "worshiped their eagles" recorded in the Dead Sea Scrolls. Some scholars consider him to be the "Wicker Priest" spoken of in the scrolls.

He favored the Ṣadducees, the religious party of aristocrats and priests, and thus came into conflict with the Pharisees, the religious party popular among the middle and lower classes. While Yannai was officiating at the Sukkot sacrifices, the onlookers pelted him with their *etrogim* – an aromatic yellow citron enjoyed during the weeklong festival. The previous uneasiness had escalated into hostility. This foolish action led to the massacre and crucifixion of more than 800 Pharisees in 83 BCE. Hundreds were forced to seek refuge in neighboring countries. Among the refugees was Rabbi Yehoshua ben Peraḥya and his disciples. With them was a young scholar known as Yeshu haNotzri.

King Yannai's eldest son, Hyrcanus II, was high priest (74 – 65 BCE) during the nine-year reign of his mother, Salome. From this point, the Jerusalem temple was under the control of Pharisaic priests. Aristobulus II, Yannai's younger son, defeated his brother in battle and ruled as both king and high priest for two years, three months (65-63 BCE). Infighting is a sign of weakness and the Roman general, Pompey, was looking for an excuse to claim this territory for Rome. He entered Jerusalem under the pretense of brokering peace between the brothers. Instead, his army marched in unopposed and occupied the city, while the people were celebrating the holiday of Shavuot. He then reinstated Hyrcanus II as high priest, who held power for the next 24 years.

Afterward, the Parthians took Hyrcanus captive and gave the position to his brother's son, Antigonus. After holding office for three years, three months, he was taken prisoner by Herod and murdered by Marc Anthony. Herod married the granddaughter of Hyrcanus II, Mariamme, and secretively ordered the murder of her brother, Aristobulus III. After a twenty-year marriage and having four children, two sons and two daughters, Herod had Mariamme executed on a false charge of adultery. Thus, ended the rule of the Hasmonean King-Priests, the descendants of the heroic Maccabeans.

II-5.6 The G-d Fearers

When Pompey brought Judaea under Roman control, he made one costly mistake – he entered the Holy of Holies of the Jerusalem Temple. (*Antq.* XIV. 71-72) To the Jews, this was an unforgivable transgression. Consequently, the Jews aided Caesar in his war against Pompey in 48-7 BCE. (*Antq.* XIV. 127-136) As a reward for their loyalty, Caesar granted them special rights, most of which were regarding the Shabbat. The most important of which was the exemption for all Jewish men from conscription into the Roman army. (*Antq.* XIV. 185-267)

This ruling made the Jews the envy of the Empire, for all other provinces were required to give up their sons. It also may have been the catalyst for the remarkable increase in conversions to Judaism over the following century. Josephus tells us that in his days (37 – ca.100 CE), there was not a community in the Roman Empire that did not have a synagogue. (*Wars* 2.16..4.398) During the reign of Tiberius, it is estimated that six to seven million Jews were living in the Roman empire. Abandoning their pagan temples, non-Jews flocked to learn Torah. (*Apion*, II, 122-123; 281-286) These proselytes were known as "G-d~worshipers" or

"G-d~fearers", (ὁι Θεοσέβεῖς, φοβούμενοι or σεβόμενοι τὸν θεόν, and *metuentes*).[90]

Seneca complained about how widespread keeping Shabbat had become. "The practice of that damnable people has become so prevalent that it has already been adopted in all lands. The conquered have given laws to their conquerors!" (Augustine: *De Civ. Dei*, 6.11) Juvenal upbraided his generation for scorning the laws of Rome and observing those of Moses by abstaining from swine as if it were human flesh and even circumcising themselves. (3, 12-16)

For many, it was simply faddist to follow occasionally a few Jewish customs. For instance, Emperor Augustus Caesar boasted in a letter to Tiberius that he fasted on the Jewish Shabbat for longer than the Jews. (Suet. *Aug.* 76.2) This, of course, is referring to the Day of Atonement, Yom Kippur, which is also known as שבת השבתון – "Shabbat of the Shabbats"). Many were G-d~fearers who drifted between their traditions and Judaism – one day in the synagogue and the next in a pagan temple. Some were enthralled with Judaism, performing many good deeds, but could not fully embrace Judaism – like Nero's wife, Poppaea Sabina, that is before her husband kicked her to death. (*Antq.* XX. 195, 252) Then some were righteous converts (גרים צדיקים), even enduring martyrdom. The first cousin

---

90 Harry J. Leon, The Jews of Ancient Rome (Philadelphia: Jewish Publication Society of America, 1960) pp. 135, 245.

of the Emperors Titus and Domitian, Flavius Clemens, and his wife, Flavia Domitilla, who was the niece of these emperors. Clemens was executed and Domitilla was exiled because they refused to renounce Judaism. (Suet. *Domit.* 15.1 and Dio Cassius 67.14.1-2) It has been suggested that roughly one-fourth of the Roman Empire was involved to one degree or another with ὁι Θεοσέβεῖς.[91]

They continued to convert even after Vespasian punished all Jews with the imposition of the infamous "Jew-tax", forcing them to compensate Rome for the expense of the first revolt. The funds were deposited directly to the Temple of Jupiter. By this maneuver, the Jews were being forced to pay homage to the supreme god of Rome.

As stated, those who were born to Judaism enjoyed the special status of exemption from conscription into the Roman army. The laws emplaced by the great Caesar prevented the authorities from persecuting them. However, those who wished to convert were considered "draft-dodgers" and suffered severe punishment if discovered, beginning during the rule of Tiberius. Titus' brother, Domitian (81 – 96 CE), tried to stop all Jewish conversions by declaring a death penalty on any Roman man who was found to have been circumcised. The Roman historian, Suetonius, witnessed the examination of a ninety-year-old nobleman charged with the crime.

---

91 Leon, pp. 33-35; 250-251, 257.

186

(*Domit.* 12.2) This decree horrified the rabbis, who issued a ruling that forbade Jews to proselytize. Since that time, anyone seeking conversion must be turned away at least twice before they can be permitted to begin studying Judaism.

Blaming it on the Bar Kochba revolt, Hadrian actually did persecute the Jews living in Judaea. Later, these negative Roman rulings were reversed by successive emperors. The only other decree detrimental to the Jews, in general, was that Septimius Severus and his dynasty (193-235 CE) forbade the conversion of Romans to either Judaism or Christianity. (*Scriptores Historiae Augustae,* Spartianus, *Severus* 17.1)

II-5.7 Yeshivat Hillel vs Yeshivat Shammai

After Pompey's conquests, a young man named Hillel left his home in Babylon and journeyed to Jerusalem. He was from a good family, for his mother was a descendant of the House of David. We do not have details of his journey; but, by the time he arrived, he was impoverished. Fortunately, he found refuge in the Yeshiva (school) of Shmaya and Avtalyon.

Shmaya is best known for teaching: "Love work and hate office and do not introduce yourself to the ruling class." Avtalyon taught: "Scholars, be careful with your words lest you incur the penalty of exile and be exiled to the place of evil waters, and the

187

students following you drink therefrom and die, and the name of G-d be desecrated." (Pirkei Avot 1:10-11)[92] Of course, these statements have profound philosophical and spiritual interpretations, but they also indicate a precarious political environment.

Hillel became the most beloved of Jewish sagas, and, without a doubt, the most influential. He and his descendants built upon the ancient foundation laid by Abraham, Moses, David, and Isaiah a dazzling spiritual and intellectual edifice – Judaism.

He taught:

- Be of the disciples of Aaron – loving peace, pursuing peace, loving people, and bringing them closer to the Torah. (Pirkei Avot 1:12)
- A name made great is a name lost. He who does not increase [in Torah], decreases. He who does not study deserves death; and he who makes use of the crown will perish. (Pirkei Avot 1:13)
- If I am not for myself, who will be for me? And if I am only for myself, what am I? And if not now, when? (Pirkei Avot 1:14)
- Don't trust yourself until the day you die; and do not judge your fellow until you are in his place. (Pirkei Avot 2:4)
- Where there are no men, strive to be a man! (Pirkei Avot 2:5)

---

92 Paul Forchheimer, trans., The Mishna of Avoth: Living Judaism of Moses Maimonides, (Jerusalem: Feldheim Publishing, 1974) pp. 38-42.

- Whosoever destroys one soul, it is as though he has destroyed the entire world. And whosoever saves a life, it is as though he has saved the entire world. (Jerusalem Talmud, Sanhedrin 4:1 (22a))
- My humiliation is my exaltation; my exaltation is my humiliation. (Leviticus Rabba 1:5)

Among the other students studying with Hillel was one named Shammai. He stressed: "Fix for your Torah-study a definite time. Say little and do much; and receive everybody with a friendly expression." (Pirkei Avot 1:15) In time these two scholars established their own schools. Hillel began his leadership 100 years before the destruction of the Second Temple (Shabbat 15a), which indicates that his school was established by 30 BCE.

In *Eruvin* 13b, a disagreement is mentioned between the two schools, on whether it was better that man was created, or if it would have been better for him not to have been created. The *Yeshiva* of Shammai argued that it would have been preferable if man had not been created. The *Yeshiva* of Hillel replied that since we have been, we must make the best of our situation by pursuing righteousness. Regrettably, their world was soon to descend into chaos due to the ascension of power-hungry individuals.

The Romans made the nobleman, Antipater, governor of the Idumeans. His son, Herod, who was educated in Rome, was a close friend of Mark Antony. When Antony and Octavius took control of

Rome, after the death of Julius Caesar, Herod used his friendships to gain control of Judaea, for the "security of Rome". The Jews rebelled against this arrangement. Herod together with his friend, Sossius, laid siege to Jerusalem in 40 BCE. They took the city the following June -39; and, the 185th Olympic Games were held the next month. The Senate confirmed Herod as king of Judea in Jan of 38 BCE. (*Antq.* XIV. 475, 487)

Yeshiva Shammai followed the traditional strict interpretation of the Law of Shimon ben Satakh and Yehoshua ben Perahya. Whereas, Hillel's approach was, for the most part, more lenient. Yeshiva Shammai considered only worthy students for admission to study Torah. Yeshiva Hillel held that Torah should be taught to anyone interested in learning, since this would bring him to repent and, thereby, become worthy. (Talmud, Ketubot 16b–17a) Yeshiva Shammai was very strict regarding divorce. A man may only divorce his wife for a serious transgression. Yeshiva Hillel was very lenient and allowed divorce for even trivial faults, such as burning a meal. (Shabbat 21b) Though both willingly accepted converts, they differed on how to handle G-d~fearers. The classic example is when a non-Jew approached Shammai with the demand, "Tell me all of the Torah while I am standing on one foot." Shammai threw him out. He then went to Hillel with the same statement. Hillel responded, "That which is hateful to you, do not do unto your fellow. That is the whole Torah; the rest is commentary; now go and learn." (Babylonian Talmud, Shabbat

31a) In time the split between them became so deep that it seemed as if two very different Torahs were being taught. (Avot of Rabbi Natan 2:9) The people loved the doctrines of Hillel the Elder. His teachings inspired a widespread religious movement based on compassion. Due to the remarkable growth among G-d~worshippers during this period, we suggest that his doctrines were instrumental in the international popularity of Judaism.

It is very puzzling that Josephus does not mention Hillel the Elder in his writings. But then, it is understandable that he would prefer not to reopen old wounds and expose the schism to foreign critics. Josephus' referring to Caiaphas as a Sadducean high-priestly leader is problematic. First, the Sadducees lost power after the death of King Yannai. Josephus characterized the Sadducees as boorish and argumentative. Caiaphas is remembered as cruel and heartless, as were the Sadducees during the reign of Yannai. It is therefore no stretch to suggest that he was not a Sadducee, but instead was a Pharisee of the Yeshivat Shammai and that Josephus wished to conceal this embarrassing fact.

Shabbat 17a records one of the many disputes between Hillel and Shammai. Their argument, regarding the purity of grapes, became so heated that Shammai rudely silenced Hillel by threatening to extend his prohibition to olives. "Hillel, who was the Nasi, was forced to sit in submission before Shammai, and the opinion of Yeshiva Shammai prevailed in the vote conducted that day. And Shammai and Hillel issued the decree, and the people did not accept it from them. And their students came and issued the decree, and the people accepted it from them." Hillel was the Nasi, "Prince", of the Sanhedrin. However, to oppose Shammai could have created a breach that might have led to bloodshed, so he withdrew. This marked a turning for the worse in Judaea. When Hillel died in 10 BCE, the situation was further destabilized and radical elements became more vocal.

Herod died in 3 BCE. The issue of succession had to wait for the decision of the Roman Senate. It was the next year before they confirmed Herod's and gave the kingdom to his son, Archelaus. However, Augustus removed and exiled him to Gaul in 6 CE. The Romans used this excuse to reduce Judaea to a province, and the power to inflict capital punishment was from that time reserved exclusively for the Roman authorities. Coponius was sent as the first procurator with the instructions to take a full census and property assessment of the Jews. (*Antq.* XVIII, 26)[93]

A Galilaean, named Judas, found this unbearable and together with a Pharisee, named Ṣaddok, incited his countrymen to revolt. Upbraiding as cowards anyone who consented to pay tribute to the Romans. He insisted that Jews should serve no mortal masters, but instead should acknowledge only G-d as their ruler.

---

93 The taxation took place in the 37th year after Augustus Caesar's defeat of Anthony at Actium.

Josephus described him as a sophist who founded a new sect that had nothing in common with the other three. (*Wars* II, 117-118) He and his many followers, asserting that Roman taxation would reduce them to the status of slaves, appealed to the nation to fight for their independence. The High Priest Joazar, the son of Beothus, quieted the people, and thus a full-scale revolt was avoided. (Ant. XVIII, 1-4 and 23-25) Though the taxation continued uninterrupted, the insult festered in the hearts of the people. Yeshiva Shammai were political sympathizers of these Zealots and the two meshed[94] into what Josephus termed the "Fourth Philosophy". Sadly, unlike the third, it was neither silent nor prophetic.

Augustus Octavius Caesar died on 19-August 14 CE and Tiberius Nero was confirmed emperor on 16-November. He sent Valerius Gratus as procurator of Judaea, who held the office for eleven years. (Spring 15 CE – 26 CE) After which, he sent Pontius Pilate, who probably arrived in about May. (*Antq.* XVIII, 33-35) Whenever someone asked Tiberius why he was so reluctant to change procurators, he would tell them of an encounter he had with a dying soldier whose wound was covered with flies. He asked the young man why he tolerated this. He replied that, since these were now full, they did not disturb him so much; but should he shoo

---

94 Steven Fine, A Call from Hazal for Mutual Respect in Times of Bitter Dispute (www.yutorah.org/professor-steven-fine , 2021 Tisha B'Av 5781) see also https://en.wikipedia.org/wiki/Houses_of_Hillel_and_Shammai

them away, new ones would come who, being hungrier, would cause him more suffering. Thus, out of compassion for the people, Tiberius appointed only two procurators during his reign, Gratus, and Pilate. (*Antq.* XVIII, 174-177)

Early in Gratus' rule, he changed the high priesthood three times before finding a man he could work with, Joseph Caiaphas, who held the office from 18 to 36 CE.[95] On the surface, Gratus' procuratorship was relatively peaceful, yet seething anger and frustration were simmering beneath the surface. The procurators controlled the High Priest and hamstrunged the Sanhedrin. What little power it retained was dissipated in endless quarrels between the two schools, which the Romans exploited. They had always engaged in vigorous discussions, but, when the Zealots joined the Yeshiva Shammai and the more peaceful factions followed Yeshiva Hillel, their disputes became more heated and less productive.

> From the time that the disciples of Shammai and Hillel grew in number, and they were disciples who did not attend to their masters to the requisite degree, dispute proliferated among the Jewish people and the Torah became like two Torahs. Two disparate systems of *halakha* developed, and there was no

---

95 Caiaphas was the son-in-law of Ananus or Annias, the son of Seth, High Priest 6–15 CE and his family were notorious for their greed and thirst for power; see Bab. Talmud Pesaḥim 57a; Tosefta Menaḥot xiii. 18; Mishnah Keritot i. 7; Yerushalmi Pesaḥim ii. 16 c and Sifre Deut. xiv. 22.

longer a ḥalakhic consensus with regard to every matter. (Sanhedrin 88b)

In roughly another forty years, the ever-widening rift between the students of Yeshiva Shammai and Yeshiva Hillel reached an impasse on eighteen points of law that resulted in the tragic loss of 3000 lives. (Tosefta Shabbat 1:17) Eventually, this senseless political conflict dragged the entire nation into a full-blown revolt against Roman divide-and-conquer tactics.

According to Mishnah Shabbat 1:4, disciples of Yeshiva Hillel and Yeshiva Shammai met to vote on the practices which were pronounced on the upper floor of Ḥananiah ben Ḥizqiah ben Garon to make them binding upon Israel. We learn from Rabbi Ono that the students of Yeshiva Shammai stood downstairs and killed the students of Yeshiva Hillel. Only six of Hillel were allowed to go up. The remainder were surrounded by students of Shammai, who held swords and lances. When the voting started upstairs, the ones below tried to force their way up, and several were murdered.

The details of Gratus' last years of rule are hazy, but he was astute enough to know that it was a good time to retire and returned to Rome. (*Antq.* XVIII 34-35)[96] Into this hornet's nest

---

96 The footnotes to Josephus give us as a source P.L. Hadley, "Pilate's Arrival in Judaea" (Jour. Of Theol. Stud. XXXV, 1934), pp. 56-57, which informs us

stepped Pontius Pilate, who probably arrived in the summer of 26 CE.

II-5.8 *Testimonium Flavianum*

We arrive now at a short paragraph that for centuries was accepted as a primary source supporting not only the validity of the anti-Jewish missionaries' "*New Testament*", but also of the purported conversion of Josephus to Christianity. Let's begin with Louis H. Feldman's footnotes and then proceed to his translation of the text.

> Ever since Scaliger in the sixteenth century first suspected the authenticity of this so called *Testimonium Flavianum,* an enormous literature (for which see especially Schürer I, 544-545 and Eisler, op cit. pp 36ff) has developed concerning it. Those against its genuineness include Schürer, Niese, Norden, Zeitlin, Lewy, and Juster. The principal arguments for its authenticity are that it is found in all the MSS., that it is cited by Eusebius, *Hist. Essl.* i. 11 and *Dem. Egang.* iii 5. 105, and that the vocabulary and style are basically Josephan.
> The principal arguments against genuineness are: (1) Josephus, as a loyal Pharisaic Jew, could not have written that Jesus was the Messiah. (The references

---

that upon examining the extant procuratorial coins, Hadley notes that "the coin-type that emerges in 17-18 CE is still supreme in 24-26, whereas the coins of the 29-32 are of an entirely different type, thus indicating, he believes, the advent of a new procurator between 24 and 26 CE."

to Jesus in the Slavonic Josephus can hardly be used as evidence of Josephus' attitude towards Christianity since the authenticity of the Slavonic version is so widely questioned); (2) Origen (*Contra Celsum* i. 47 and *Comment. in Matt.* xiii. 55) explicitly states (c. A.D. 280) that Josephus did not believe in Jesus as the Christ. Eusebius, however, c. A.D. 324, does have our passage: hence, ever since the seventeenth century, when Richard Montague, bishop of Norwich, declared the phrase "he was the Messiah" a Christian gloss, some scholars have argued that the passage was forged, in whole or in part, during the interval between 280-324, perhaps, though there is no evidence, by Eusebius himself; (3) The passage breaks the continuity of the narrative, which tells of a series of riots. §65 seems to belong directly after §62; (4) There are several stylistic peculiarities (*e.g.*, τῶν πρώτων ἀνδρῶν παρ' ἡμῖν is not the way that Josephus refers to the Jews), though Thackeray and Richards and Shutt have noted a number of Josephan idioms, ... The most probable view seems to be that our text represents substantially what Josephus wrote, but that some alterations have been made by a Christian interpolator.[97]

We will address each of Feldman's concerns but in reverse order, beginning with the fourth. Marking (*) the two Greek quotes, ὁ χριστὸς οὗτος ἦν and τῶν πρώτων ἀνδρῶν παρ' ἡμῖν as examples of Christian interpolation, we notice below that they are

---

97 Louis H. Feldman. Trans., *Flavius Josephus: Complete Works* (Harvard University Press, 1966), p. 49.

separated by καὶ αὐτὸν ἐνδείξει σταυρῷ ἐπιτετιμηκότος Πιλάτου, "When Pilate, upon hearing him accused, had condemned him to be crucified" – which is known to be historically accurate. Could this indicate a pattern? By breaking the account into individual lines and italicizing each alternating line, we arrive at the following.

1. Γίνεται δὲ κατὰ τοῦτον τὸν χρόνον Ἰνσοῦς σοφὸς ἀνήρ,
   About this time there lived Jesus (Greek for Yoshua), a wise man,

2. *εἴγε ἄνδρα αὐτὸν λέγειν χρή· ἦν γὰρ παραδόξων ἔργων ποιητής,*
   if indeed one ought to call him a man. For he was one who wrought surprising feats (for he was a performer of miraculous deeds)

3. //ἦν// διδάσκαλος ἀνθρώπον τῶν ἡδονῇ τἀληθῆ δεχομένων, καὶ πολλοὺς μὲν Ἰουδαίους, πολλοὺς δὲ καὶ τοῦ Ἑλληνικοῦ ἐπηγάγετο·
   and was a teacher of such people as accept the truth gladly. He won over many Jews and many of the Greeks.

4. * *ὁ Χριστὸς οὗτος ἦν.*
   He was the Messiah.

5. καὶ αὐτὸν ἐνδείξει σταυρῷ ἐπιτετιμηκότος Πιλάτου.
   When Pilate, upon hearing him accused, had condemned him to be crucified,

6. *τῶν πρώτων ἀνδρῶν παρ' ἡμῖν.*
   by men of the highest standing amongst us,

7. *οὐκ ἐπαύσαντο οἱ τὸ πρῶτον ἀγαπήσαντες·*
   those who had in the first place come to love
   him did not give up their affection for him.

8. *ἐφάνη γὰρ αὐτοῖς τρίτην ἔχων ἡμέραν πάλιν
   ζῶν τῶν θείων προφητῶν ταῦτά τε καὶ ἄλλα
   μυρία περὶ αὐτοῦ θαυμάσια εἰρηκότων.*
   On the third day, he appeared to them
   restored to life, for the prophets of God had
   prophesied these and countless other
   marvelous things about him.

9. *εἰς ἔτι τε νῦν τῶν Χριστιανῶν ἀπὸ τοῦδε
   ὠνομασμένον οὐκ ἐπέλιπε τὸ φῦλον.*
   And the tribe of the Christians, so called
   after him, has still to this day not
   disappeared. (Antq. XVIII, 63-64) [98]

Thus, the interpolations are easily identified as:

*2. if indeed one ought to call him a man. For he
was one who wrought surprising feats (or for he
was a performer of miraculous deeds)*

4. He was the Messiah.

6. by men of the highest standing amongst us

*8. On the third day he appeared to them
restored to life, for the prophets of
God had prophesied these and countless other
marvelous things about him.*

---

98 Due to the inclusion of this paragraph and a few lesser issues, Orthodox Jews
are forbidden to read the histories of Josephus.

Feldman's third comment has two parts. He states that the passage on Kristos breaks the continuity of the narrative sequence, which seems to focus on riots. In the first part (*Antq. 18:55-59 (iii 1)*, Pilate sends troops to Jerusalem to arrange winter quarters [autumn 26 CE], taking with them engraved images of Caesar and carrying the military standards that had engraved images of eagles. The Jews protested daily in Caesarea until Pilate threatened them to cease or die. οἱ δὲ πρηνεις ῥίψαντες ἑαυτοὺς καὶ γυμνουντες τὰς σφαγὰς ἡδονη δέξασθαι τὸν Θάνατον ἔλεγον ἢ τολμήσειν τὴν σοφίαν παραβήσεσθαι των νόμων. "They, throwing themselves down prone and baring their necks, stated that they accepted the death with pleasure, rather than to endure the wisdom of the laws to be transgressed." Pilate relented and removed them.

The second, *Antq. 18:60-62 (iii 2)*, which probably refers to the spring of 27 CE, Pilate misappropriates sacred funds from the Temple to construct an aqueduct to bring water to Jerusalem. Again, the people rioted. This time he uses force to end the uprising and continued to misuse the funds. Such an act was sacrilegious by Roman as well as Jewish standards. The Jews protested, just as the Romans would have protested had the funds of the Temple of Jupiter been used for a mundane project. This time Pilate did not relent and many died.

Since the passage regarding CT-Yeshu says nothing about a riot, it seems to be out of place. However, since there is evidence that the passage has been corrupted, we can question if perhaps the original text included a riot during the short public career of Yeshu-Ḳristos.

The second concern of Feldman is the statement translated as "He was the Messiah." As we stated earlier, a Jew may believe that anyone is a messiah. However, to state that someone is or was "The Messiah" is too emphatic to be acceptable. Since Josephus was so anti-Zealot and encouraged G-d~fearers, we can deduce that he belonged to Hillel's branch of Pharisaic Judaism, and would have avoided such blatantly offensive terminology. Hence, the evidence favors the scholars who argue that the passage was probably forged between 280-324 CE.[99] The remaining five lines in sections 63 through 64 can be considered original. Therefore, we can reconstruct the text as follows:

> 1. About this time there lived Jesus (Greek for Yoshua), a wise man, a teacher of such people as accept the truth gladly.

> 3. He won over many Jews and many of the Greeks.

> 5. When Pilate, upon hearing him accused that "he was the so-called Messiah"[100] «ὁ χριστός λεγόμενος οὗτος ἦν», condemned him to be crucified,

---

99 Since I have very little knowledge of the "Slavonic Josephus", I fully accept the opinion of those who, having the necessary expertise reject its authenticity.

100 Feldman's footnote: Variant (Richards' and Shutt's emendation in Class. Quart. xxi, 1937, p. 176) "the so-called Christ".

7. those who had in the first place come to love him did not give up their affection for him.

9. And the tribe of the Christians, so called after him, has still to this day[101] not disappeared.

The reconstruction of the line regarding Pilate is based on the terminology Josephus uses in reference to James, the brother of Yeshu-Ḳristos (*Antq.* XX, 200) in contrast to that of John the Baptist (*Antq.* XVIII, 116). The term ὁ λεγόμενος means "so-called" while ὁ ἐπικαλούμενος means someone who is addressed or characterized by a special term, called, or give a surname.[102] Since he did not use the later term for both, then it weakens the argument that Josephus believed Yeshu-Ḳristos was the Mashiaḥ.

The root for *Mashiah* reaches back to the ancient Akkadian *mashā'u* and Aramaic-Syriac מְשַׁח, *m'shaah*, "to spread or smear oil over, to anoint", while מְשַׁחָא, *meshaha*, is the oil used for it. Likewise, in ancient Greek, χρῖσις, *ḳrisis,* is "smearing, anointing", while χρῖσμα, *ḳrisma,* is the oil used for it. Hence, *Mashiah* has the same meaning as Ḳristos and the followers are called *Meshiḥim* or Ḳristianoi, respectively. We find in Tacitus:

"Nero fastened the guilt (for the great fire in Rome in 64 CE) and inflicted the most exquisite tortures on a class hated for their abominations, called Christians by the populace. Christus, from whom the name had

---

101 Josephus completed The Antiquities of the Jews in 95 CE.
102 Danker, pp. 590 (4) and 373 (2).

its origin, suffered the extreme penalty during the reign of Tiberius at the hands of one of our procurators, Pontius Pilatus, and a most mischievous superstition, thus checked for the moment, again broke out not only in Judaea, the first source of the evil but even in Rome, where all things hideous and shameful from every part of the world find their center and become popular." (*Annals* 15:44)

Roman historians, such as Tacitus, [103] had access to official reports kept in the Imperial Library. Thus, Pilate's report must have given his name only as Ķristus, indicating that this was the primary charge that resulted in his execution. In the CT, Matt. 3:13-17, Mark 1:9-11, Luke 3:21-22, and John 1:29-39 relate how he was "anointed" by the Holy Spirit. I cannot understand how anyone could be called Mashiah unless he had been anointed with oil by a priest or prophet. The title simply does not make sense unless it involves oil. However, the CT does inform us that his mother's relative was a priest (Luke 1:36-40), so it is not impossible that a priest poured oil on him to please his followers. But Josephus seems to doubt this.

---

103 Tacitus was the son-in-law of Agricola (Tacitus *Agricola*, IX.9), who benefited from the friendship and patronage of all three Flavian emperors. (Tacitus, *Histories*, I.1; his *Histories* written 100-110 CE and *Annals* 112-116 CE) However, Tacitus seems to have used Apion instead of Josephus' history as a source when writing about the origin of the Jews (*Hist.* 5. 2-5), which may have been a catalyst for Josephus' *Against Apion*.

II-5.9 Josephus and the Historic Yeshu-Ḳristos

Feldman commented that, since the account in *Testimonium Flavianum* (63-64) does not mention riots, then the events of Paulina thru Fulvia (65-84) should follow directly after that of the aqueduct (60-62). Rioting is not described in the stories of the noblewomen, but it is implied. However, we do find in the story of Barabbas (Mark 15:7 – τῇ στάσει φόνον πεποιήκεισαν; Luke 23:25 – διὰ στάσιν καὶ φόνον) references to rioting and murder in the CT.[104]

It seems odd that Josephus dedicated such an unusual amount of space to the story of Paulina and Mundus [65-80 (iii 4)], but then it is an intriguing story. Mundus, a love-sick Roman knight, bribed the priests of the Temple of Isis to assist him in impersonating the Egyptian god Anubis, simply so he could spend one night with the woman he loved. So blind was poor Paulina's faith in this cult that afterward she proudly boasted to her husband and friends how marvelously the god had honored her. When the deception was discovered, she was equally infuriated. She demanded that her husband right the wrong. Saturninus, a close friend of Tiberius, appealed to the emperor for justice. He ordered the Temple of Isis destroyed and its priests crucified, while the still enamored Mundus was exiled far from Paulina.

---

104 https://www.logosapostolic.org/bibles/interlinear_nt.htm

The inclusion of the next story [81-84 (iii 5)] is more germane. Another noble Roman lady, Fulvia, had converted to Judaism. It is difficult to determine at what level of commitment, but she was obviously a sincere G-d~worshipper. A Jewish scoundrel, "a fugitive from his own land due to charges of transgression of some laws," joined with three others of equal character. Professing to be experts in Jewish teachings, they defrauded Fulvia by stealing the gifts that they had convinced her to donate to the Temple in Jerusalem. Since Fulvia's husband was also called Saturninus, they are thought to have been the two Sentii Saturnini brothers – Gaius (consul in 4 CE) and Lucius.[105] Upon hearing the details of this second case, Tiberius ordered the expulsion of both Jews and Egyptians. Suetonius (*Tib.* 36), Tacitus (*Ann.* ii.85), and Dio Cassius (lvii.18.5a) give proselytism as the cause of the expulsion. In particular, 4000 young Jewish men, probably converts, were sent to military service. Archeological evidence firmly sets this persecution in 19 CE.

Both contextually and chronologically, the stories of Paulina and Fulvia seem out of place. Beginning with the phrase "At about this same time", the misadventures of these unfortunate women follow closely on the heels of the account of Yeshu-Kristos. Yet, Christian scholars set a date for his execution as 33

---

105 Feldman's footnote: a plausible conjecture by E. Groag, Prosopog. Imp. Rom. ii A. 1528.

CE, which was 14 years after the expulsions from Rome. If we give credit to the use of this phrase and place his death in the early years of Pilate's tenure, possibly as early as 28 CE, then these incidences would be separated by only seven years. It should also be noted that in the ancient layout of Josephus' Book XVII of *Antiquities of the Jews*, chapter three begins with Pilate's assumption of power and continues through the story of Fulvia, Thus, they form a single block of events, which further support an earlier date for the execution of Yeshu, the so-called Ḳristos.

In Greco-Roman religious thought, any intimacy with a god always resulted in the birth of a son. Thus, Paulina was boasting that, due to her piety and chaste nature, she most certainly would give birth to a great hero. This is reminiscent of the claim made for the Yeshu of the Christian Texts. Therefore, we can surmise that Josephus included the story of Paulina because he was cognizant of the story of the miraculous conception and birth of CT-Yeshu in the Book of Matthew. Fluvial was a noble lady of equal honorable character, yet she and the Samaritans were deceived by religious charlatans. Josephus, therefore, was warning his readers not to be deceived by such stories. This also suggests that the missing sections of the story of Yeshu-Ḳristos tell of the deception of innocent individuals, using fantastic, fraudulent, and miraculous stories by charlatans.

Another tantalizing point is that, in contrast to the Christian account, Josephus informs us that John the Baptist died after the

206

CT-Yeshu. Also, he states that the Essenes wore only white linen. Whereas, the Christian Text has John wearing a garment made out of camel's hair. (Mark 1:6) Since the camel is a non-kosher animal, it would be offensive for a religious Jew to wear such a garment.

Herod, the tetrarch of Galilee, fell in love with his half-brother's wife, Herodias, who was the daughter of another son of King Herod, Aristobulus. As Josephus reports: "Herodias, taking it into her head to flout the way of our fathers, married Herod, her husband's brother by the same father; to do this she parted from a living husband," after having given birth to a daughter. (*Antq.* XVIII:136-137) Her husband, Philip, died in the 20th year of Tiberius, which places his demise between 16-Nov 34 CE and 15-Nov 35 CE. Since Philip was still alive when Herodias left him (106-108), then she must have married Herod during that interval. John the Baptist denounced their sin in his sermons; therefore, he was imprisoned and beheaded in 35 CE. Hence the evidence upholds that the historic Yeshu-Ḳristos died before John the Baptist.

Herodias had told Herod that she would marry him only if he agreed to divorce his current wife, the daughter of Aretas, king of Petra. His wife learned about their plot and secretively fled to her father. After Herod and Herodias returned from Rome, Aretas attacked and destroyed his former son-in-law's army. Many Jews considered the destruction of Herod's army as divine justice for the murder of John, a righteous man. (117-119) This battle was probably in the summer of 36 CE, for Herod had time to complain to Tiberius and for Vitellius, the governor of Syria, to receive imperial instructions to punish the aggressor. (120-124).

Also, in this last year of Pilate's rule, a multitude of Samaritans agreed to follow a man to Mt Gerizim. He promised to show them the sacred vessels that, according to their tradition, were believed to have been buried there by Moses. Josephus describes him as a man who was unscrupulous regarding lies. Being informed of their plans, Pilate blocked the way up the mountain and killed a great many of them. This must have occurred early in 37 CE. (85-89) The Samaritans appealed directly to Vitellius, charging Pilate with the slaughter of innocent victims. He dispatched his friend, Marcellus, to take charge of Judaea and ordered Pilate to return to Rome to answer these charges.

In the meantime, Vitellius prepared to attack Aretas; but, in deference to Jewish sensitivity regarding the engraved insignias, had his army detour off the direct route from Damascus to Petra, because it went through Jewish territory. While waiting for them, he and Herod went up to Jerusalem to enjoy the Passover festival, which was on 18-April in 37 CE. It was there he was informed that Tiberius had died on the 16th of March. He immediately sent a message to dismiss the troops. Vitellius knew that tension in Judaea had reached a dangerous level. He removed Caiaphas from the office of high priest. The reason is not given, but it is safe to infer that it was due to collaboration in the crimes of Pilate. He also returned access to the priestly apparel to those in charge of the services. Such actions alleviated the anxiety of the masses.

Those were tense times and the people turned to any would-be *mashiah* who promised them relief from the stress and uncertainty of Roman occupation. These included charlatans, such as the Samaritan and later Theudas, who, when Fadus was procurator (44-46 CE), brought about yet another Jewish massacre by the Romans (*Antq.* XX, 97-98). On the other hand, there were those like John the Baptist, who sought only to turn the heart of people towards physical and spiritual purification.

Above we quoted Rabbi Ulla's statement that the gentile authorities were interested in acquitting this Yeshu. This shows that he was familiar with the CT story where Pilate freed him and washed his hands of the matter. However, the CT portrayal of Pilate does not fit the historical person period of Yeshu haNotzri nor that of Yeshu-Kristos. During the days of the former, Queen Salome ruled Judaea. During the days of the latter, only Pilate had the power to call for the death penalty. From the beginning to the end of his tenure, his first reaction to each challenge by the Jews or Samaritans was brutal and resulted in the loss of a great many lives. For this reason, most scholars view the CT account of Pilate washing his hands of the guilt for Yeshu-Kristos death as propaganda. Rabbi Ulla lived later, when the Christians stripped the Jews of the last semblance of independence. Thus, he would have been aware of the basic claims of the Christian Texts, which had been in public circulation for roughly 250 years by then.

In the purported *Testimonium Flavianum,* we are informed that Yeshu-Ḳristos was a wise man, who readily taught both Jews and non-Jews. Thus, he was a talented student of the school/*Yeshiva* of Hillel the Elder. According to Josephus, there were hundreds of teachers, representatives of all three Jewish sects, touring the country teaching Torah. Hence, his popularity would have excited the jealousy of the Shammai Pharisees, and we suggest that it was they who continuously argued with him regarding the law.

From the insertion of the stories of the two noblewomen, we can add that, charlatans, noticing his success, and due to his naivety, gained his trust. Fantastic stories, claiming that he performed miraculous deeds, which included "faith-healing" – a very ancient and widespread belief spread throughout the country. Some went as far as claiming that one should not call him a mere man, and his following increased remarkably. Rumors grew out of proportion and became more and more fantastic. Like poor, misguided Pauline, the simple-minded came to believe that his real father was none other than the Deity.

210

II-5.10 Revolt and Reconstruction

Both the Jerusalem and Babylonian Talmuds attribute the breakdown in civil order to sectarian divisions. The Romans were experts in the tactics of divide-and-conquer and agitated the situation at every opportunity. Thus, it was divisiveness that brought about the disastrous revolt of 66 CE. Josephus, like other followers of Yeshiva Hillel, detested the Zealots, who hijacked the Yeshiva Shammai, blaming them for the destruction of the nation. Likewise, confused missionaries have blamed those of Yeshiva Hillel for the crimes of Yeshiva Shammai for the last 2000 years. Just when the Zealots thought that they had the upper hand, the Romans sent reinforcements to reestablish "peace" in Judaea.

At this time, Yosef ben Matthias (*Wars*.I.3; *Apion* I.54) was commissioned by Simon b. Gamaliel b. Hillel the Elder to command the defensive efforts in the Galilee (*Wars* II.568-584) against the advancing army of General Titus Flavius Vespasian, the Elder. Despite the valiant efforts of the Galileans, the Romans conquered the city of Yodfat (Jotapata), and Yosef, its commander, was taken prisoner. Acting on a dream he had had, he greeted Vespasian the Elder, as emperor. Since Nero was still alive, the general ordered his execution, but his son, Titus Flavius Vespasian, the Younger, advised him to wait to see if it would perhaps come true. So, Yosef was imprisoned for two years (*Wars* III.141-339;

211

Life 412). After the death of Nero, civil war broke out between the supporters of Aulus Vitellius, son of the former governor of Syria, and those of Vespasian in their claims to power. After an eight-month rule by Vitellius, the Flavians were victorious. Vespasian, the Elder, left for Rome, while his son, better known as Titus, (Suetonius, *Titus, I*) was left in charge of the war against the Jews (*Wars*, v. 358-9). He needed a translator; and, remembering Yosef, he took him from prison as his personal slave (*Apion* I, 48).

During the long siege of Jerusalem, students of Yeshiva Hillel smuggled their sage, Yohanan ben Zakai, out of the city in a coffin, claiming that their rabbi had died. Yosef translated for him as he greeted Titus Flavius Vespasian the Younger as emperor. Yosef explained to Titus that the sage had just predicted that the young general would be the next emperor. Titus allowed the sage to establish a school in the small village of Yavne.

News that the former commander of the Galilee was collaborating with the Roman infuriated the Zealots. They murdered his father and threw his body off the walls of the city. When the Temple was taken, Yosef begged Titus to allow him to save some of the priests who had taken refuge in the Temple. Those whom he chose were sent to Yavne; but, to his dismay, both his mother and wife had starved to death in prison and his only brother had gone insane.

With the destruction of the Temple and the slaughter or enslavement of countless Jews, the conquest of the country was completed. Titus returned to Rome and paraded his captives in his father's triumph. After this, Titus freed Yosef and commissioned him to write the history of the war (*Wars*, v. 361, 363, 416). Since it was customary for freed slaves to be given the family name of their former owner and now patron, he was then entered into the Roman census as Flavius Josephus.

The village of Yavne grew as more refugees gathered to learn. Gamaliel II, the great-great-grandson of Hillel the Elder, became head of the reinstituted Sanhedrin. They reviewed all the points disputed by Yeshiva Hillel, and this time it was their opinions that won the vote because they were more agreeable and forbearing. The laws of the harsh Yeshiva Shammai were now null and void. All Jews since have followed the teachings of Yeshiva Hillel.

The destruction of the Temple sent shockwaves throughout the world. We can only imagine the effect it had on G-d~fearers. Yet, there is evidence, as given above regarding Clemens and Domitilla, that their numbers continued to increase. However, there must also have been those who, expecting Hashem to perform a great miracle and save the Temple, faced a crisis of faith. It is reasonable to consider that the writings of Paul and the authors of the first four books of the Christian Texts, the so-called "Gospels" were all the works of G-d~fearers. For instance, in the Book of Acts, we are informed that Paul's father was Jewish, but nothing is said of his mother. The city of Tarsus, where he was born, was an ancient center of multiple pagan cults. It is possible that he was given a Jewish education; but, judging from his writings, it must have been very limited.

It should be noted that of all the Christian Texts, the Book of James is the closest to Judaism. The others were written by creative, evangelical editors.

> What then must be borne in mind when reading the canonical gospels for historical information about Jesus of Nazareth? First, the impression of orderliness conveyed by their connected narratives should not deceive us about their true nature: these are composite documents, the final products of long and creative traditions in which old material was reworked and new material interpolated. As they now stand, they are witnesses first of all to the father of their individual writers and their late first-century, largely Gentile communities.[106]

In the oldest surviving manuscripts of the CT's "Four Gospels", the authors are all anonymous. The names that were given to them appear much later. Most scholars agree that Mark was composed around 66 to 74 CE. They believe that the author had at hand a few sources of stories and parables. The early Church derived most of its opinions of Yeshu-Ḳristos from the author of *Matthew*.[107] Even though the *Book of John* contains

---

106 Paula Fredriksen, *From Jesus to Christ*, 2nd ed. (New Haven: Yale University Press, 2000), p. 4.
107 https://en.wikipedia.org/wiki/Gospel_of_Mark

evidence of originating around 70 CE or perhaps earlier, most scholars agree that it reached its final form around 90 to 110 CE.[108] The majority of scholars agree that the *Book of Matthew* was composed between 80 to 90 CE, and allows a range possibly from 70 to 110 CE.[109] Matthew and Luke used Mark and other source material – Q-Matthew and Q-Luke. Most scholars agree that the Book of Luke was composed between 80 and 110 CE. There is evidence that it was still being revised well into the 2nd century.[110]

The greater consensus of scholars is that none of them were written by either the companions of Yeshu-Ḳristos or Paul. The surviving texts are third-generation copies and no two are completely identical. Thus, we find that most of the originals were published during the reigns of Domitian, Nerva, Trajan, and Hadrian.

It is not surprising that the *Christian Texts* were composed and promoted during the reign of Domitian. During the civil war between Vitellus and Vespasian 68-69 CE, Vitellus cornered Sabinus, Vespasian's brother in the Temple of Jupiter with other supporters. During the night Sabinus' younger son, Clemens, and Vespasian's younger son, Domitian escaped by swimming across the Tiber and hiding in the Temple of Isis on 20th December. The

---

108 https://en.wikipedia.org/wiki/Gospel_of_John
109 https://en.wikipedia.org/wiki/Gospel_of_Matthew
110 https://en.wikipedia.org/wiki/Gospel_of_Luke

215

priests were beginning their Winter Solstice celebration of the birth
of Horus. Domitian was deeply affected by this night. He believed
that the virgin goddess Isis/Minerva/Athena saved him from
certain death at the hands of his family's enemy. Flavius Sabinus,
the Elder, was captured and beheaded. Sabinus, the Younger,
Clemens' older brother liberated the city of Rome from the forces
of Vitellus. The aged Nerva became the next emperor. One of his
first acts was to revoke the "Jew tax". Nerva's reign was short, 96-
98 CE.

The next emperor, Trajan, (98-117 CE) admired Titus,
since his father had fought alongside him in Judaea. He favored
honoring Titus' promise to Josephus to rebuild the Temple in
Jerusalem. However, the murder of a "princess" that was blamed
on the Jews, caused him to withdraw his support for the project.
Then in 115, the Jews revolted in the North African city of Cyrene,
on the island of Cyprus, and in Alexandria. At the time, Trajan was
campaigning deep in Parthian territory. Hadrian was involved in
Rome's brutal response. After Trajan's death, Hadrian became the
next emperor (117-138 CE). He was a Grecophile and promoted
the worship of the old gods. Thus, we find that the four emperors
who followed Titus each had reasons to show more favor towards
Christianity than Judaism.

There are numerous differences between the Book of John
(the fourth book of the CT canon) and the Synoptic volumes (the
first three books). John's CT-Yeshu reflects a more Dionysian

216

persona, where it seems that the Shammai Pharisees are cast in the role of his Theban relatives. Therein he is portrayed as Δίος ὁ Ἐπιφανής, "the God/Zeus Manifested".

> "John's Jesus is not the wandering charismatic Galilean who appears in the Synoptics, but an enigmatic visitor from the cosmos above the cosmos, the preexistent, supremely divine Son (e.g., 1:1-4; 8:23, 42, 58; 17:5; 20:28). As *he travels repeatedly between Jerusalem and the Galilee*, this Jesus encounters, not fellow Jews, but sons of darkness, denizens of the lower cosmos who can never receive the word of God (8:23, 43-47; 10:25; 12:34; cf. 15:19-22). To those divinely chosen to receive it, Jesus brings the message of eternal life, of the glory of the Son and the Father, pronounced in the elliptical idiom of this gospel as much by Jesus' wondrous signs as by his own mysterious speech (e.g., 3:15, 36; 4:14; 5:24; 6:35-53; 11:1-4). The topic of his address is, most frequently, himself. An image of Jesus thus does not emerge from John's gospel: it dominates his entire presentation.[111] (emphasis added)

Since the Book of John is so remarkably different from the other CT texts, it is viewed as having developed from a unique source (*Quelle*).[112] Q-John is essentially the story of Yeshu HaNotzri as preserved by his followers after his death in 73 BCE. On the other hand, the Q of the Synoptic texts – Books of Mark, Matthew, and Luke – was written not long after the death of

---

111 Fredriksen, p. 199.
112 Fredriksen, p. 3.

Yeshu-Ḳristos and preserved by his brother, James (Yaʿaqov), who was put to death by the High Priest, Ananus ben Ananus, in 62 CE. Since he only held the office for three months, it seems that Festus had appointed Ananus to the office shortly before his death. Taking advantage of the hiatus between the demise of Festus and the arrival of Albinus, he ordered the execution by stoning of "James the brother of Jesus", who was the leader of the *Meshiḥim.* Josephus informs us: "Those of the inhabitants of the city who were considered the most fair-minded and who were strict in the observance of the law were offended at this." Some went to meet Albinus who was on his way from Alexandria, while others appealed to King Agrippa. Ananus was immediately removed from office. (*Antq.* XX, 200-203) He later resurfaces as a leader of the Zealots during the revolt.

For the first 300 years after the death of Yeshu-Ḳristos, those who considered themselves Christians were divided into many sects. They often quarreled among themselves, which degenerated into open warfare with many victims – non-Jewish Christians, Jewish *Meshiḥim,* and traditional Jews. During these years many Christian texts were written and many burned by their rivals. Finally, in 325 CE, the Roman emperor, Constantine, called the First Council of Nicaea to settle the multitude of Christian sectarian disputes, define heresy, and establish an orthodox version of the life and teachings of Yeshu-Ḳristos. The Council of Nicaea declared in clear terms the doctrine that the CT-Yeshu was the "incarnate," "immutable," and "essence of God." The teachings of Arius (250-336 CE), presented him as a human intermediary who, unlike G-d, had a point of origin, were declared heresy.

11-6 Return to the Present

Now that we have explored the historical context of both Judaism and Christianity, we are ready to examine our current issues with a deeper understanding of the forces that formed them. So, we will return to where we left off at the end of Part I.

As you remember, the JfJ website reader has been carefully directed to the threshold of Christianity with the welcoming statement: "Next, we'll look at what the New Testament has to say about Isaiah 53." The reader is then directed to download the *Book of Matthew*, where the reader discovers the genealogy of CT-Yeshu beginning with Adam, through Abraham and King David, and until his father, Joseph. The posted testimonials of those who had gone through this process, previous readers, were very impressed by "how Jewish" the Yeshu as found in CT was. After reading the *Book of Matthew*, they are gently encouraged to read also *Luke*, which presents a slightly different perspective and is considered a supportive account of *Matthew*. After that, the reader is encouraged to turn to the *Book of John. The Book of Mark* is not as important in the process and is considered more as additional reading material.

This is a well-thought-out sequence. Everything on the website is designed with one purpose in mind – to convince you that the content you are reading is authentic Judaism. Let's analyze their source material, then you can determine for yourself if it is true or not.

Part III: Why we reject Christianity

III-1 *Matthew* – Gateway to Christianity

On their website, the JfJ authors proudly display testimonials of those members who wish to share their personal stories of conversion to Christianity. To my ears, they seem to be young Jews[113] with limited knowledge or experience in comparative religious studies. They express how surprised and touched they were by the Yeshu presented in the Christian Texts (CT), especially the *"Book of Matthew"*.

> 1: "So, I decided to read the New Testament, and I was very surprised. I read through *Matthew*'s Gospel and by the end, I had tears in my eyes. It was not what I had expected."

> **2: Jesus was a Jewish person through and through**. He had a Jewish family tree. His parents named him Yeshua, which means "salvation" in Hebrew. He was called "rabbi" by his followers and contemporaries. He went to shul. He taught from the Hebrew Scriptures. He celebrated Hanukkah, Passover, and Sukkot. All of his first followers were Jewish. In fact, they were later called "Christians" because the Greek word *christos* is a translation of the Hebrew word "Messiah." **The word Christian literally means "follower of the Messiah."**

> 3: I searched for "Christianity" and found the New Testament in Hebrew. I expected it to be an antisemitic book with stories about Santa Claus! But in the first pages, the *Gospel of Matthew*, I read the genealogy of Jesus and saw

---

113 Again, we do not wish to identify these individuals so as not to cause them embarrassment when they return to Torah – may we soon see that happy day.

all these Hebrew names. It felt so familiar. Then **I realized that I was reading a book written by Jews about Jews, here in Israel.** That really surprised me! You cannot help but like him – his wisdom, compassion, and love. **Every time I read Jesus' words and learned about his deeds, I wanted more.**

4: I went to my local library and I read the gospels in the New Testament for the first time. **I was dumbfounded to see so much familiarity in it and just how Jewish it was.** Hummm... so Santa Claus is an antisemite?

Before answering them, let me clarify that Rabbis, Rabbanits and Rabbetzens do not usually read the Christian Texts. The traditional response has always been a straight forward hands-off policy. Unfortunately, the missionaries chose to raise the stakes in their game by translating the CT into our sacred language, Hebrew and brazenly peddle it in our heart of hearts – Jerusalem. Combining this outrage with their heightened levels of deception, as described above, requires a much stronger response than those of past generations. Desperate times require desperate measures. The following are the thoughts and insights I gathered over my life-time.

Missionaries prefer to refer novice converts to the *Book of Matthew* first because it is an enchanting composition filled with charming stories and rich in fantastic claims.

III-1.1 The Genealogy of the CT-Yeshu

Since the commentators quoted above seem to be awed by the "Genealogy of Jesus", let's begin there. Below is a table of the three genealogies in question. The lists of names in the first two columns are found in I Chronicles 3:1-24. The names in the first are transliterated from the Hebrew of the Masoretic Text (MT), while the second are from the *Septuagint* (LXX). The names in the third column (blue) are found in Matthew 1:1-17. Those in the last column (green) are found in *Luke* 3:23-34. Each begins with David, and the generations are counted as the interval between each name – David to Solomon, Solomon to Rehoboam, etc. Thus, we have 30 generations in the MT and LXX texts. *Matthew*'s text lacks of the four names provided in the first two, giving us 28 generations. The author follows the MT through Zerubbabel, minus four generations, but adds two for Joseph and this Yeshu. *Luke* was the most ambitious, giving us 42 generations.

#	Mesoretic (Hebrew)	LXX (Greek)	#	Matthew (Gk)	#	Luke (Gk)
	David	David		David		David
1	Shlomo	Solomon	1	Solomon	1	Nathan
2	Reḥav'am	Roboam	2	Rehoboam	2	Mattatha
3	Aviyah	Abia	3	Abijah	3	Menna
4	Asa	Asa	4	Asa	4	Melea
5	Yehoshafat	Josaphat	5	Jehoshaphat	5	Eliakim
6	Yoram	Joram	6	Jehoram	6	Jonam
7	Aḥazyahu	Ochozias		(Aḥazyahu)	7	Joseph
8	Yoash	Joas		(Yoash)	8	Judah
9	Amatzyahu	Amasias		(Amatzyahu)	9	Simeon
10	'Azaryah	Azarias	7	Uzziah	10	Levi
11	Yotam	Joatham	8	Jotham	11	Matthat
12	Aḥaz	Achaz	9	Ahaz	12	Jorim
13	Ḥezqiyahu	Ezekias	10	Hezekiah	13	Eliezer
14	Manasseh	Manasses	11	Manasseh	14	Joshua
15	Amon	Amon	12	Amon	15	Er
16	Yoshiyahu	Josia	13	Josiah	16	Elmadam
17	Yehoyaqim	Joakim	14	Joakim	17	Cosam
18	Yekanyah	Jechonias	15	Jeconiah	18	Addi
19	Shealtiel	Salathiel	16	Shealtiel	19	Melki
20	Pedayah	Phadaias		(Pedayah)	20	Neri
21	Zerubbabel	Zorobabel	17	Zerubbabel	21	Shealtiel
22	Ḥananyah	Anania	18	Abihud	22	Zerubbabel
23	Yesh'ayah	Jesias	19	Eliakim	23	Rhesa
24	Refayah	Raphal	20	Azor	24	Joanan
25	Arnan	Orna	21	Zadok	25	Joda
26	'Ovadyah	Abdia	22	Akim	26	Josek
27	Shekanyah	Sechenias	23	Elihud	27	Semein
28	N'aryah	Noadia	24	Eleazar	28	Mattathias
29	Elyo'enai	Elithenan	25	Matthan	29	Maath
30	Hodavyahu, Elyashiv Playah, 'Aqquv, Yoḥanan, Dalayah, 'Anani	Odolia, Heliasebon, Phadaia, Akub, Joanan, Dalaaia, Anan	26	Jacob	30	Naggai
			27	Joseph	31	Esli
	Notes:		28	Jesus	32	Nahum
					33	Amos
	30 gens. X 30 yrs ea. = 900; 1070 BCE - 900 yrs = 170 BCE				34	Mattathias
					35	Joseph
	28 gens. X 30 yrs ea. = 840 yrs - 30 CE = 810 BCE >David				36	Jannai
	(2 sets x 14 gens = 28 gens.)				37	Melki
					38	Levi
	42 gens. X 30 yrs@ = 1260 yrs - 30 CE = 1230 BCE >David				39	Matthat
	(3 sets x 14 gens = 42 gens.)				40	Heli
					41	Joseph
					42	Jesus

We have allowed 30 years per generation as an average

between the standard suggestions of 20 or 40 years per generation.

For the **MT** and **LXX** accounts, we find 900 years from David to

the seven sons of Elyoʿenai/Elithenan. Though there are many

opinions regarding when David was born, I suggest using 1070

BCE. By subtracting 900 years from this date, we find that with

these men we have reached a terminal date of 170 BCE for the

recorded lineage of David in Scripture. It may be simply

coincidental, but, since seven names are given here, one is tempted

to connect them to the martyrdom of Ḥannah and her seven sons.

HANNAH AND HER SEVEN SONS, a story told
in II Maccabees, Chapter 7,of seven brothers who were
seized along with their mother by Antiochus IV Epiphanes,
presumably shortly after the beginning of the religious
persecutions in 167/166 B.C.E., and commanded to prove
their obedience to the king by partaking of swine's flesh. The
brothers defiantly refused to do so. Encouraged in their
resolve by their mother, they were executed after being put
to frightful tortures. When the mother was appealed to by the
king to spare the youngest child's life by prevailing upon him
to comply, she urged the child instead to follow in the path
of his brothers, and she herself died shortly thereafter.[114]

---

114 https://www.jewishvirtuallibrary.org/hannah-and-her-seven-sons

Matthew records 28 generations, which gives us 840 years. The traditional date for the CT-Yeshu's death is 33 CE, while I suggest 28 CE, so, just to keep the math simple, we can compromise at 30 CE. Since we are calculating back, we must subtract this from 840 years, which gives us the year 810 BCE for the birth of David. On the other hand, *Luke* presents us with 42 generation, which would equal 1260 years and give 1230 BCE as the year David was born. Perhaps there are those who would accept either of these dates, but let's just say that they would represent the minority opinions.

The author of the letters to Timothy and Titus (traditionally identified as Paul) was not very impressed with the stories and genealogies of *Matthew* and *Luke*. He seems to consider them simply as a waste of time.

> "Neither give heed to fables and endless genealogies, which minister questions, rather than Godly edifying which is in faith: *so do.*" (1 Tim. 1:4.)

> "But avoid foolish questions, and genealogies, and contentions, and strivings about the law; for they are unprofitable and vain. (Titus 3:9)[115]

The most obvious difference between the two Christian genealogies is that *Matthew*'s begins with David's son, Solomon, while *Luke*'s begins with his son, Nathan; but, each end with CT-

---

115 http://thekingsbible.com/

Yeshu's father, Joseph. The standard answer to this corundum is that *Matthew*'s is for Joseph's side of the family, while *Luke*'s is for his wife, Mary's. There are two issues with this answer.

1) This is not what it says. 2) There is a difference of 420 years between the genealogies (*Luke*=1230 yrs. minus *Matthew*=810 yrs.). Does this mean that Joseph was roughly 420 years older than Mary? That's quite an age gap! Of course, this debate always come back a primary question. Since Mary was still a virgin at CT-Yeshu's birth (Matt. 1:18-25 & *Luke* 1:26-56), then why are we even discussing these genealogies?

III-1.2 Virgin-Birth

We have already touched on the topic of "Virgin-birth", but since it is such a fundamental belief in Christianity, it is worth a quick revisit.

1) All gods, goddesses, and demi-gods were conceived by miraculous means, usually involving virgin-birth. (Should I put this in all-caps and bold type?)

2) A *na'ar* is a young girl, who is assumed to be a virgin. An *'almah* is a young woman of marriageable age, who, if she is not yet married, is also assumed to a virgin. *Betulah* is a girl of marriageable age who has never been intimate with a man. All three terms are used in describing Rebecca (Rifkah).

Below are verses from both the Hebrew and Greek scriptures related to this subject. In Genesis 24:16 we find *na'ar* and *betulah,* while in verse 43, where Eleazar is speaking to her family, we find *'almah.* However, in the Greek text we find only the term *parthenos* (παρθένος), "virgin", for all three terms. In Isaiah 14:7, we find the same substitution – *'almah* is rendered as *parthenos.* But, when we dig deeper, it gets very interesting. Proverbs 30:19 has *'almah* in the Hebrew, but Proverbs 30:1 thru 31:9 are not found at all in the LXX. It's been removed. Also, note that Exodus 2:8, Psalms 68:26, and Song of Songs 1:3, 6:8 all have *'almah* or the plural form *'almoth.* The LXX for these verses uses the correct Greek forms of the term <u>νεᾶνις</u>, <u>νεανίδων</u> or <u>νεάνιδες</u>, which like *'almah* means "maiden" or "damsel", who usually is in her teens. Therefore, Genesis 24:16 and 43, Isaiah 14:7, and Proverbs 30:19 in the LXX originally used forms of νεᾶνις, and that they were deliberately altered by early Christian scribes for the purpose of deifying CT-Yeshu and "elevate" Mary to the stature of a virgin-goddess in the eyes of neophytes.

טז **וְהַנַּעֲרָ**, טֹבַת מַרְאֶה מְאֹד--**בְּתוּלָה**, וְאִישׁ לֹא יְדָעָהּ; וַתֵּרֶד הָעַיְנָה, וַתְּמַלֵּא כַדָּהּ וַתָּעַל.

Gen. 24:16 And the **damsel** was very fair to look upon, a **virgin**, *neither had any man known her*; and she went down to the fountain, and filled her pitcher, and came up.
Gen. 24:16 ἡ δὲ **παρθένος** ἦν καλὴ τῇ ὄψει σφόδρα· **παρθένος** ἦν, ἀνὴρ οὐκ ἔγνω αὐτήν. καταβᾶσα δὲ ἐπὶ τὴν πηγὴν ἔπλησε τὴν ὑδρίαν αὐτῆς καὶ ἀνέβη.

16 And the **virgin** was very beautiful in appearance, she was a **virgin**, a man had not known her; and she went down to the well, and filled her water-pot, and came up.

מג הִנֵּה אָנֹכִי נִצָּב, עַל-עֵין הַמָּיִם; וְהָיָה **הָעַלְמָה**, הַיֹּצֵאת לִשְׁאֹב, וְאָמַרְתִּי אֵלֶיהָ, הַשְׁקִינִי-נָא מְעַט-מַיִם מִכַּדֵּךְ.

Gen. 24:43 behold, I stand by the fountain of water; and let it come to pass, that the **maiden** that cometh forth to draw, to whom I shall say: Give me, I pray thee, a little water from thy pitcher to drink;

Gen. 24:43 ἰδοὺ ἐγὼ ἐφέστηκα ἐπὶ τῆς πηγῆς τοῦ ὕδατος, καὶ αἱ θυγατέρες τῶν ἀνθρώπων τῆς πόλεως ἐκπορεύονται ἀντλῆσαι ὕδωρ, καὶ ἔσται ἡ **παρθένος**, ᾗ ἂν ἐγὼ εἴπω, πότισόν με ἐκ τῆς ὑδρίας σου μικρὸν ὕδωρ,

43 behold, I stand by the well of water, and the daughters of the men of the city come forth to draw water, and it shall be [that] the **damsel** to whom I shall say, Give me a little water to drink out of thy pitcher,

יד לָכֵן יִתֵּן אֲדֹנָי הוּא, לָכֶם--אוֹת: הִנֵּה **הָעַלְמָה**, הָרָה וְיֹלֶדֶת בֵּן, וְקָרָאת שְׁמוֹ, עִמָּנוּ אֵל.

Is. 7:14 Therefore the Lord Himself shall give you a sign: behold, **the young woman** has conceived, and has born a son, and shall call his name Immanuel.

Is. 7:14 διὰ τοῦτο δώσει Κύριος αὐτὸς ὑμῖν σημεῖον· ἰδοὺ ἡ **παρθένος** ἐν γαστρὶ ἕξει, καὶ τέξεται υἱόν, καὶ καλέσεις τὸ ὄνομα αὐτοῦ Ἐμμανουήλ·

14 Therefore the Lord himself shall give you a sign; behold, **a virgin** shall conceive in the womb, and shall bring forth a son, and thou shalt call his name Emmanuel.

יט דֶּרֶךְ הַנֶּשֶׁר, בַּשָּׁמַיִם-- דֶּרֶךְ נָחָשׁ, עֲלֵי-צוּר; דֶּרֶךְ-אֳנִיָּה בְלֶב-יָם-- וְדֶרֶךְ גֶּבֶר בְּעַלְמָה.

Prv. 30:19 The way of an eagle in the air; the way of a serpent upon a rock; {N}

the way of a ship in the midst of the sea; and the way of a man with a **young woman**.

ח וַתֹּאמֶר-לָהּ בַּת-פַּרְעֹה, לְכִי; וַתֵּלֶךְ, **הָעַלְמָה**, וַתִּקְרָא, אֶת-אֵם הַיָּלֶד.
Ex. 2:8 And Pharaoh's daughter said to her: 'Go.' And **the maiden** went and called the child's mother.
Ex. 2:8 ἡ δὲ εἶπεν ἡ θυγάτηρ Φαραώ· πορεύου. ἐλθοῦσα δὲ ἡ **νεᾶνις** ἐκάλεσε τὴν μητέρα τοῦ παιδίου.
8 And the daughter of Pharao said, Go: and **the young woman** went, and called the mother of the child.

כו קִדְּמוּ שָׁרִים, אַחַר נֹגְנִים;   בְּתוֹךְ **עֲלָמוֹת**, תּוֹפֵפוֹת.
Ps.68:26 The singers go before, the minstrels follow after, in the midst of **damsels** playing upon timbrels.
Ps.68:26 προέφθασαν ἄρχοντες ἐχόμενοι ψαλλόντων ἐν μέσῳ **νεανίδων** τυμπανιστριῶν.
26 The princes went first, next before the players on instruments, in the midst of **damsels** playing on timbrels.

ג לְרֵיחַ שְׁמָנֶיךָ טוֹבִים, שֶׁמֶן תּוּרַק שְׁמֶךָ; עַל-כֵּן, **עֲלָמוֹת אֲהֵבוּךָ**.
Songs 1:3 Thine ointments have a goodly fragrance; thy name is as ointment poured forth; therefore, do the **maidens** love thee.
Songs 1:3 καὶ ὀσμὴ μύρων σου ὑπὲρ πάντα τὰ ἀρώματα· μῦρον ἐκκενωθὲν ὄνομά σου. διὰ τοῦτο **νεάνιδες** ἠγάπησάν σε,
3 And the smell of thine ointments is better than all spices: thy name is ointment poured forth; therefore, do the **young maidens** love thee.

ח שִׁשִּׁים הֵמָּה מְלָכוֹת, וּשְׁמֹנִים פִּילַגְשִׁים; **וַעֲלָמוֹת**, אֵין מִסְפָּר.
Song 6:8 There are threescore queens, and fourscore concubines, and **maidens** without number.
Song 6:8 ἑξήκοντά εἰσι βασίλισσαι, καὶ ὀγδοήκοντα παλλακαί, καὶ **νεάνιδες** ὧν οὐκ ἔστιν ἀριθμός.

8 There are sixty queens, and eighty concubines, and **maidens** without number.

Since we follow the Torah, we find such stories nonsensical, but to the non-Jewish world at that time, these were crucial issues. Physical and spiritual purity have always been essential foci and goals in each individual Jewish life that also manifest in our national persona. On this level, we can understand the concept behind the ancient, innate reverence for the state of innocence. Yet, CT stories take nature reverence to an unnatural level. For most of history of Christianity countless individuals, Jews and non-Jews were senselessly murdered because they could not accept this doctrine.

Personally, I do not believe that she was raped by a Roman soldier as some rabbis portray her, though, of course, that is possible. I am confident that the historic mothers of both Yeshu haNotzri and Yeshu-Ḳristos were virgins when they stood under the wedding canopy, but that neither was such when they gave birth to their beloved, first-born sons (Matt. 1:25). But then, if people are gullible enough to believe that either mother was virgin when her son was born, then they should have no problem accepting the proposition that his father was over 400 years old when he was born.

III-1.3 The Magi

The "Adoration of the Magi", "Flight to Egypt", "Massacre of the Innocents and death of King Herod are only recorded in Matt. 2:1-23. and are claimed by some to be historical –, which actually did occur, is included in this set and is used by scholars to set the date of CT-Yeshu's birth. However, the date they use is correct if, and only if, this connection is correct; but, at this time, we are not concerned with this issue. Here is the sequence of events.

The "Adoration of the Magi" This is a charming story that follows the miraculous birth of CT-Yeshu. The Magi (μάγοι – the plural for Magus) were Zoroastrian priests, famous for magic and astrology. Upon arriving in Jerusalem, they wander about the city asking people: "Where is he that is born King of the Jews? For we have seen his star in the east, and are come to worship him." This is odd for two reasons. Since they are priests, wouldn't they have asked "Where does your high priest live?" Also, they are telling us that they traveled hundreds of miles to a politically insignificant, country that has lost its independence in order to *worship* a foreign newborn. This is an effective dramatic expression that successfully appeals to emotions of those who love the under-dog. The word got around; soon, Herod was informed. He and *all* of Jerusalem were alarmed. He gathered *all* of the chief priests and inquires: "From where is the "Ḳristos" (ὁ χριστὸς) to come?" They informed he that he will come from Bethlehem. Then, even though by now the entire city knew what was going on, still he met them secretively. Mostly, he wanted to know when the sign appeared. [the plot thickens!] Then he sent them to Bethlehem. "Go and search diligently for the young child; and when ye have found him, bring me word again, that I may come and worship him also… and, lo, the star, which they saw in the east, went before them, till it came and stood over where the young child was." Really? It is five and a half miles from Jerusalem to Bethlehem. So, they find the young family and bow down and worship the baby and mother. Then they presented to the parents – gold, frankincense, and myrrh. Having been warned in a dream, they did not return to Herod, instead they happily return home. Joseph also has a dream warning him to take them and seek refuge in Egypt. Seeing that the Magi did not return, Herod, anxious to destroy this dangerous rival, has all infant boys in Judaea murdered. The question that comes to mind is – If Herod was so alarmed by their mission, wouldn't he have sent his own men with them to report back to him?

As well as the internal issues, there are also exterior ones. After Alexander destroyed the Old Persian empire, they were under Greek rule for 84 years and then under Parthian for 470 more years. Ardashir I, appalled at the state his country and temples, rallied his people and defeated the Parthians in 224 CE, establishing the Sassanid Persian Empire. *Matthew* was written roughly 130 years earlier, when the Persian religion was at a low point. If Zoroastrian Magi were looking for a savior-king, why would they wander about the Middle East, searching for one in a politically insignificant, conquered nation that was on the brink of self-destruction? Wouldn't they have searched for a royal Persian infant, who would become an earlier version of Ardashir? It is more realistic to suggest that this set of stories were add after the revitalization of the Persian empire and Zoroastrian religion as global powers? Thus, it's purpose was to reassure the struggling Christian sectarians that they, like the Persians would one day unite and ascend to great power. At that time even the Persian Magi would bow before their god, CT-Yeshu.

It is not our desire to demean this or any other charming story in the Christian Texts. Every culture has expressions reflect their emotional experience more so than their physical history. Such accounts do not need to be factual to possess meaningful significance for their people. No one has the right to ridicule the legends others. We are only commenting on them here because missionaries insist that we must accept them as historically true – which we cannot do.

III-2 Yeshu as Everything

> **JfJ:** That Scripture testifies to more than one
> possibility for qualification as a Son of God is not
> disputed. That it points toward one individual
> who was to be glorified as the Son of God is also
> quite clear. The Jewish followers of Jesus in his
> day were on the alert for just this One. Thus, the
> Galilean skeptic, Nathaniel, blurted on first
> meeting Yeshua, "Rabbi, you are the Son of God;
> You are the King of Israel." (John 1:49.)

This statement is entirely misleading, and it is still highly disputed. Since we are all the children of G-d, everyone meets this requirement from birth. From Judaism's Torah central perspective, the Mashiah is no more *the* son of G-d than my husband is. However, he is unique. He is Hashem's chosen-one for extremely critical responsibilities. My husband is a devout, dedicated and talented Jew, but he does not qualify for the position of Mashiah. For one to hold that position, he must possess the qualifying characteristic required by that job description.

There were Greeks and Romans living in Judaea who very possibly were waiting for the anticipated return of Alexander the Great. There were many, perhaps even the majority of Jews, who were praying for a great military leader to free them of Roman oppression. Yet, the Mashiah must not only be a military genius, he must, more importantly, be an administrative and political genius. Obviously, none of the would-be-messiahs to date have possessed the necessary qualifications. The Jews of that time may have believed with all their heart that one or both Yeshu was the Mashiaḥ, but, as we have noted, simply believing that something is true does not magically transform it into an actual truth.

It is a well-known fact that from the inception of Christianity missionaries have cherry-picked verses, taking them out of context and then twisting the meanings to support their illusions. *The Book of Matthew* is an excellent example of this activity. I am certain that this author and its redactors were totally convinced that the ends justified the means. Afterall, theirs was a righteous cause, since they were altering the texts to save lost souls and impart to them eternal life. I have no doubts that they were totally convinced that their teachings reflected "The Truth" that, due to their devout and strict lifestyle, god had revealed to them. Therefore, whenever the author or editors of Matthew happened upon a passage in the LXX that related something inspirational, they knew that it must be referring to CT-Yeshu, their "Lord and Savior". The author or editors inserted these "proofs" throughout their Texts with variants of such phrases as "That it might be fulfilled which was spoken of the Lord by the prophet, saying…" These references are characteristic in the *Book of Matthew*, where the largest number can be found. The purpose is not only to deify CT-Yeshu but to incorporate in his persona those characteristics most greatly admired by followers of all traditional pagan gods. In like manner, they identify him as not only the predicted descendant of David, the Mashiaḥ, but also the incarnate of everyone other important person in Jewish history, including Avraham, MelḵeiTzadiq, Joseph, Moshe, Aharon, King David, Eliyahu, etc. Let it suffice to quote: "When you try to be everything to everyone, you accomplish being nothing to anyone."[116]

Of course, the most important role that Yeshu plays in the CT is that as "*The* Son of God". As usual, they start with the Jewish perspective and quote well known Torah verses; however, you must watch carefully for the "***But***". This is the turning point in their persuasive argument, when they try to redirect you towards Christianity.

> **JfJ:** When God instructed Moses preparing him to speak before Pharaoh, He said, "Israel is my firstborn son... Let my son go." (Exodus 4:22-23) It was God who "fathered Israel." The Lord called Israel into existence through the Gentile, Abraham. To him was promised blessing and the privilege of being a blessing to all the nations. Israel then is God's own, a sanctified treasure, a pre-eminent son. For as a people, Israel is called to accomplish God's purpose. Through Israel's posterity would come Messiah.
>
> While Israel has prayed to "God, our Father," our people do not claim divine equality. Sonship is

---

[116] https://quotefancy.com/quote/1783612/Bonnie-Gillespie-When-you-try-to-be-everything-to-everyone-you-accomplish-being-nothing

understood as a relationship to the Creator, an example of the creature beloved by a gracious God. This relationship is demonstrated again when Moses reminds Israel of God's fatherly love for the nation in his farewell speech. (Deuteronomy 32:6)

The prophet Hosea adds another sense to the idea of sonship. Not only is the nation regarded as God's son (*i.e.* **"When Israel was a child, I loved him, and out of Egypt I called my son." Hosea 11:1**), but the prophet adds that each of the Israelites are **"...the sons of the living God." (Hosea 1:10.)** *But this latter picture is of an internally united Israel and comprised of people who, having been chastened, have returned to the fear and love of God.*

But of all the Israelites, is there not *one special son of God*? Through the family of David and the line of the tribe of Judah, a son would come whose throne would be eternal. "When your days are over and you go to be with your fathers, I will raise up your offspring to succeed you, one of your own sons, and I will establish his kingdom." (1 Chronicles 17:11) Of *this one*, God says, **"I will be his father, and he will be my son." (I Chronicles 17:13.)**

Notice that the bold italicized line very subtly implies that Israel currently lacks the character required to be called Hashem's son. I completely disagree with this message. For 2000 years, *Am Israel* has suffered from the canonized slander of anti-Jewish missionaries. It is time that

236

we stand-up and firmly protest: די – Enough! Though we are multifaceted, yet we are united; and, though we don't shout it publicly, yet we do fear and love Hashem – in a way that despotic missionaries cannot phantom. In your heart, you know this is true. Also, I would add that we do believe that Hashem had a "son" – his name was Adam.

III-2.1 Yeshu haNotzri

In 1965, Hugh J. Schonfield publish his bestseller, *The Passover Plot,* in which he presents the thesis that the CT-Yeshu plotted and enacted his own crucifixion in order to gain recognition as the Suffering Servant-Messiah and thus unite the people against the Roman. Yet, Schonfield overlooked one very important fact. The historic Yeshu haNotzri (ישעו הנוצרי, aka "Jesus of Nazareth"), was executed by stoning at the order of the Sanhedrin in Jerusalem 100 years before Pontius Pilate ordered Yeshu-Ḳristos (Ἰησοῦς, ὁ Χριστὸς, aka "Jesus the Christos") executed by crucifixion. Thus, these were two very different people, each with his own agenda. How did their stories become meshed into one? Since the CT account is well known, let's begin with that of Yeshu haNotzri, which is found in the Babylonian Talmud.

Sanhedrin 103a:

237

דבר אחר לא תאונה אליך רעה שלא יבעתוך חלומות רעים
והרהורים רעים ונגע לא יקרב באהלך שלא יהא לך בן או
תלמיד שמקדיח תבשילו ברבים [כגון ישו הנוצרי]

Alternatively, the phrase "no evil shall befall you" means that you will be frightened neither by bad dreams nor by evil thoughts. "Nor shall any plague come near your tent" means that you will not have a child or student who overcooks his food in public, i.e., sins in public and causes others to sin, such as in the well-known case of Yeshu haNotzri.[117]

Sanhedrin 107b:

תנו רבנן לעולם תהא שמאל דוחה וימין מקרבת לא כאלישע
שדחפו לגחזי בשתי ידים [ולא כרבי יהושע בן פרחיה שדחפו
ל**יש"ו** בשתי ידים] הוספה מחסרונות הש"ס: רבי יהושע בן
פרחיה מאי הוא כדקטלינהו ינאי מלכא לרבנן אזל רבי יהושע בן
פרחיה **ויש"ו** לאלכסנדריא של מצרים כי הוה שלמא שלח לי'
שמעון בן שטח מני ירושלים עיר הקודש ליכי אלכסנדרי' של
מצרים אחותי בעלי שרוי בתוכך ואנכי יושבת שוממה קם אתא
ואתרמי ליה ההוא אושפיזא עבדו ליה יקרא טובא אמר כמה יפה
אכסניא זו אמר ליה רבי **עיניה טרוטות** אמר ליה רשע בכך
אתה עוסק אפיק ארבע מאה שיפורי ושמתיה אתא לקמיה כמה
זמנין אמר ליה קבלן לא הוי קא משגח ביה יומא חד הוה קא קרי
קריאת שמע אתא לקמיה סבר לקבולי אחוי ליה בידיה הוא
סבר מידחא דחי ליה אזל זקף לבינתא והשתחוה לה אמר ליה
הדר בך אמר ליה כך מקובלני ממך כל החוטא ומחטיא את
הרבים אין מספיקין בידו לעשות תשובה ואמר מר **יש"ו** כישף
והסית והדיח את ישראל:

The Sages taught: Always have the left-hand drive sinners away and the right draw them near, so that the sinner will not totally despair of atonement. This is unlike Elisha, who pushed away Gehaze with his

[117] https://www.sefaria.org/Sanhedrin.103a.14?lang=bi&with=all&lang2=en

two hands and caused him to lose his share in the World-to-Come, and unlike Yehoshua ben Peraḥya, who pushed away **Yeshu HaNotzri** with his two hands.

What is the incident involving Yehoshua ben Peraḥya? The Gemara relates: When King Yannai was killing the Sages, Yehoshua ben Peraḥya and **Yeshu HaNotzri**, his student, went to Alexandria of Egypt. When there was peace between King Yannai and the Sages, Shimon ben Shataḥ sent a message to Yehoshua ben Peraḥya: "From me, Jerusalem, the holy city, to you, Alexandria of Egypt: My sister, my husband is located among you and I sit desolate. The head of the Sages of Israel is out of the country and Jerusalem requires his return."

He (Yehoshua ben Peraḥya) understood the message, arose, came, and happened to arrive at a certain inn on the way to Jerusalem. They treated him with great honor. He (Yehoshua ben Peraḥya) said: "How beautiful is this inn." His student (Yeshu) said to him: "My teacher, her eyes (of the innkeeper's wife) are narrow." He (Yehoshua ben Peraḥya) said to him: "Wicked one! Do you involve yourself with regard to that matter, the appearance of a married woman?" He produced four hundred *shofarot* and ostracized him.

He (Yeshu) came before him (Yehoshua ben Peraḥya) several times and said to him: Accept our (i.e. my) repentance. He (Yehoshua ben Peraḥya) took no notice of him. One day he (Yehoshua ben Peraḥya) was reciting Shema and he (Yeshu) came before him with the same request. He (Yehoshua ben Peraḥya) intended to accept his request, and signaled him with his hand to wait until he completed his prayer. He (Yeshu) did not understand the signal and thought: "He is driving me away." He went and stood a brick upright to serve as an idol and he bowed to it. He (Yehoshua ben Peraḥya) then said to him (Yeshu): "Repent." He (Yeshu) said to him: "This is the tradition that I received from you: Whoever sins and causes the masses to sin is not given the opportunity to repent." And the Master says: **Yeshu HaNotzri** sorcery, incited Jews to engage in idolatry, and led Israel astray. Had Yehoshua ben Peraḥya not caused him to despair of atonement, he would not have taken the path of evil.[118]

The rabbis inform us that on his deathbed King Yannai repented of his persecution of the Pharisees (88-76 BCE) and asked that Queen Salome bring them back and set them as her chief advisors. It is understandable that the king would repent for the atrocities he had committed; but, considering the sociopolitical distance between the two parties, it is difficult to accept that he instructed her to hand all power over to his adversaries. The pieces do not seem to fit. Let's step back and review these cryptic statements within a political matrix.

In 76 BCE, his young queen suddenly finds herself a widow with two young sons. Her warrior husband has left them with recently expanded but currently strong bounders. After roughly a decade of internal instability, she wants peace. So, she calls the

---

[118] https://www.sefaria.org/Sanhedrin.107b.8?lang=bi&with=all&lang2=en

leader of the opposition, Shimon ben Satakh, to her palace. He
accepts her offer of peace and writes to the exiles that it is safe to
return.

On his return trip, Yehoshua ben Peraḥya stopped at an inn,
where the proprietors show them great honor and concern. He
turned to his disciple and stated, "She is lovely inn." Yeshu
haNotzi replied, "Yes, but she (the innkeeper's wife) has
[*terutot=bleary-eyed*] "bleary eyes." Squinting, narrow eyes carries
negative connotations that the individual is shrewd and greedy. He
may have been implying to be cautious of the couple's flattery.
For this statement the student was placed under *ḥerem*
(excommunication). This seems like a harsh penalty for such a
simply comment. Yet, he was criticizing their host, who had shown
them only respect. Yehoshua ben Peraḥya found his statement and
fact that he looked at a married woman offensive and beneath the
dignity of a student. Besides, one gets the feeling that Yeshu
haNotzi was already on probation and that this was the last-straw.
Ḥerem was a very serious punishment. Not only was he cast-out of
his study community but also no one was permitted to speak to
him, aid him, or conduct business with him.

After arriving home, the student repeatedly came to his
teacher begging forgiveness but was refused. Yeshu decided to try
one last time. Yehoshua ben Peraḥya had decided to forgive him,
but he was praying when Yeshu entered. He motioned for him to
wait. The student misunderstanding the gesture, stormed out.

After finishing his prayers, the teacher sought him out, but it was too late. v "stood a brick upright to serve as an idol and he bowed to it." The Talmud reprimands Yehoshua ben Peraḥya's mishandling of the situation meaning that it had dire consequences.

This is very odd. It is such an extreme reversal to go from a monotheistic scholar one day to worshipping a stone the next. Note that "he stood a brick upright". We find such a statement in the account of Jacob journey from Beir Sheva to Ḥaran. (Gen. 28:10-18) "Jacob rose up early in the morning, and took the stone that he had put under his head, and set it up for a pillar (מַצֵּבָה), and poured oil upon the top of it." Before the giving of the Torah at Mount Sinai, this was the mode of worship, but, after the Mishkan was constructed, it was forbidden to do so. This probably indicates that Yeshu haNotzi, suffering from the acute pain of rejection, decided to revive this ancient custom. The act of setting up a *matzevah*, stone pillar implies that he went about the land teaching a revitalization doctrine that contained elements contradicting accepts of both the written and oral Law. At any rate, the novelty of a new movement would be enough to attract an initial following. We return now to the Talmud, Sanhedrin 43a, for evidence of his teachings.

וכרוז יוצא לפניו לפניו אין מעיקרא לא והתניא **בערב הפסח**
תלאוהו **לישו והכרוז** יוצא לפניו מ' יום **ישו** יוצא ליסקל על
שכישף והסית והדיח את ישראל כל מי שיודע לו זכות יבא
וילמד עליו ולא מצאו לו זכות ותלאוהו **בערב הפסח**

The Mishna teaches that a crier goes out before the condemned man. This indicates that it is only before him, i.e., while he is being led to his execution, that yes, the crier goes out, but from the outset, before the accused is convicted, he does not go out. The Gemara raises a difficulty: But isn't it taught in a *baraita*: **On Passover Eve** they hung the corpse of Yeshu after they killed him by way of stoning. And a crier went out before him for **forty days**, publicly proclaiming: "Yeshu is going out to be stoned because he practiced sorcery, incited people to idol worship, and led the Jewish people astray. Anyone who knows of a reason to acquit him should come forward and teach it on his behalf." And the court did not find a reason to acquit him, and so they stoned him and hung his corpse on Passover eve.

אמר עולא ותסברא בר הפוכי זכות הוא מסית הוא ורחמנא אמר (דברים יג, ט) לא תחמול ולא תכסה עליו אלא שאני **ישו דקרוב למלכות הוה**

Ulla said: And how can you understand this proof? Was Yeshu worthy of conducting a search for a reason to acquit him? He was an inciter to idol worship, and the Merciful One states with regard to an inciter to idol worship: "Neither shall you spare, neither shall you conceal him" (Deuteronomy 13:9). Rather, Yeshu was different, as **he had close ties with the government**, and the gentile authorities were interested in his acquittal. Consequently, the court gave him every opportunity to clear himself, so that it could not be claimed that he was falsely convicted.

Rabbi Ulla [ca. 275-325 CE] was a leader among the Amoraim scholars. He lived in the land but also traveled to

243

Babylon to discuss and teach religious law. Here he says: 1) Yeshu haNotzi had close ties with the government (למלכות, *i.e.* monarchy). However, he does not elaborate on which monarchy. 2) The gentile authorities were interested in his acquittal.

1) Yeshu is a shortened form of the name Yoshua. The term *hanotzri*, הנוצרי, is interesting. The ה of course is the article "the". The masculine noun, נֵצֶר, means "a sprout, shoot". There are four *pesukim* in Isaiah where it is used in reference to the Suffering Servant. The first two verses refer to an individual, while the last two are distinctly speaking of Israel as a nation. We turn again to the JPS online translation.

2) יא:א וְיָצָא חֹטֶר, מִגֵּזַע יִשָׁי; **וְנֵצֶר**, מִשָּׁרָשָׁיו יִפְרֶה.

11:1 And there shall come forth a shoot out of the stock of Jesse, **and a twig** shall grow forth out of his roots.

יד:יט וְאַתָּה הָשְׁלַכְתָּ מִקִּבְרְךָ, **כְּנֵצֶר נִתְעָב**--לְבֻשׁ הֲרֻגִים, מְטֹעֲנֵי חָרֶב; יוֹרְדֵי אֶל-אַבְנֵי-בוֹר, כְּפֶגֶר מוּבָס.

14:19 But thou art cast forth away from thy grave **like an abhorred offshoot**, in the raiment of the slain, that are thrust through with the sword, that go down to the pavement of the pit, as a carcass trodden under foot.

מט:ו וַיֹּאמֶר, נָקֵל מִהְיוֹתְךָ לִי עֶבֶד, לְהָקִים אֶת-שִׁבְטֵי יַעֲקֹב, **וּנְצִירֵי (וּנְצוּרֵי) יִשְׂרָאֵל** לְהָשִׁיב; וּנְתַתִּיךָ לְאוֹר גּוֹיִם, לִהְיוֹת יְשׁוּעָתִי עַד-קְצֵה הָאָרֶץ.

49:6 Yea, He saith: 'It is too light a thing that thou shouldest be My servant to raise up the tribes of Jacob, and to restore the **offspring of Israel**; I will also give thee for a light of the nations, that My salvation may be unto the end of the earth.'

ס:כא וְעַמֵּךְ כֻּלָּם צַדִּיקִים, לְעוֹלָם יִירְשׁוּ אָרֶץ; **נֵצֶר מַטָּעוֹ** (מַטָּעַי) מַעֲשֵׂה יָדַי,
לְהִתְפָּאֵר.

60:21 Thy people also shall be all righteous, they shall inherit the
land for ever; **the branch of My planting**, the work of My hands,
wherein I glory.

Hence, the name Yeshu haNotzri means, Yoshua the "shoot
or branch" of the root of David. Thus, this Yeshu was a direct
descendant of King David. However, he could also have been,
through the marriage of a forefather to a daughter of one of the
Maccabean warrior-priests, related to the Hasmonean rulers as
well.

3) The statement that the gentile authorities were interested in
his acquittal does not fit for the period of Yeshu haNotzri, since the
government was still in the hand of Jewish king/priests in his time.
Rabbi Ulla lived in the years of the rule of the Nasi Hillel II, before
the Christians stripped the Jews of the last semblance of
independence. Thus, he would have been aware of the basic claims
of the Christian Texts, which had been in public circulation for
roughly 250 years by then. Therefore, we will address this
statement when we discuss Yeshu, who was called Ḵristos.

ת"ר **חמשה תלמידים היו לו לישו** מתאי נקאי נצר ובוני
ותודה אתיוהו למתי אמר להו מתי יהרג הכתיב (תהלים מב, ג)
מתי אבוא ואראה פני אלהים אמרו לו אין מתי יהרג דכתיב
(שם מא, ו) מתי ימות ואבד שמו. אתיוהו לנקאי אמר להו נקאי
יהרג הכתיב (שמות כג, ז) ונקי וצדיק אל תהרוג אמרו לו אין
נקאי יהרג דכתיב (תהלים י, ח) במסתרים יהרג נקי. אתיוהו

לנצר אמר נצר יהרג הכתיב (ישעיה יא, א) ונצר משרשיו יפרה
אמרו לו אין נצר יהרג דכתיב (שם יד, יט) ואתה השלכת
מקברך כנצר נתעב. אתיוהו לבוני אמר אמר בוני יהרג הכתיב
(שמות ד, כב) בני בכורי ישראל אמרו לי' אין בוני יהרג דכתיב
(שם, כג) הנה אנכי הורג את בנך בכורך. אתיוהו לתודה אמר
תודה יהרג הכתיב (תהלים ק, א) מזמור לתודה אמרו לו אין
תודה יהרג דכתיב (שם נ, כג) זובח תודה יכבדנני.

Apropos the trial of Yeshu, the Gemara cites
another *baraita*, where the Sages taught: **Yeshu
HaNotzri had five disciples**: Mattai, Nakai, Netzer,
Buni, and Toda. They brought Mattai in to stand trial.
Mattai said to the judges: Shall Mattai be executed?
But isn't it written: "When [*matai*] shall I come and
appear before G-d?" (Psalms 42:3). Mattai claimed
that this verse alludes to the fact he is righteous. They
said to him: Yes, Mattai shall be executed, as it is
written: "When [*matai*] shall he die, and his name
perish?" (Psalms 41:6).

Then they brought Nakai in to stand trial. Nakai
said to the judges: Shall Nakai be executed? But isn't
it written: "And the innocent [*naki*] and righteous
you shall not slay" (Exodus 23:7)? They said to him:
Yes, Nakai shall be executed, as it is written: "In
secret places he kills the innocent [*naki*]" (Psalms
10:8).

Then they brought Netzer in to stand trial. He said
to the judges: Shall Netzer be executed? But isn't it
written: "And a branch [*netzer*] shall grow out of his
roots" (Isaiah 11:1)? They said to him: Yes, Netzer
shall be executed, as it is written: "But you are cast
out of your grave like an abhorred branch [*netzer*]"
(Isaiah 14:19).

Then they brought Buni in to stand trial. Buni said
to the judges: Shall Buni be executed? But isn't it
written: "My firstborn son [*beni*] is Israel" (Exodus

4:22)? They said to him: Yes, Buni shall be executed, as it is written: "Behold, I shall kill your firstborn son [*binkha*]" (Exodus 4:23).

Then they brought Toda in to stand trial. Toda said to the judges: Shall Toda be executed? But isn't it written: "A psalm of thanksgiving [*toda*]" (Psalms 100:1)? They said to him: Yes, Toda shall be executed, as it is written: "Whoever slaughters a thanks-offering [*toda*] honors Me" Psalms (Psalms 50:23).[119]

Perhaps the terms חמשה תלמידים, "five students" should be read instead חמשה למודים, "five teachings" of Yeshu haNotzi. If we take each teaching and position next to the response of the rabbis we find following philosophical argument.

Teaching: "*When [matai] shall I come and appear before G-d?*" When should the Mashiaḥ come? Isn't now as good of a time as any?
Rabbis: "*When [matai] shall he die, and his name perish?*" Since the Mashiaḥ is human, after he comes, he will die and in time his name will perish. Or, when Yeshu came, he brought troubles for the nation, and now he must appear for judgement before G-d.

Teachings: "And the *innocent [naki]* and righteous you shall not slay."
Yeshu claimed to be completely innocent and pure.
Rabbis: "In secret places he kills the *innocent [naki]*."
Yet, his political aspirations caused the slaughter of many innocent people, whose blood is on his hands.

Teachings: "And a *branch [netzer]* shall grow out of his roots."
Yeshu claimed to be the branch from the root of David and, therefore, the true ruler of Israel, not the sons of King Yannai.

---

[119] https://www.sefaria.org/Sanhedrin.43a.26?lang=bi&with=all&lang2=en

Rabbis: "But you are cast out of your grave like an abhorred *branch* [*netzer*]".

But, since he brought rebellion and opened the door for foolish people to mix Torah with pagan beliefs, he has become an abhorrent leader, who will be stoned and his grave left empty while his corpse is publicly hanged until sunset.

Teachings: "My *firstborn son* [*beni*] is Israel"
As the Mashiaḥ he is Israel and, thus, the firstborn son of G-d.
Rabbis: "Behold, I shall kill your *firstborn son* [*binkha*]"
If this is his belief and teaching, then it is better that G-d has handed him over to the authorities for execution.

Teachings: "A psalm of *thanksgiving* [*toda*]"
As a descendant of King David, he attracted followers by singing his psalms of *thanksgiving* and playing the lyre.
Rabbis: "Whoever slaughters *a thanksgiving-offering* [*toda*] honors Me".
We give a thanks-offering to G-d that He has permitted us to restore peace to His land and people.

Therefore, we can take the meaning of each name and form this question posed by his followers. Then the meaning of each reply by the rabbis would be more comprehendible.

Shall he be executed *when* [*Matai*] he is an *innocent* [*Naki*] *branch* [*Netzer*] and G-d's *firstborn son* [*Beni*] and sang psalms of *thanksgiving* [*Toda*] for his followers?

"*When* [*matai*] his name perishes because of the *innocent* [*naki*] ones he killed, he will be known as an abhorred *branch* [*netzer*], since he claimed to be G-d's *firstborn son* [*binkha*]and, thus, by his death, we have honored and *give thanks* to G-d.

As we mentioned earlier, many non-Jews had been settled there by Ptolemy I. By the time of Yeshu haNotzi, they had lived there for 234 years. These Greeks and Egyptians had absorbed elements of Jewish culture; and, it is worth noting that the LXX had by then been in circulation for 206 years. Thus, this Yeshu's movement would have struck a very different chord with the non-Jews. One that involved the king of the gods – Amon-Re, Zeus, Jupiter; the virgin mother goddess – Isis, Kebele, Athena/Minerva; the divine suffering son – Osiris, Dionysos, Attis, Baʿal; and the Holy-Spirit – the *Shehinah* that they had discovered in the LXX.

Included among the non-Jews were a large number of Roman mercenaries who made up a large portion of King Yanni's army. They revered Orpheus and Mithra, who was the "Sun of Righteousness" and bull-slayer, and, upon receiving baptismal in the blood of the bull, were reborn and assured of eternal life. To this we must add the association of David with Orpheus, which continued to be made for another six centuries.[120]

> The figure of Orpheus as a spiritual master of the lyre posed a challenge to Jews at a fairly early date, they found a creative solution: in the second century BCE, Aristobulus of Alexandria in his commentary on the Pentateuch identified Moses with the Greek Musaeus, making the latter the teacher of Orpheus, thereby subordinating the Greek sage, songster, and shaman to the greatest of men, the lawgiver of Israel, who spoke with God awake and face to face (more on Moses and David presently). And in a pseudepigraphon, Orpheus is made to abandon his inconvenient polytheism for belief in the one true

---

[120] Jaś Elsner, "Orpheus as David. Orpheus as Christ?" *Biblical Archaeology Review*, Vol. 35 No. 2, March/April 2009. Pp. 34-45.

God. The loose ends are neatly tied. Early Christians adopted as a matter of course various images of earlier gods and philosophers to portray their Savior. Among these was the figure of Orpheus and his lyre (or with a little lamb), employed to depict Christ the good shepherd; and the episode of Orpheus and Eurydice was taken as an obvious foreshadowing of Christ's own harrowing of hell and liberation of the souls of the righteous. But Christ was not to the best of our knowledge a musician. The pre-eminent harpist of the Bible is King David; so that musical aspect of Orpheus was diverted to the Psalmist.[121]

Simeon ben Shetach's court sentenced eighty women from Askelon to death on the charged of witchcraft. (Talmud *Yerushalmi Sanhedrin 6:6 and Hagigah 2:2,* 11a–b). This brings to the scene the additional component of the Maenads, the frenzied followers of Dionysos. This fits because Orpheus was often thought of as another manifestation of Dionysos; and, like these revered deities, Yeshu haNotzi purportedly performed acts of magic and sorcery.

Another factor is that Romans were always suspicious of a female ruler. Queen Salome would not have been able to hold the mercenary troops together without a substantial increase in their pay and even then, not without difficulties. They would have been more inclined to follow the young descendant of King David, who,

---

[121]

https://dash.harvard.edu/bitstream/handle/1/37143010/The_Lyre_of_King_David_and_the_Greeks.pdf?sequence=1 thanks to the LXX, was an internationally renowned warrior-king of near mythological stature.

The fact that Queen Salome had made peace with the Pharisees and warmly received in Jerusalem could not have sat well with the Ṣadducees. Above we suggested that the Ḥalakhic Letter may indicate that the sectarians assumed responsibility for the temple services during the seven-year period in which the high priest's position was reported "vacant" and that the sectarians were force to flee when Jonathan Hasmonean returned. Thus, there would have been many Ṣadducees and sectarians who would have been inclined to support a scion of David as a new king.

As a queen, Salome was concerned about losing the throne for their father's heirs. As a mother she feared for their lives. With these motivations, it would be easy to understand her decision to turn to the Pharisees for support and guidance. To Shimon ben Satakh and Yehoshua ben Peraḥya the solution was simple. The source of current turbulence was Yeshu HaNotzri. To end they turmoil the needed to remove its source. The people had suffered immensely during the past ten years of civil strife. It must end. Here we turn to the CT for the method they used – bribery. It is therefore reasonable that the Judas account orginated with the history of Yeshu HaNotzri.

There is a Medieval story that the rabbis despaired of apprehending this Yeshu, because he knew the secrets of manipulating the holy Name and, by so doing, could fly. So, they entrusted this occult knowledge to a friend of his, who, using it, flew above him. Once well positioned, he peed on him. Having become defiled, Yeshu haNotzi fell to the ground and was easily captured.[122] Of course, this was composed much later, during a period after despotic missionaries had decimated the Jews in Alexandria and displaced most Jews from their homeland. Therefore, it is understandable that they would write disparaging stories about the one who seemed most responsible for their misfortunes.

Because he was of royal lineage a decree was posted for forty days before his execution, asking for anyone who could bring a good testimony before the court, giving the evidence in his favor, to come forward, and his life would be spared. No one responded. Just before Passover, Yeshu HaNotzri and his five disciples were stoned to death. Is it only a coincident that the Catholic ritual of Lent is 40 days before the holiday of Easter?

This Yeshu traveled several times between the Galilee and Jerusalem, had time to develop a following strong enough to shake the power-that-be and seal his own fate. Therefore, his revolt probably covered the years from 76 to 73 BCE. He died on *erev*

---

[122] https://dovbear.blogspot.com/2012/07/the-strange-story-of-flying-jesus.html and
https://www.mohrsiebeck.com/uploads/tx_sgpublisher/produkte/leseproben/9783161534812.pdf and
https://archive.org/stream/ToledotYeshuTheLifeStoryOfJesus_201812/Toledot%20Yeshu%20The%20Life%20Story%20of%20Jesus_djvu.txt

Pesah. In those days, Passover began with each family bring it lamb or kid to be sacrificed in the Temple (14-Nisan); therefore, his death occurred on 13-Nisan, which in -73 was on 4-April. He was stoned to death in the morning, his body was hanged for public viewing until afternoon, but buried before sundown.

Hence the Talmud has preserved clues as to what Yeshu haNotzri taught and the reason that he was executed. It also gives evidence as to why the Hebrew term *Notzrim* was given to those who,.

But what of Yeshu, who was called Ḵristos? Before we can understand this second messianic personality and his movement, we must have a sound understanding the dynamics that led to the deification of the CT-Yeshu.

John 14:26 ὁ δὲ **παράκλητος** (one who is called to someone's aid; chosen), **τὸ πνεῦμα** (wind, air; breath; life; spirit, mind; inspiration; ghost. Spiritual being; Holy Spirit), **τὸ ἅγιον** (dedicated, consecrated, holy, or sacred to the service of God)**,** ὃ πέμψει ὁ πατὴρ ἐν τῷ ὀνόματί μου, ἐκεῖνος ὑμᾶς διδάξει πάντα καὶ ὑπομνήσει ὑμᾶς πάντα ἃ εἶπον ὑμῖν.

The translation given online for this verse has:

John 14:26 But **the Comforter**, which is the **Holy Ghost**, whom the Father will send in my name, he shall teach you all things, and bring all things to your remembrance, whatsoever I have said unto you.

This is more of an interpretation not a translation. The Greek term δὲ here is a marker connecting a series of closely related data or terms. A more accurate translation would be:

John 14:26 **The Chosen One**, the **Inspired**, and **Consecrated One**, who the Father will send in my name, and bring all things to your remembrance, whatsoever I have said unto you.

John 16:7 ἀλλ᾽ ἐγὼ τὴν ἀλήθειαν λέγω ὑμῖν συμφέρει ὑμῖν ἵνα ἐγὼ ἀπέλθω ἐὰν γὰρ μὴ ἀπέλθω **ὁ παράκλητος** οὐκ ἐλεύσεται πρὸς ὑμᾶς ἐὰν δὲ πορευθῶ πέμψω αὐτὸν πρὸς ὑμᾶς.
16:7 Nevertheless I tell you the truth; It is expedient for you that I go away: for if I go not away, **the Comforter [the Called or Chosen One]** will not come unto you; but if I depart, I will send him unto you.

16:8 καὶ ἐλθὼν ἐκεῖνος ἐλέγξει τὸν κόσμον περὶ ἁμαρτίας καὶ περὶ δικαιοσύνης καὶ περὶ κρίσεως:
16:8 And when he is come, he will reprove the world of sin, and of righteousness, and of judgment:

16:13 ὅταν δὲ ἔλθῃ ἐκεῖνος **τὸ πνεῦμα τῆς ἀληθείας** ὁδηγήσει ὑμᾶς εἰς πᾶσαν τὴν ἀληθείαν οὐ γὰρ λαλήσει ἀφ᾽ ἑαυτοῦ ἀλλ᾽ ὅσα ἂν ἀκούσῃ λαλήσει καὶ τὰ ἐρχόμενα ἀναγγελεῖ ὑμῖν.
16:13 Howbeit when he, **the Spirit of truth**, is come, he will guide you into all truth: for he shall not speak of himself; but whatsoever he shall hear, that shall he speak: and he will shew you things to come.

16:14 ἐκεῖνος ἐμὲ δοξάσει ὅτι ἐκ τοῦ ἐμοῦ λήψεται, καὶ ἀναγγελεῖ ὑμῖν.
16:14 He shall glorify me: for he shall receive of mine, and shall shew it unto you.

Here Yeshu haNotzri is informing the faithful followers to watch for another who will come to them and that they are to listen and follow him, as they had him. This is a strong indication that these were two distinctive individuals. It follows that he Notzrim of Damascus would have traveled to the Galilee to hear Yeshu-Ḳristos speak, and ultimately the two sects were intertwined.

III-2.2 Yeshu "Ḳristos"

Based on a criterion of plausibility from the scant pieces of available evidence, we can reconstruction a reasonable account of the short life of Yeshu-"Ḳristos". He was conceived naturally and enjoyed a happy, normal childhood in nurturing Torah observant home. Educated in the Yeshivat Hillel, he was singled out for his learning and compassionate heart. The central theme of the *Book of James* is *ḥesed*, loving-kindness, and *tzadaq*, righteous behavior. Hillel, the Elder, was noted for his personal acts and emphasis of *ḥesed* and *tzadaq*. However, charity of the Synoptic texts' expressions of charity are seem more extreme – "if your neighbor asks of you your cloak, give him also your coat." Judaism requires that we compassionately and respectfully give charity and behavior righteously towards all men especially the needy. Yet, we are warned not to take these to an extreme, since it does help society if a person foolishly impoverish himself. On the other hand, the Rambam does advise a very stingy person to go to the extreme of giving too much as a means of reaching a balanced level of giving.

In the purported *Testimonium Flavianum,* we are informed that he was a wise man, who readily taught both Jews and non-

Jews. Thus, he was a talented student of the school/*Yeshiva* of Hillel the Elder. According to Josephus, there were hundreds of teachers, representatives of all Jewish sects, who toured the country teaching Torah at this time. His popularity excited the jealousy of the other sectarians, who continuously argued with him regarding the law. From this perspective, Yeshu-Ḵristos, a charismatic and egalitarian teacher of Hillel's doctrine of peace, which conflicted with the two polarized, dominate parties – the Fourth Philosophy party of Yeshivat Shammai with its strong Zealot component (the "Pharisees") and the corrupt High Priest, Caiaphas, (the "priests and scribes") who was a Roman agent.

Greedy individuals, such as are common to all cultures, saw an opportunity in the popularity of the young rabbi and attached themselves to his inner group. In order to prey upon the desperation of the poor and ill, the charlatans spread rumors that he was a great healer and worker of miracles. By planting fake lame and blind persons among them, they tricked the crowd into believing the rumors. Without his knowledge they extorted coins and goods from people who could barely afford the necessities of life to support the ministry. Such deception of innocent individuals, using fantastic, fraudulent, and miraculous stories are evident even today in many countries and many cultures. Their illusions were so cleverly executed that they convinced even this Yeshu. Yet, these went so far as to claim that one should not call him a mere man. Once sparking the thought, the rumor spread like a wild-fire and his following increased remarkably. Rumors grew out of proportion and became more and more fantastic. Like poor, misguided Pauline, the simple-minded came to believe that his real father was none other than the Deity.

With the failure of his opponents – Yeshivat Shammai Zealots and the Romanized sector of the priests – to deter his followers, hotheads on both sides started a quarrel that escalated into a riot. The large crowds surrounding him panicked, resulting in total chaos. Upon hearing that the people called him Messiah/King, Pilate and Caiaphas took notice. Upon hearing that people were calling him a demi-god, the Shammai Pharisees took notice. The powers-that-be decided that it was time to put an end to this bothersome student of Yeshivat Hillel.

There is evidence within the Christian Text for the meshing together of that the two Yeshu personalities – Yeshu haNotzri, who was put to death by the Sanheidrin in ca. 73 BCE, and Yeshu, who was called the Ḳristos, who was put to death by the Romans in ca. 33 CE. The evidence is found in the celebration of Palm Sunday. The story in the Christian Texts tells how that Yeshu entered Jerusalem to celebrate the Passover,[123] the Jews laid their palm branches on the ground before him,

> [8]Many people *spread their cloaks on the road, and others spread leafy branches* that they had cut in the

---

[123] https://bible.oremus.org/

fields. ⁹Then those who went ahead and those who followed were shouting,
"*Hosanna!* Blessed is the one who comes in the name of the Lord!
¹⁰Blessed is the coming kingdom of our ancestor David!
Hosanna in the highest heaven!" (Mark 11:8-10)

"⁸A very large crowd *spread their cloaks on the road, and others cut branches from the trees and spread them on the road.* ⁹The crowds that went ahead of him and that followed were shouting, "*Hosanna* to the Son of David! Blessed is the one who comes in the name of the Lord! *Hosanna* in the highest heaven!" (Matt. 21:8-9).

¹³So they *took branches of palm trees* and went out to meet him, shouting, "*Hosanna!* Blessed is the one who comes in the name of the Lord— the King of Israel!" ¹⁴Jesus found a young donkey and sat on it; as it is written: ¹⁵"Do not be afraid, daughter of Zion. Look, your king is coming, sitting on a donkey's colt!" (John 12:13-15)

The name of the palm branch in Hebrew is *lulav*. The only time of the year in which Jews carry the *lulav* is during the autumn harvest festival of Sukkot. To this day, Jews circle the sanctuary carrying their *lulavim* and chanting the *Hosha'ana* – "Please, Hashem, save now!" In the Books of Matthew and Mark have "leafy branches". Two sources state that they were "leafy branches", which could also refer to the *lulavim*. Or, they could mean the סְכָךְ *sakak,* which are the branches placed as a make-shift

258

roof on the *sukkot,* the temporary dwelling that we build each year for this festival.[124] Since the people were chanting *Hosha'ana* and carrying branches, we have evidence that Yeshu-Kristos was crucified in the autumn, not in the spring. We suggest that he died on the day before the holiday began on 14-Tishrei and that this was 2-October in 28 CE.

The name Ponitus suggests that his family may have come from southern central Italy and probably of plebeian origin. Like all but one other governor of Judaea, he was of the equestrian order, a middle rank of the Roman nobility. According to the *cursus honorum,* an office holders of equestrian rank would have needed to distinguish himself as a military command before becoming a prefect.[125] The name Pilate means "skilled with the javelin" and his appointment as the prefect of Judaea, suggesting that he had a successful military career. Alexander Demandt suggests that Pilate could have been stationed on the Danube for much of his military career.[126]

There is another intriguing account found in the CT that also connects to an autumn execution for Yeshu-Kristos. It regards the mockery he endured at the hands of the Roman guards before being led away.

---

[124] Known among the Christians as the Feast of the Tabernacles.
[125] https://en.wikipedia.org/wiki/Pontius_Pilate

[126] Alexander Demandt, *Pontius Pilatus* (Munich: C. H. Beck, 2012).

⁶Now at the festival he used to release a prisoner for them, anyone for whom they asked... ¹⁶Then the soldiers led him into the courtyard of the palace (that is, the governor's headquarters); and they called together the whole cohort. ¹⁷And they clothed him in a purple cloak; and after twisting some thorns into a crown, they put it on him. ¹⁸And they began saluting him, "Hail, King of the Jews!" ¹⁹They struck his head with a reed, spat upon him, and knelt down in homage to him. (Mark 15: 6-20)

¹⁵Now at the festival the governor was accustomed to release a prisoner for the crowd, anyone whom they wanted... ²⁷Then the soldiers of the governor took Jesus into the governor's headquarters, and they gathered the whole cohort around him. ²⁸They stripped him and put a scarlet robe on him, ²⁹and after twisting some thorns into a crown, they put it on his head. They put a reed in his right hand and knelt before him and mocked him, saying, "Hail, King of the Jews!" ³⁰They spat on him, and took the reed and struck him on the head. ³¹After mocking him, they stripped him of the robe and put his own clothes on him. Then they led him away to crucify him. (Matt. 27:15, 27-31)

¹Then Pilate took Jesus and had him flogged. ²And the soldiers wove a crown of thorns and put it on his head, and they dressed him in a purple robe. ³They kept coming up to him, saying, "Hail, King of the Jews!" and striking him on the face. (John 19:1-3)

Both Matthew and Mark inform us that Pilate was accustomed to releasing a prisoner at the demand of the people before a festival. This claim is enigmatic since no such custom has found in either Jewish or Roman law. Then the Roman guards dressed him in a red or purple (*i.e.* an fit for royalty) cloak[127] and place a mock crown made of thorns on his head. Generally, these actions are viewed as an example of Roman cruelty, but there could be more to it. This strange behavior brings to mind the crowning of a "King of the Saturnalia". Chosen by lots, even a slave could live like a king and his capricious commands obeyed from 17th-19th of December.[128]

According to the *Acta Dasii* (4th century CE), Christians soldiers in the Roman army were given a choice between joining in pagan ritual or face death. Dasius refused to participate in the Imperial cult. The text is odd because about a third of it is dedicated to describing the celebration of the Saturnalia by legionaries stationed in Durostorum, which is near the border of modern Romania and Bulgaria where the Danube empties into the Black Sea. It seems that the "king" of the festival was chosen one month before the festival and given a month of special privileges and license. But, in the end, he was sacrificed before the altar of Saturn. Romans abhorred human sacrifice, so this may be a drama

---

[127] Luke 23:10-12 has Herod and his soldiers mocking him and "then he put an elegant robe on him."
[128] https://en.wikipedia.org/wiki/Saturnalia

device. After all, Dasius was already convicted and sentenced to death. [129]

This may well have been the source of Pilate's strange custom. The condemned men would have drawn lots whereby one was freed and another became to "king". Which is similar to the two goats on Yom Kippur, where one is sacrificed while the other was set free in the wilderness. By releasing a prisoner, Pilate flaunted the fact that only he held the power of life and death in Judaea, thus expressing contempt for the G-d of Israel.

After a hurried trial on the morning before Sukkot, Pilate condemned him to be crucified. Then Pilate asked those gathered in the courtyard, who he should release before the festival. The Zealots and Shammai Pharisees cried out for one of their own who was also imprisoned, Barabbas (meaning "son of our fathers"), who had actually committed murder during the previous riot. (Matt. 27:16-26) Which to Pilate meant that Yeshu-Kristos should be the "King of the Saturnalia". He was turned over to the prison guards. Since he had been accused of leading the Jews in rebellion against Rome and had been proclaimed King of the Jews by many who followed him, he was a most delectable catch for them. It is understandable that he would have chosen, as Dasius later did, to accept torture and execution rather than spend the next two months

---

[129] James G. Frazer, *The Golden Bough: a Study in Magic and Religion*, a new abridgement from the 2nd and 3rd editions. (Oxford: Oxford University Press, 2009) pp. 632-633; and https://en.wikipedia.org/wiki/Dasius_of_Durostorum

in fornication and idolatry. They spat on and beat him. Thus, it is no stretch that Yeshu-Ḳristos was crucified by Pontius Pilate, one day before Sukkot, on 14-Tishrei, which was the morning of 20-October in 28 CE.

In 1828, Heinrich E.G. Paulus proposed the swoon-theory in his work, *The Life of Jesus*. Therein he states that the CT-Yeshu was not actually dead when he was removed from the Cross. Instead, he had fallen into a coma-like state and was unconscious when entombed. Later he revived, rolled away the stone that sealed the tomb from the inside, evaded the Roman guards, and escaped. As soon as possible, he appeared to his disciples and proclaimed that he had conquered death. But rather than making a full recovery from his wounds, the CT-Yeshu died soon thereafter.

In Schonfield's version, the CT-Yeshu was aid by Joseph of Arimathea in the execution of an elaborate hoax. After he was crucified, Joseph had an unidentified person gave him a drugged drink that cause him to lose consciousness and appear to be dead, hoping to trick the guards. However, they did not anticipate the thoroughness of the Romans in fulfilling their duty. Before permitting them to remove his body, the soldier pierced his liver to ensure that, if he were not already dead, he would soon die. He was then placed in the tomb until the next day. At which time, he briefly regaining consciousness, convinced his disciples that he had resurrected, died of the spear wound, and was reburied elsewhere

I agree with the swoon-theory with a few reservations. Paulus' scenario is unrealistic. Even without having suffered serious internal injuries, he would not have had the strength to roll a huge stone away, especially from aside the tomb. Likewise, and Schonfield's conspiracy-theory is too fancifully irrational, and even unnecessary. To begin with, such a hoax was too risky and fool-hardy. Leaving a critically injured man in a cold stone-cut tomb over-night, is irresponsible. To expect him to survive is delusional.

Before the body could have been placed buried, by Jewish law it would have to be prepared. It would have been claimed by his family before sunset, when all the city was busy with last minute preparation for the holiday. However, as they were washing his body for burial, he took a sharp breath, causing those present to believe that he had returned to life. He asked them to send for his disciples. He survived long enough for them to gather about and to hear his last words. Binding those who still loved him to continue his teaching, he forgave those who had betrayed him and died of loss of blood. Living until the third morning, discovered hi tomb empty, and multiple sighting were rumors spread by grief-stricken followers – similar to the sightings of Elvis Presley since his death in 1977.

Belief in the general resurrect of the dead is deeply rooted in Judaism. It is easy to understand how many would hope to meet him again in the Galilee. There is ample evidence that his followers respected his memory and continued his teachings of peace, charity, and brotherhood after his death. Until he would return, they were to spread the good news of his resurrection.

The authors of *Matthew* and *Luke*, embellishing *Mark*'s account, each created a masterpiece for their particular audiences. Between 250 and 350 CE, devout monks edited the four "gospels" adding or adjusting phrases to balance essential doctrines, just as they did with the *Testimonium Flavianum*. However, the *Book of John* is distinct from the *Synoptics* Christian Texts. The tangent where Christianity meets Judaism was then and is now Hillel the Elder. He is the source of the righteous teachings that inspired Yeshu-Kristos, who was memorialized in the Christian Texts.

III-2.3 Natzrat or Nazaret

Thus far, we have identified three messianic characters – Yeshu "haNotzri", Yeshu-Kristos, and the CT-Yeshu, the Nazarite. In the CT, we find that he took an oath of a *nazir*. "But I say unto you, I will not drink henceforth of this fruit of the vine, until that day when I drink it new with you in my Father's kingdom." (Matt. 26:29, Mark 14:25, Luke 26:29) When we compare the spelling of the term, used in instructions given to Samson's parents, with that of the name of the city where the CT-Yeshu grew up, we find that the Hebrew root matches the Greek stem – נָזִיר (*nazir*) and ναζὶρ (*nazir*) – match, confirming the connection. Compare the following verses.

Among these fantastic accolades is a claim that is worth the effort. They claim, that he was, like Shimshon and Shmuel, a *nazir*. When we compare the spelling of the term, used in instructions given to Shimshon's parents, with that of the name of the city where the CT-Yeshu[130] grew up, we find that the Hebrew root matches the Greek stem – נָזִיר (*nazir*) and ναζὶρ (*nazir*) – match, confirming the connection. Compare the following verses.

Judges 14:5

ה כִּי הִנָּךְ הָרָה וְיֹלַדְתְּ בֵּן, וּמוֹרָה לֹא-יַעֲלֶה עַל-רֹאשׁוֹ--כִּי-**נְזִיר** אֱלֹהִים יִהְיֶה הַנַּעַר, מִן-הַבָּטֶן; וְהוּא, יָחֵל לְהוֹשִׁיעַ אֶת-יִשְׂרָאֵל--מִיַּד פְּלִשְׁתִּים.

Judges 14:5 For, lo, thou shalt conceive, and bear a son; and no razor shall come upon his head; for the child shall be a **Nazirite** unto G-d from the womb; and he shall begin to save Israel out of the hand of the Philistines.'

Judges 14:5 ὅτι ἰδοὺ σὺ ἐν γαστρὶ ἔχεις καὶ τέξῃ υἱόν, καὶ σίδηρος ἐπὶ τὴν κεφαλὴν αὐτοῦ οὐκ ἀναβήσεται, ὅτι **ναζὶρ** Θεοῦ ἔσται τὸ παιδάριον ἀπὸ τῆς κοιλίας, καὶ αὐτὸς ἄρξεται σῶσαι τὸν Ἰσραὴλ ἐκ χειρὸς Φυλιστιΐμ.

Judges 14:5 for behold, thou art with child, and shalt bring forth a son; and there shall come no razor upon his head, for the child

---

[130] For this section, we will use the following site for the Greek and English translations of the Christian Texts.
https://www.logosapostolic.org/bibles/textus_receptus_king_james/greek_englis h_kjv_index.htm

shall be a **Nazarite** to G-d from the womb; and he shall begin to save Israel from the hand of the Phylistines.

Matt. 2:23 καὶ ἐλθὼν κατῴκησεν εἰς πόλιν λεγομένην **ναζαρὲτ** ὅπως πληρωθῇ τὸ ῥηθὲν διὰ τῶν προφητῶν ὅτι **ναζωραῖος** κληθήσεται
Matt. 2:23 And he came and dwelt in a city called **Nazareth**: *that it might be fulfilled which was spoken by the prophets, He shall be called* a **Nazarene.**

Thus, the CT identifies the village of Nazareth as a settlement of *nazarites/nazarim*, individuals who have taken an oath to abstain from drinking wine and contact with the dead. Earlier, we discussed the prediction in Isaiah 11:1 that the Mashiaḥ would be a וְנֵצֶר "shoot" from the "root" of Jesse, meaning, of course, that he would be a descendant of King David. Generally, the term צִיּוֹן is written in English as Zion. Here we generally use the phonetic expression "tz" for the צ and render it *tzion*, while scholars prefer to use ṣ. Yet, notice that in both the LXX and CT the צ is transliterated from Hebrew into Greek using a sigma Σσ.

ט:ט גִּילִי מְאֹד בַּת-**צִיּוֹן**, הָרִיעִי בַּת יְרוּשָׁלַם, הִנֵּה מַלְכֵּךְ יָבוֹא לָךְ, צַדִּיק וְנוֹשָׁע הוּא; עָנִי וְרֹכֵב עַל-חֲמוֹר, וְעַל-עַיִר בֶּן-אֲתֹנוֹת.
Zech. 9:9 Rejoice greatly, O daughter of **Zion**, shout, O daughter of Jerusalem; behold, thy king cometh unto thee, he is triumphant, and victorious, lowly, and riding upon an ass, even upon a colt the foal of an ass.

Zech. 9:9 Χαῖρε σφόδρα, θύγατερ **Σιών**· κήρυσσε, θύγατερ Ἰερουσαλήμ· ἰδοὺ ὁ βασιλεὺς σου ἔρχεταί σοι, δίκαιος καὶ σῴζων αὐτός, πραΰς καὶ ἐπιβεβηκὼς ἐπὶ ὑποζύγιον καὶ πῶλον νέον.

Zech. 9:9 Rejoice greatly, O daughter of **Sion**; proclaim [it] aloud, O daughter of Jerusalem; behold, the King is coming to thee, just, and a Saviour; he is meek and riding on an ass, and a young foal.

Matt. 21:4 τοῦτο δὲ ὅλον γέγονεν ἵνα πληρωθῇ τὸ ῥηθὲν διὰ τοῦ προφήτου λέγοντος
Matt. 21:5 εἴπατε τῇ θυγατρὶ **Σιών** ἰδού ὁ βασιλεύς σου ἔρχεταί σοι πραΰς καὶ ἐπιβεβηκὼς ἐπὶ ὄνον καὶ πῶλον υἱὸν ὑποζυγίου

Matt. 21:4 *All this was done, that it might be fulfilled which was spoken by the prophet, saying,*
Matt. 21:5 Tell ye the daughter of **Sion**, Behold, thy King cometh unto thee, meek, and sitting upon an ass, and a colt the foal of an ass.

Hence, we conclude that, when the CT authors and redactors state that their Yeshu was a **ναζὶρ** *nazarite*, intentionally identifying him as a נָזִיר *nazir*. In contrast, all Jewish sources refer to him as Yeshu as haNotzri, thus identifying him as the נֵצֶר *natzer* "shoot" – in other words a descendant of King David. Hence, to Jews the city in northern Israel where this Yeshu lived is called נָצְרַת Natzrat, while the Christians consistently identify it as ναζαρὲτ, Nazaret. Of course, it is possible that these were two different villages in the Galilee at that time.[131]

Over the subsequent 100+ years, the followers of Yeshu-Ḳristos, haNazir, intertwined their stories with the followers of Yeshu haNotzri, whose doctrine by this time had developed a gnostic dimension. There may have been follower of Yeshu

---

[131] See also, https://en.wikipedia.org/wiki/Nazareth

haNotzri who considered Yeshu-Ḳristos as a resurrected or
returning Yeshu haNotzri. For we find in Sanhedrin 106a the
statement "Woe for him who resurrects himself with the title of G-
d."

Of course, both Yeshu HaNotzri and Yeshu-Ḳristos were
Jewish. Both believed in Hashem. Both taught Jews and non-
Jews to the best of their understanding. Certainly, both were
very friendly and knowledgeable young men, who sincerely
believed that what they were doing was right. Yet, both
destabilized the country and caused the death of many Jews. If
anyone chooses to believe that one, or both of them, was a
mashiah, that's fine. However, the JfJ commentator number four
quoted above is mistaken. The notions promoted in the Christian
Texts are not Jewish, nor are they acceptable to knowledgeable
Jews – not in the past, not today, and at no time in the future.

III-2.4 Early Jewish Meshiḥim

Renowned Professor of Religious Studies, Bart Erhman,
provides us a vivid description of early Christianity and among
them the Jewish *meshiḥim*.

> Christianity in the second and third centuries was in
> a remarkable state of flux. To be sure, at no point in
> its history has the religion constituted a monolith.
> But the diverse manifestations of its first three

hundred years – whether in terms of social structures, religious practice, or ideologies – have never been replicated.[132]

During these formative years, the consensus among the Christian sects was that their Yeshu was *the* "Son of God"; however, there was no consensus of what "sonship" actually meant. Though opinions varied, it seems that most held that he was must have been fully divine, otherwise how could he bring salvation to the world if he were a mere mortal. At the opposite end of the spectrum were the Adoptionists, who espoused the conviction that he was a flesh and blood human being, who had been adopted by G-d and destined to bring about salvation of mankind.[133] Though all early Christian sects claimed to base their credos on the authentic teachings of his original disciples, Erhman has demonstrated that the adoptionistic Christologies are traceable to sources that predate the surviving Christian Texts.

Paul was of the opinion that the CT-Yeshu was appointed G-d's son at his resurrection. Yet, those adoptionists for whom we have primary records – the Ebionites, Theodotus, and Artemon – held that this honor was conveyed on him at his baptism. The CT bear witness to the adoptionistic doctrine but most of these have been "corrected" by later editors of the texts. The *Book of Mark* is

---

[132] Bart D. Ehrman, *The Orthodox Corruption of Scripture: The Effect of Early Christological Controversies on the Text of the New Testament* (Oxford: Oxford University Press, 1993) p. 3.
[133] Ehrman, p. 47-48.

the nearest of their teachings. It indicates that their Yeshu was "made" *the* "son of God" at his baptism and lacks references to his pre-existence, deification, or "virginal conception".

The early Jewish *meshiḥim*, the Ebionites, were a diverse sect. What has come down to us, concerning these early Jewish sects, are the perception of their opponents. Thus, most of what we know about them is from their critics. Ehrman convincing argues via textual analyses of the surviving manuscripts preserved by the early Christian orthodox indicates that they altered *meshihim* passages that suggested that Yeshu had a human father (Joseph). They also doctored other verses in order to accentuate their own orthodox faith in his divinity, pre-existence, and virgin-birth.[134]

Hence, we know that the Ebionites believed in the following precepts.

1. They supported the validity of the Mosaic Law
2. Practiced circumcision and Jewish customs
3. Kept Shabbat and kashrut – the dietary laws
4. Considered Yeshu-Ḳristos as a "normal", human being – not a deity to worship
5. Rejected the notions of Yeshu-Ḳristos as pre-existent (*John*)
6. Rejected he was born via virgin-birth (*Matthew* and *Luke*).
7. Believed that he was remarkably righteous, due to his personal development of character

---

[134] Ehrman, p. 54.

8. G-d adopted him for his messianic mission at his baptism (immersion as in a mikvah – a natural source of fresh water such as a river)
9. That his death was part of his messianic mission
10. after his death, he was temporarily resurrected from the dead and then returned to (*i.e.* was exalted to) his father in Heaven.

Compare this with JfJ – "Statement of Faith" published on their website.

1. That the BIBLE, consisting of the Tenach (Old Covenant/Testament) and the later writings commonly known as the *B'rit Hadasha* (New Testament/Covenant), is the only infallible and authoritative word of God. We recognize its divine inspiration, and accept its teachings as our final authority in all matters of faith and practice.
2. We believe that the Shema, "Hear O Israel, the Lord our God, the Lord is one" (Deuteronomy 6:4), teaches that God is *Echad*, as so declared: "a united one, a composite unity, eternally existent in plural oneness; that He is a personal God who created us and that He exists forever in three persons: Father, Son, and Holy Spirit."
3. God does have a Son who was and is and will return.
4. Yeshua (Jesus) came to this world born of a virgin.
5. The Son is God (Deity), and is worshiped as God, having existed eternally.
6. This One is the promised Mashiach (Messiah) of Israel He is the root and offspring of David.

7. In the Tenach, the Spirit of God came upon individuals during the times of our forefathers, like Moses, David, and the Prophets, for the specific purposes.

8. In the New Covenant, the Messiah Yeshua, promised His disciples that "the Comforter" would come to them after He was gone. Yeshua further declared that the Spirit of Truth, would guide us into all truth and would glorify Him – the Messiah – not Himself. He empowers us. The Spirit of God seals us.

9. Men and women are created in the image of God, however because of disobedience, mankind fell from the first state and became separated from God. Therefore, according to the Scriptures, all humans are born with a sinful nature.

10. Our only hope for redemption (salvation) is through the atonement made by the Messiah, resulting in regeneration by the Holy Spirit, which is the new birth. For by grace, we are saved through faith, it is a gift of God.

11. We believe in the resurrection of both the redeemed and the lost: the former to everlasting life and the latter to eternal separation from God, a state of everlasting punishment.

12. The Anointed One and Redeemer: The Scriptures promised two "comings" of the Messiah.

13. The initial coming's purpose was to make atonement—as the Suffering Messiah. The Redeemer shall come to Zion.

14. Second Coming: The Messiah Yeshua will return to the earth as King. Upon His return, a many wonderful things will happen: He will bring with Him an army of the Heavenly hosts, and those who went on before us and those who

are still on earth will meet in the air to receive
the believers to Himself.

It is obvious that the JfJ and other such "Messianic Jewish"
organizations are completely Christian and promote the same
orthodox dogma of those who persecuted the early Jewish
meshihim. Thus, it is the JfJ's version of CT-Yeshu, not that of that
the Ebionites, that the Rambam refers to in his *Mishneh Torah* as a
"stumbling block" who makes "the majority of the world to err and
serve a god other than the L-rd".

In addition, since the early Jewish *meshihim* did not believe
that Yeshu-Ḳristos was a deity, then all accounts in the CT
portraying the Jews as trying to kill him for blasphemy must have
been mendacious inventions to promote distain for Jews and
Judaism. An excellent example of this is in John 10:30-39 that was
cited above. The most apparent reason for promoting such
vehement anti-Jewish propaganda would have been to "knock the
competition". Judaism was then as it is today a powerful, vibrant
religion and culture that has always intimidated others.

III-2.5 Paul, the Chameleon

Why did Paul have such a vendetta against the Meshihim?

There are Christian scholars who question the integrity of
both the *Book of Acts* and the epistles of Paul. Paula Fredriksen

informs us that serious controversies exist regarding whether the text of Paul's letters, as handed down to us, preserve the actual words dictated by him. Many scholars have identified evidences of textual corruption in sections of the present versions of Philippians, 2 Corinthians, Romans, and 1 Thessalonians. Additionally, multiple contradictions are identifiable between the account in Acts and those in his letters. Generally, Romans, I & 2 Corinthians, Galatians, Philippian, 1 Thessalonian, and Philemon are almost universally accepted as penned by Paul and are considered the best sources for information regarding his life and thoughts, while the others were possibly written by later followers of Paul.[135]

He is first mentioned in the *Book of Acts* as the one responsible for the stoning of Stephen. (7:58-60; 22:20) In Romans 16:7, he states that his nephew, Andronicus along with Junia (presumably his wife), were Meshihim before he was and that they were prominent among the Apostles. It is possible that Paul was of a wealthy merchant family who dealt in leather crafts and tent-making. (Acts 18:1-3). It is probable that Andronicus was his older brother's son and heir. If it was Stephen who introduced the young couple to either Yeshu-Kristos personally or to his disciples, then we would have a motive for Paul's intense distain for Meshihim.

---

[135] See also the contributions to Wikipedia on these topics.

Roughly eight years after the evil High Priest, Caiaphas, successfully eliminated Yeshu-Ḳristos, Paul, an assimilated Jew, arrived in Jerusalem in search of his runaway nephew. As a young man of means, he was granted an audience with Caiaphas, and was introduced by his Hebrew name, Shaul. Andronicus and Junia, where discovered living among the early Meshiḥim of Jerusalem. (Romans 16:7) They refused to return with him to Tarsus. Therefore, he testified against Stephen before the High Priest and his court. Following the stoning of Stephen, his nephew agreed to return home to stop Shaul's persecutions, which he agreed to do. However, at his request, Caiaphas granted him papers with authority to travel to Damascus and destroy the community of Notzrim, who were living there.

Something dramatic happened to Shaul on his way to Damascus. It has often been suggested that he had an epileptic seizure while traveling. However, if he was epileptic, he would have experienced more seizures resulting in additional accounts of visions. *Acts* provides us with a full description the event. Since it occurred at noon, while he was traveling, he suffered a Near Death Experience due to a heat-stroke. The following NDE descriptions are very similar to Paul's experience. (Galatians 1:16, 1 Corinthians 15:8, Acts 9:1–22, 2 Corith. 12)

Common traits that have been reported by NDErs:[136]

- A sense/awareness of being dead.
- A sense of peace, well-being, and painlessness. Positive emotions. A sense of removal from the world.
- An out-of-body experience. A perception of one's body from an outside position, sometimes observing medical professionals performing resuscitation efforts.
- A "tunnel experience" or entering a darkness. A sense of moving up, or through, a passageway or staircase.
- A rapid movement toward and/or sudden immersion in a powerful light (or "Being of Light") which communicates telepathically with the person.
- An intense feeling of unconditional love and acceptance.
- Encountering "Beings of Light", "Beings dressed in white", or similar. Also, the possibility of being reunited with deceased loved ones.
- Experiencing euphoric environments
- Receiving a life review, commonly referred to as "seeing one's life flash before one's eyes".
- Approaching a border or a decision by oneself or others to return to one's body, often accompanied by a reluctance to return.
- Suddenly finding oneself back inside one's body.
- Connection to the cultural beliefs held by the individual, which seem to dictate some of the phenomena experienced in the NDE and particularly the later interpretation thereof.
- Meeting the dead and hallucinating ghosts in an after-life environment

Generally, scholars place Paul's conversion between 31 and

36 CE. It is possible that it occurred in 36 CE, the summer before

---

[136] https://en.wikipedia.org/wiki/Near-death_experience

Vitellius removed Caiaphas from office. In Galatians 1:16, Paul writes that "God was pleased to reveal his son to me." In 1 Corinthians 15:8, as he lists the order in which CT-Yeshu appeared to his disciples after his resurrection, Paul writes, "last of all, as to one untimely born, He appeared to me also."

Ironically, those who nursed him back to health were followers of Yeshu-Ḳristos, who had fled to the safety of the Notzrim community in Damascus. Touched by their kindness and awed by his near-death-experience, Shaul's perspective took a 180° turn. (Acts 8:1-9:14) He tried to convince the Jewish Meshiḥim to trust him, but with little success. Consequently, Paul turned to the gentiles, especially the G-d~fearers.

In Philippians 3:5, he claims that he was "circumcised on the eighth day, a member of the people of Israel, of the tribe of Benjamin, a Hebrew born of Hebrews; as to the law, a Pharisee." He states several times that he was born a Jew in the city of Tarsus in the provence of Cilicia, and that he was "brought up in this city [Jerusalem ?] at the feet of Gamaliel, *and* taught according to the perfect manner of the law of the fathers, and was zealous toward God, as ye all are this day." (Acts 21:39 and 22:3-8) However, in Paul's own writings, he never states that he studied under Gamaliel.[137]

---

[137] Fredriksen, p. 55.

Personally, I don't buy it. I find very little that is distinguishably Jewish about Paul actions or philosophy – though he is well versed in the doctrine of the Stoics. He most certainly did not study under the grandson of Hillel the Elder. He may have been aware of some of their teachings, but, if he studied at all, it must have been a very shallow and brief exposure. Honestly, he comes across more as an enthusiastic G-d~fearer than a student of Hillel the Elder. If this was more than simply a boast aimed at gaining more converts, then perhaps it was another Gamaliel from the school of Shammai. Forgive me for being so blunt, but there are few things as profound as Paul's lack of Torah knowledge.

In his writings, Paul makes it abundantly clear that he was a chameleon. He colored his words to match his surroundings. If he spoke to Jews, he employed terms and concepts acceptable to Jews. If he spoke to Greeks, he used terms and concepts acceptable to Greeks.

> For though I be free from all men, yet have I made myself servant unto all, that I might gain the more; And unto the Jews I became as a Jew, that I might gain the Jews; to them that are under the law, as under the law, that I might gain them that are under the law; To them that are without law, as without law, (being not without law to God, but under the law to Christ,) that I might gain them that are without law. To the weak became I as weak, that I might gain the weak: I am made all things to all men, that I might by all means save some. And this I do for the gospel's sake, that I might be partaker thereof with you. (1 Corinthians 9:19-23)

Paul was a merchant, and salvation was his merchandise. He traveled extensively and spoke the colloquial, cultural, and religious language of each city he entered in order to make a sale. He recreated himself and his savior to each person he met. His purpose was to save as many people as he could before the imminent return of Yeshu-Ḵristos and the catastrophic destruction of the world. All of which he expected to happen any day. Hence, for Paul the ends definitely justified the means. Like a chameleon, his identity changed with his environment. He was totally convinced that he would live to see the evil Roman Empire vanquished and the "Kingdom of God" established. The more souls he and his followers could save from their inevitable fate, the more please would God (as he understood Him) be with them and the greater their reward would be for saving so many lost "sheep".

It was a "good-new", "bad-news" approach. The good-news that the messiah had finally arrived. The bad-news was that he had died. The good-news was that he had risen from the dead. The bad-news was that this meant they were living in the "End of Times". The good-news was that all who believed Paul's teachings would take part in the great "Parousia", the transformation into purified individuals, and witness the resurrection of righteous dead. The bad-news was that anyone who did not accept his teachings would burn eternally, since his sins had not been forgiven. The good-news was that, if they hurried, they could still make it. The bad-news was time was running out. It was a great shock to his followers when some of their faithful members died. Paul reassured them that those good believers were just asleep and that very soon they would awaken with the great resurrection of the dead. (1 Thes. 4:13-16; 1 Cor. 15:35-52; Phil. 3:20; Rom. 16:20; 1 Cor. 3:19)

Actually, the belief that the resurrection of the dead is to be preceded by the arrival of the Mashiah is an authentic Jewish concept. Superficially, it appears that Christians and Jews are awaiting the same person. However, the Christians are expecting second coming of a divine messiah, the reappearance of their god, who will float down to earth in a cloud of glory. We await the initial appearance of a normal man, but one of exceptional abilities, who will correct the flaws of this world in a very real and practical manner. Ours expectations are more realistic.

III-3 The Christian Texts (CT)

With the exception of the *Book of James,* the Christian Texts were all written by G-d~fearers. As noted, they were a conglomerate of various non-Jewish ethnicities, religious affiliations, and socio-economic circumstances. Ranging from single individuals to organized groups, they represented a full spectrum of commitment to Judaism. They may have attended synagogues, praying devoutly to Hashem, on Shabbat and festivals but display equal reverence to Zeus/Amon-Re on the next day in their ancestral temples. They learned the Scriptures from reading the LXX and attending lectures and services. The frequent errors found in the CT supports the position that it was written by persons with limited knowledge of the history, geography, and religion of Israel.

III-3.1 The *Book of Mark*

The original text of the *Book of Mark*, like those of *Matthew* and *Luke*, is anonymous. It was a vital source for both *Matthew* and *Luke*. However, it does not trace CT-Yeshu's genealogy back to David, nor does it contain a fantasy of miraculous or virgin birth. The oldest copy of *Mark* ends after 16:1-8 that is with his followers discovering his empty tomb and being told that he will meet them again in the Galilee. Until he returns, they are to spread the good news of his resurrection.

Most scholars date *Book of Mark* to ca. 66–74 CE, at roughly the time of the destruction of the Second Temple.[138] The *Mark* was most likely written by one who either had direct access to Q-Yeshu "Ḳristos" or knew someone who was well versed in it – such as a surviving follower of James, the brother of Yeshu-Ḳristos. *Mark* has been characterized as a three-act drama and Greek tragedy; therefore, he was probably a Roman G-d~fearer, educated as a private secretary, who had a love for the theater.[139]

While *Matthew* and *Luke* accent his divinity, *Mark* portrays him as the Suffering Servant. In all three he is a teacher, a faith-healer, and an exorcist. But, in *Mark*, he only refers to himself as the "Son of Man", not as a deity, and he tries to keep his messianic mission a secret. Of course, later redactors doctored this text as well, giving him an aurora of something more than human.

When studying the Pastoral Epistles, scholars found themselves at a crossroad. According to the *Book of Acts*, the trailblazer, Paul, died during the persecutions of Nero in 64

---

[138] https://en.wikipedia.org/wiki/Gospel_of_Mark

[139] *R.T. France, The Gospel of Mark: A commentary on the Greek text (Wm. B. Eerdmans Publishing, 2002); and* Smith, Stephen H, "A Divine Tragedy: Some Observations on the Dramatic Structure of Mark's Gospel", *Novum Testamentum* **37** (3) (Leiden: E.J. Brill, 1995), pp. 209–31.

CE, so aptly described by Tacitus above. However, these letters contain terms like" overseers" (ἐπίσκοποι), which is traditionally translated as bishops, "deacons" (διάκονοι), and "elder" (πρεσβύτερος), which is root source for the English word priest; and also, their main concerned is with forms of worship and organization of the church, which points to a much later period than when Paul lived. Thus, either they were written by another, later Paul, or the founder of Christianity lived for roughly another 30 or 40 years, making him 60 or 70 years old at his death. At any rate, the last date they were written no later than 144 CE.[140] The Book of *Mark* was probably the primary source used by the sect whose author wrote the letters to Timothy and Titus.

III-3.2 The *Books of Matthew* and *Luke*

Matthew's parents were Hellenistic G-d~fearers, who formerly had worshipped Zeus and the virgin-goddesses Athena and Kebele. It is possible that they were from the island of Cyprus or Crete. After the destruction of the Temple, the faith of many G-d~fearers was undoubtably severely shaken or entirely destroyed. When the author of Matthew and his family heard the teachings of Paul and read *Mark*'s text, they found a new source of inspiration.

---

[140] https://en.wikipedia.org/wiki/Pastoral_epistles

It was obvious to them that this was no ordinary man. Here they found what they needed a new interpretation that brought together the old and the new. Freed from the well-defined structure of Judaism, they yearned for the old traditions but still revered the beauty of Torah. Taking the account of *Mark* and the letters of Paul as the foundation, they resolved to include the evidence that *Mark* had neglected. *Matthew's* elaboration is well calculated and decisively purposeful. content.

Luke, who was probably from Alexandria, Egypt, was another G-d~fearer, whose faith had been shaken by the destruction of the Temple and enslavement of the Jews people. In Christian tradition, he was a friend and companion of Paul, but modern scholarship questions this. He used both *Mark* & *Matthew*'s texts but like *Matthew* added his own personal perspective of the events. His concept of God is informed by the still popular worship of Amon-Re/Zeus, Isis/Athena and the divine Horus/Dionysos. There is also evidence of Buddhism influence in some of his stories of CT-Yeshu. As mentioned above, both texts were heavily redated by later monks. After the rise to power of Constantine, the monks became especially animated, intent on spreading the truth as they saw it.

III-3.3 The *Book of John*

The texts of *John,* like that of *Mark,* was written between 65 and 85 CE. Thus, their authors would most likely second-generation G-d~fearers whose parents had either known Paul or were members of the communities that corresponded with him. The view that Christianity began with Paul is well known. The author of *John,* like those of the Dead Sea Sect, was strongly influenced by gnostic doctrines and Second Temple Era Jewish thought. Hence, we suggest that he was from either from Antioch or Damascus.

III-3.4 CT-Yeshu as Dionysus

It cannot be an accident that the personae of *John's* Yeshu bear a striking resemblance to Euripides' *Bacchus*, for both characters come across as bazaar and rather delusional.

> **I am Dionysus, the child of Zeus,** and I have come to this land of the Thebans, where Kadmos' daughter Semele once bore me, delivered by a lightning-blast. Having assumed a mortal form in place of my divine one,... **20** In Hellenic territory I have come here to Thebes first, having already established my *khoroi* (χόροι – "favor, graciousness, goodwill") and mysteries in those other lands so that I might be a *daimôn* (a divinity) manifest among mortals, and have raised my cry here, fitting a fawn-skin to my body and **25** taking a thyrsos in my hand, a dart of ivy. **For my mother's sisters**—*the very ones for*

whom it was least becoming—**claimed that I was not the child of Zeus**, but that *Semele had conceived a child from a mortal father and then blamed her sexual misconduct on Zeus[141]*,...

35 as many as are women, I have made to leave the house with madness, and they, mingled with the sons of Kadmos, sit on roofless rocks beneath green pines. It is necessary that this *polis* learn, even though it should not wish to, **40** that it is not an initiate into my Bacchic rites, and that I plead the case of my mother, Semele, in making myself manifest to mortals as a *daimôn*, whom she bore to Zeus. ... Kadmos then gave his office and his tyranny to Pentheus, his daughter's son, **45 who fights against the gods in my person and drives me away from treaties, never making mention of me in his prayers.** For which reasons I will show him and all the Thebans that **I am a god**. And when I have arranged the situation here to my satisfaction I will move on to another land, **50** revealing myself. But if ever **the polis (city) of Thebes should in anger** seek to drive the Bacchae down from the mountains with arms, I, leading on my Maenads, will join battle with them. For these reasons **I have assumed a mortal form, altering my shape into the nature of a man.**[142]

---

[141] This statement regarding Dionysos birth brings to mind the much later accusations made by an anonymous, early Medieval Jewish author concerning the birth of Yeshu haNotzri. Of course, there is no actual connection. However, the infamous apostate, Pablo Christiani, brought the rabbinic views of Yeshu haNotzri as written in the Talmud and this later story, both referenced above, to the attention of the Inquisition clergy in Spain. This brought about the "Great Disputation" between him and Rabbi Moses ben Nachman in 1262, which resulted in the Ramban's exile from Spain and, soon afterwards, his death.

[142] T.A. Buckley, Alex Sens, and Gregory Nagy, "Euripides', *Bacchae*" (support material, University of Houston, 2003).

John's Yeshu:

"**I and my Father are one.**" Then the **Jews took up stones again to stone him**. Jesus answered them, "Many good works have I shewed you **from my Father**; for which of those works do ye stone me?" The Jews answered him, saying, "For a good work we stone thee not; but for blasphemy; and **because that thou, being a man, makest thyself God.**"

Jesus answered them, "Is it not written in *your* law, I said, 'Ye are gods?' If he called them G-ds, unto whom the word of god came, and the scripture cannot be broken; Say ye of him, **whom the Father hath sanctified,** and sent into the world, 'Thou blasphemest;' because I said, '**I am *the* son of God**?' If I do not the works of my Father, believe me not. But if I do, though ye believe not me, believe the works: that ye may know, and believe, that the **Father is in me, and I in him.**" Therefore, **they sought again to take him: but he escaped out of their hand**. (John 10:30-39)

Also…

And he said unto them, Ye are from beneath; **I am from above**: ye are of this world; **I am not of this world**. I said therefore unto you, that ye shall die in your sins: **for if ye believe not that I am *He***, ye shall die in your sins. (John 8:23-24)

For both the CT-Yeshu and Dionysos,[143] the primary concern is to be recognized as the son of Dios/God and that all

---

[143] This connection between Dionysos and CT-Yeshu seems so obvious to me. Therefore, other must have published on it before me. However, to date, I am

288

people should worship him. From the content of *John,* we can surmise that the author did not distinguish between the Dios (another name for Zeus) of the Greeks and the G-d of Israel. For the Jews, the issue is that this Yeshu identifies himself as *The* Son of G-d. Had he said that he was *a* son of G-d, as we find David stating in Psalms, there would be no problem. For the Jewish reader, *John's* Yeshu is denying the divine breath that is innate to us all and bombastically claiming that only he is righteous.

אֲנִי-אָמַרְתִּי, אֱלֹהִים אַתֶּם; וּבְנֵי עֶלְיוֹן כֻּלְּכֶם

Ps. 82:6 I said: Ye are god like beings [or empowered persons], and all of you sons of the Most High.

Like Dionysus, CT-Yeshu demands the respect of the officials and is accused of being insolent when he denounces them.

> **515 Dionysus:** I will go, since I need not suffer [*paskhô*] that which is not necessary. But Dionysus, who you claim does not exist, will pursue you for this hubris. For in treating us without dikê (justice) you are leading him into chains. *Dionysus is led away by the attendants. Pentheus exits into the palace.*
> **Pentheus:** You must pay the penalty for your evil devices.
> **Dionysus:** And you for your ignorance and impiety toward the god.
> **Pentheus:** Seize him, he insults me and Thebes!
> **Dionysus:** I warn you not to bind me, since I am balanced [*sôphrôn*] and you are not.
> **Pentheus:** Shut him up near the horse stable, **510** so that he may see only darkness.

---

only aware of the references in Sir James G. Frazer, *The Golden Bough: A study in Magic and Religion* editor Robert Frazer, pp. 396-404.

Dionysus: He found a bull by the stable where he shut me up, and threw shackles around its legs and hooves, **620** breathing out *thûmos*, dripping sweat from his body, biting his lips. And I, present nearby, sat serenely [*hêsukhos*] and looked on. Meanwhile, Bacchus came; he shook the house and set fire to his mother's tomb. When Pentheus saw this, **625** he ran here and there, thinking that the house was burning, and ordered the slaves to bring water; every servant was at work, toiling in vain.

Dionysus: In this too I mocked him, since thinking that he was chaining me he neither touched nor handled me, but fed on hopes.

Pentheus: I have suffered [*paskhô*] a terrible disaster: the stranger, who was recently imprisoned, has escaped me. Ah! **645** Here is the man. What is this? How do you appear in front of the house, having come out?

Dionysus: Why? Do gods not pass even over walls?

Peter and John (Acts 5:17-23) and Paul and Silas (Acts 16:25-30) were also imprisoned and miraculously released, mimicking the release of Dionysos. Yeshu, as Dionysos, was unjustly persecuted by his kinsmen:

> Now both the chief priests and the Pharisees had given a commandment, that, if any man knew where he was, he should shew *it*, that they might take him. (John 11:57)

> The high priest then asked Jesus of his disciples, and of his doctrine.
> Jesus answered him, "I spake openly to the world; I ever taught in the synagogue, and in the temple,

whither the Jews always resort; and in secret have I said nothing. Why askest thou me? ask them which heard me, what I have said unto them: behold, they know what I said." And when he had thus spoken, one of the officers which stood by struck Jesus with the palm of his hand, saying, "Answerest thou the high priest so?" Jesus answered him, If I have spoken evil, bear witness of the evil: but if well, why smitest thou me?" (John 18:19-23)

At this point in both stories, the focus shifts to punishment. Pentheus fails to catch Dionysos, who taking the offensive extract revenge on his cousin. Yet, how is it possible that mere humans could punish a god?

> **Messenger:** His own mother, as priestess, began the slaughter, **1115** and fell upon him. He threw the miter from his head so that wretched Agave might recognize and not kill him. Touching her cheek, he said: "It is I, mother, your son Pentheus, whom you bore in the house of Ekhion. **1120** Pity me, mother! Do not kill me, your child, for my errors!"
> But she, foaming at the mouth and rolling her eyes all about, with her *phrenes* (φρήνες, intellect, mind) not as they should be, was under the control of Bacchus, and he did not convince her...[144]

What follows is the dismemberment of poor Pentheus depicted earlier. His delusional mother then carries his head back to her father, convinced that her trophy is a lion's head. Dionysos via his *Maenads* has taken revenge on his kinsmen for their lack of

---

[144] T.A. Buckley, et.al.

piety towards him. Thus, Dionysos has accomplished his mission. He has established his divinity among the Thebans. No one will dare challenge his divinity again.

According to the CT, Yeshu also experiences recognition as a divinity by his followers.

> ***Mark***: And Jesus went out, and his disciples, into the towns of Caesarea Philippi: and by the way he asked his disciples, saying unto them, "Whom do men say that I am?" And they answered, "John the Baptist: but some *say*, Elias; and others, One of the prophets." And he saith unto them, "But you, who do you say I am?" Peter answers that he is the Christ, and Jesus commands him to silence; he began to teach them, that the Son of man must suffer many things... (Mark 8:27-31);

> ***Matthew:*** "But whom say ye that I am?" and Simon Peter answered and said, "Thou art the Christ, the Son of the living God." And Jesus answered and said unto him, "Blessed art thou, Simon Barjona: for flesh and blood hath not revealed *it* unto thee, but my Father which is in heaven." (Matt. 16:15-17)

> ***Luke***: "But whom say ye that I am? Peter answering said, The Christ of God." he straitly charged them, and commanded *them* to tell no man that thing; Saying, The Son of man must suffer many things, and be rejected of the elders and chief priests and scribes, and be slain, and be raised the third day." (Luke 9:20-21)

> ***John***: Then Simon Peter answered him, Lord, to whom shall we go? thou hast the words of eternal

life. And we believe and are sure that thou art that Christ, the Son of the living G-d. (John 6:68-69)

III-3.5 *Eucharistía*

Isn't it amazing?

Paul and his associates spent years sermonizing and sending letters claiming that the world was coming to an end in their life-time. Even though the prediction obviously didn't come true, people still believe his message 2000 years later. Hence, it was Paul's sincerely felt and obsessively insistent claim that "The End is just around the corner" that transformed an obscure sectarian group into a religious empire.

Of course, the doomsday doctrine was a time-honored traditional theme among the followers of Attis and Mithra, so it had a long history among the non-Jews for centuries before either Yeshu was born. Likewise, the worship of Dionysos was wide-spread in the ancient world. This raises an important question. How far did Paul go in meshing pre-existing, pagan concepts with the teaching of the early Meshiḥim who he was trying to influence?

Eucharistía, (εὐχαριστία), which means "gratitude, thankfulness", is a very sacred Christian ceremony that commemorates their spiritual union with their god via ritual cannibalism, where they symbolically consumed his "flesh" and drink his "blood". His "body" is represented by a wafer of dry bread and his "blood" is epitomized by a small portion of wine. As discovered above, Dionysos was the god of wine and bread. In the CT, Yeshu is also identified by wine and bread. "I am the true vine, and my Father is the husbandman." (John 15:1) Keep in mind that Dionysus was the god of grain/bread; thus, bread is the grain-god's body. Since Dionysus was the god of wine, then wine is the grapevine-god's blood. This entire passage is directly from the Dionysian mysteries. In addition, CT-Yeshu's first miracle, recorded in the *Book of John,* was turning vats of spring water into wine – a very Dionysian activity. (John 2:1-11)

The concept is that the Passover lamb offering was replaced by their god, as a human sin-offering. (*1 Cor* 5:7) They then take part in ritual cannibalism by symbolically consuming part of their deity's body (the wafer) and his blood (the wine); thereby the individual's body is fused with the body of the consumed deity. (1 Cor. 12:13, 27). It cannot be denied that this ritual, symbolic cannibalism is an entirely foreign implant.

> The cup of blessing which we bless, is it not the communion of the blood of Christ? The bread which we break, is it not the communion of the body of Christ? For we *being* many are one bread, *and* one body: for we are all partakers of that one bread. (**1 Cor. 10:16-17**)

For I have received of the Lord that which also I delivered unto you, That the Lord Jesus the *same* night in which he was betrayed took bread: And when he had given thanks, he brake *it*, and said, "Take, eat: this is my body, which is broken for you: this do in remembrance of me." After the same manner also *he took* the cup, when he had supped, saying, "This cup is the new testament in my blood: this do ye, as oft as ye drink *it*, in remembrance of me. For as often as ye eat this bread, and drink this cup, ye do shew the Lord's death till he come." (**1 Cor 11:23-26**)

According to the CT, this ritual was initiated by Yeshu before his death. It appears in the Synoptic and the *Book of John*. Yet, it is well known that these were written decades after Paul's Epistles. In view of Paul's heavy influence on the early development of Christian, it is reasonable to consider that the *eucharistía* ritual was first introduced by him and interpolated into the texts of the Synoptics (Matt. 26:26-29, Mark 14:18-29, Luke 22:19-21) and *John* (6:47-51; 6:42-59) by later redactors whose task it was to bring the various texts into greater harmony.

One of the great beauties of our Torah laws is that they surround us like the protect protective wings of a mother eagle from the profane rituals of the pagan world. Therein, we are cautioned regarding the consumption of blood.

- And ye shall eat no manner of blood, whether it be of fowl or of beast, in any of your dwellings. Whosoever it be that eateth any blood, that soul shall be cut off from his people. (Lev. 7:26-27)

- And whatsoever man there be of the house of Israel, or of the strangers that sojourn among them, that eateth any manner of blood, I will set My face against that soul that eateth blood, and will cut him off from among his people... Therefore, I said unto the children of Israel: No soul of you shall eat blood, neither shall any stranger that sojourneth among you eat blood... And every soul that eateth that which dieth of itself, or that which is torn of beasts, whether he be home-born or a stranger, he shall wash his clothes, and bathe himself in water, and be unclean until the even; then shall he be clean. But if he wash them not, nor bathe his flesh, then he shall bear his iniquity. (Lev. 17:10, 12, 15, 16)
- Ye shall not eat with the blood; neither shall ye practice divination nor soothsaying. (Lev. 19:26)
- Only ye shall not eat the blood; thou shalt pour it out upon the earth as water. Only be stedfast in not eating the blood; for the blood is the life; and thou shalt not eat the life with the flesh. Thou shalt not eat it; that it may go well with thee, and with thy children after thee, when thou shalt do that which is right in the eyes of the LORD. (Deut. 12:16, 23, 25).
- Only thou shalt not eat the blood thereof; thou shalt pour it out upon the ground as water. (Deut. 15:23)

As you can see, our Torah is very explicit about not eating meat with blood and most certainly, not drinking blood. We may only eat meat from animals with split hooves and that also chew the cud. Of fowl and fish, and others, we may not eat predators or scavengers. Human flesh is never allowed. Therefore, a Jew may never participate in the eucharistic ritual.

I do not write this to demean Christianity. The eucharistic ritual is a very ancient tradition among many people, going back thousands is not tens of thousands of years. We have no intention of tell any other people what to or what not to believe. Our focus is and must remain on our Torah and our own people. By the same token, imperialistic missionaries have no right to try to indoctrinate our people with their traditional beliefs. Where did Paul get the *hutzpah* to declared the Abrahamic rite of circumcision null and void? (Gal 5:6) To say that Hashem will reject us and condemn us to eternal suffering because we keep his Laws and refrain from partaking in ritual cannibalism is totally ludicrous. We have just as much right to keep our traditions as they do. But by projection of a severe conscience, Greco-Roman era writers, such as Apion and Dio Cassius, resulted in their false accusations of ritual cannibalism among Jews. Their own Dionysian fixations ultimate brought about the infamous, mendacious blood-libel that has haunted Jews for centuries.

III-3.6 Death, Resurrection and Guilt

John's Yeshu, transcendent and calm, accepted his death as an unpleasant but necessary task and without a hint of revengefulness. However, at this point, *John's* Yeshu demonstrates characteristics manifestation in a combination of Tammuz, Dionysos, Ba'al, Attis, and Orpheus, each of whom also triumphed over death. To paraphrase John's account of his Yeshu's resurrection:

The first *day* of the week, Sunday, Mary Magdalene arrived just before dawn at CT-Yeshu's tomb. We are not informed why she was there at such an early hour. She sees that the stone before the sepulcher has been rolled away, and runs to tell his disciples. She tells them that someone has stolen his body. This, of course, is an assumption since it was too dark to see inside and she did not enter the tomb.

By the time his disciples arrive with her at his grave, it must have been light enough for them to see for they note that the linen wrappings were there but the body was gone. Oddly, the text states: "For as yet they knew not the scripture, that he must rise again from the dead." This is strange because he had told them that several times that his karma was to be executed. But then they are consistently presented as rather slow-witted bunch. Then they nonchalantly go home.

But Mary stood outside the sepulcher crying. Then she stooped down and, looking inside, saw two angels in white sitting at either end of where CT-Yeshu had been placed the previous Friday afternoon. They said to her, "Woman, why weepest thou?" She saith unto them, "Because they have taken away my Lord, and I know not where they have laid him." And when she had thus said, she turned around and saw him standing there. Oddly, she doesn't recognize him. He asks her the same question. "Woman, why weepest thou? whom seekest thou?"

She is so confused that she thinks he must be the gardener and answers, "Sir, if thou have borne him hence, tell me where thou hast laid him, and I will take him away." To this CT-Yeshu calls her name and suddenly she answers, "Rabboni", which the text informs us means "Master." Quickly, he tells her, "Touch me not; for I am not yet ascended to my Father: but go to my brethren, and say unto them, I ascend unto my Father, and your Father; and *to* my God, and your God." Dutifully, Mary Magdalene runs off to give them the message.

Strangely, they do nothing else until that evening, when we are informed that they must lock their doors *"for fear of the Jews"*. Then, suddenly, CT-Yeshu is standing right there in front of them – in the locked room and greets them with "Peace *be* unto you." Even with this dramatic entrance, he still needs to show them the puncture wounds on his hands and side before they recognize him. Then they were glad. Then he states, "As *my* Father hath sent me, even so send I you." And when he had said this, he breathed on *them*, and added, "Receive ye the Holy Ghost." (John 20:1-23)

In the *mythoi* of Baʿal and Attis the death experience primarily symbolizes winter and his resurrection that of the rejuvenating spring season. In the CT-Yeshu *mythos*, the winter of the old-world order is coming to an end and his devotees are now promised to witness the budding of a new world following the "Parousia" of the general resurrection of the faith dead. However, there is an inconsistency here. Since eternal live is only promised to those who have already recognized and worshiped him, and he's return is imminent, then who is to be resurrected. Those who died before his arrival obviously had done neither.

Which brings us to another inconsistency, how is the crucifixion of the CT-Yeshu, as expressed in John 3:16 a sacrifice? Of course, it would be a demeaning experience for any od to allow humans to abuse his physical form; but, if you think about it, this wouldn't be anything worse than if someone smashed a stone idol of the assumed deity. Gods, as immortal-beings, do not die or feel pain as we humans do. So, how is this such a big deal? Granted, it was a novel concept for the first century Common Era Greco-Roman world. But – News-flash – this is the twenty-first century!

Personally, I find Moses' response to Hashem's reaction to the Golden Calf incident much more poignant. Moses' offer – that his name be blotted out of Hashem's *Book* (of Life) –

300

> And Moses returned unto the LORD, and said: "Oh,
> this people have sinned a great sin, and have made
> them a G-d of gold. Yet now, if Thou wilt forgive
> their sin--; and if not, blot me, I pray Thee, out of
> Thy book which Thou hast written." And the LORD
> said unto Moses: "Whosoever hath sinned against
> Me, him will I blot out of My book." (Ex. 34:31-33)

entail the elimination of his very existence. He is not simply saying that he is will to suffer death for his people. He is offering his entire existence – past, present and future – and his immortality! This renders the death of the CT-Yeshu as a deity as entirely insignificant. In addition, Hashem makes it perfectly clear that He holds each individual accountable for his/her on transgression, which negates the notion of vicarious atonement especially as depicted in the CT.

Recently, we read *Haftorah Masei*. All Messianic Jews should reread them and reassess the path they have chosen. Here are a few excerpts from it.

Jeremiah 2:10. For pass over to the isles of the Kittites, and see, and send unto Kedar, and consider diligently, and see if there hath been such a thing.
2:11. Hath a nation changed its G-ds, which yet are no G-ds? But My people hath changed its glory for that which doth not profit.
2:12. Be astonished, O ye heavens, at this, and be horribly afraid, be ye exceeding amazed, saith the LORD.
2:13. For My people have committed two evils: they have forsaken Me, the fountain of living waters, and hewed them out cisterns, broken cisterns, that can hold no water.
2:17. thou hast forsaken the LORD thy G-d, when He led thee by the way?

2:18. And now what hast thou to do in the way to Egypt, to drink the waters of Shihor [the Nile]? Or what hast thou to do in the way to Assyria, to drink the waters of the River [Euphrates]?

2:19. Thine own wickedness shall correct thee, and thy backslidings shall reprove thee: know therefore and see that it is an evil and a bitter thing, that thou hast forsaken the LORD thy G-d, neither is My fear in thee, saith the Lord G-D of hosts.

2:21. Yet I had planted thee a noble vine, wholly a right seed; how then art thou turned into the degenerate plant of a strange vine [Dionysos/Yeshu] unto Me?

2:23. How canst thou say: 'I am not defiled, I have not gone after the Baalim'?

4:1 If thou wilt return, O Israel, saith the LORD, yea, return unto Me; and if thou wilt put away thy detestable things out of My sight, and wilt not waver;

4:2. And wilt swear: 'As the LORD liveth' in truth, in justice, and in righteousness; then shall the nations bless themselves by Him, and in Him shall they glory.

Hence, we conclude that the Christian Text is not the *Brith Hadash* spoken of by the prophets in the Tanakh. On the contrary, it is better entitled the *New Testament of Dionysus*.

302

III-4 Clarifying Misconceptions

The accusation raised against our Torah by the JfJ website are so *hutzvan* that it is mind-numbing. I was actually left speechless by their bazaar declaration that Tanak contains evidence supporting the Christian belief in the Trinity. At first, they seemed to present a strong argument; and, I admit, I was taken aback. However, I recuperated quickly and found that the "mountain" of evidence vanished like fog before the warming rays of our Torah.

First, let me give an analogy as to why Jews and Christians, who are reading the same scriptures, arrive at such conflicting conclusions as to its meaning.

An English-speaking American diligently studies the Russian language. Having reached an acceptable level of proficiency, she begins reading Russian poetry and is enthralled both with the beauty of the text and her own accomplishment. She exuberantly enters into a conversation with a native Russian speaker regarding her favorite poems. She is shocked that the Russian disagrees with her. The meaning of the poem as she has expressed it is so clear to her. The Russian is insulted that such a stupid American thinks that she understands what the author's meaning. Of course, the problem is that her interpretation of the poem reflects her American culture and linguistic constructs. On the one hand, her interpretation is not invalid even though the author herself would not recognize it. She appreciates the author's creation from a definitive American perspective. On the other hand, the Russian is also right. She does not understand the significance of the poem as does a home-born, native Russian.

This scenario illustrates the dilemma encountered when Jews and Christians debate the meaning of Hebrew Scriptures. It is impossible for the two to reach a consensus on their meaning. The most that can be accomplished is for both parties to agree that each has the right to gain spiritually from the divine beauty of Hashem's great gift – His Torah.

III-4.1 Illusions of the Trinity

> **JfJ:** It is an all-too-common assumption that the concept of the Trinity is a purely Christian idea. But the idea of a God being a three-in-one unity actually has its roots in foundational Judaism and in the Hebrew Scriptures... Even if what Christians believe is monotheistic, it does not seem to be monotheistic enough to qualify as true Jewishness.
> But if we are to examine this line of thinking, it is best to begin with the very source of Jewish theology and the only means of testing it—the Hebrew Scriptures. We should be open to exploring and understanding the nuances of the Jewish roots of the Trinity because many Jewish people do believe in the Trinity! If we go back to the Scriptures, the case is clear, and this article will walk you through that case. Our

understanding hinges on the Hebrew language, so to the Hebrew first we shall turn.

The point made, of course, is true because the Bible does teach that God is only one God, and therefore, the general pattern is to have the plural noun followed by the singular verb when it speaks of the one true God. However, there are places where the word is used of the true God and yet is followed by a plural verb.

The sacred Trinity of Ancient Egypt were Osiris, Isis, and Horus – the Holy Family. The sonship of Paul's Yeshu sonship centers on his divine mission as commissioned by "God the Father" and communicated through the *Ruaḥ haQodesh,* the "Holy Spirit". The new Christians, who came from an Egyptian tradition, insisted on the continuing the apotheosis of the feminine-mystique as manifested of Isis as the Holy Virgin-Mother, which resulted in the interpolation of Mariology into the CT.

III-4.1.1 G-d followed by a plural verb

In order to investigate this issue in depth, we turn now to examine each of these verses as they are found in the Greek translation of the Hebrew scriptures, the Septuagint (LXX). Since it is was written roughly 335 years before the earliest Christian texts and was the authoritative Scripture used by those authors, it should be an acceptable witness.

#1-JfJ: <u>Genesis 20:13</u>: "And when God [Elohim] caused me to wander [literally: **"They" caused me to wander**] from my father's house.

כ:יג וַיְהִי כַּאֲשֶׁר **הִתְעוּ אֹתִי** אֱלֹהִים מִבֵּית אָבִי,
20:13 And it came to pass, when **G-d caused me to wander** from my father's house,

20:13 ἐγένετο δέ, ἡνίκα **ἐξήγαγέ με ὁ Θεὸς** ἐκ τοῦ οἴκου τοῦ πατρός μου,
20:13 And it came to pass **when G-d [singular] brought me forth** out of the house of my father,

#2-JfJ: <u>Genesis 35:7</u>: "**There God [Elohim] had revealed himself to him**." [Literally: "They" appeared unto him.]

לה:ז וַיִּבֶן שָׁם, מִזְבֵּחַ, וַיִּקְרָא לַמָּקוֹם, אֵל בֵּית-אֵל: **כִּי שָׁם, נִגְלוּ אֵלָיו הָאֱלֹהִים**, בְּבָרְחוֹ, מִפְּנֵי אָחִיו.
And he built there an altar, and called the place El-beth-el, **because there G-d was revealed unto him**,

35:7 καὶ ᾠκοδόμησεν ἐκεῖ θυσιαστήριον καὶ ἐκάλεσε τὸ ὄνομα τοῦ τόπου Βαιθήλ. **ἐκεῖ γὰρ ἐφάνη αὐτῷ ὁ Θεὸς** ἐν τῷ ἀποδιδράσκειν αὐτὸν ἀπὸ προσώπου Ἡσαῦ τοῦ ἀδελφοῦ αὐτοῦ.
35:7 And he built there an altar, and called the name of the place Baethel; **for there God [singular] appeared to him**,

#3-JfJ: <u>2 Samuel 7:23</u>: "God [Elohim] went."" [Literally: "They" went.]

ז:כג וּמִי כְעַמְּךָ כְּיִשְׂרָאֵל, גּוֹי אֶחָד בָּאָרֶץ--אֲשֶׁר **הָלְכוּ-אֱלֹהִים לִפְדּוֹת-לוֹ** לְעָם,
7:23 And who is like Thy people, like Israel, a nation one in the earth, whom **G-d went to redeem unto Himself** for a people,

7:23 καὶ τίς ὡς ὁ λαός σου Ἰσραὴλ ἔθνος ἄλλο ἐν τῇ γῇ; ὡς ὡδήγησεν αὐτὸν **ὁ Θεὸς τοῦ λυτρώσασθαι αὐτῷ** λαόν,

 7:23 And what other nation in the earth [is] as thy people Israel? whereas **God [singular]** was his guide, **to redeem for himself** a people,

#4-JfJ: <u>Psalm</u> **58:11**: "Surely **there is a God** [Elohim] **who judges.**" [Literally: "They" judge.]

נח:יב וְיֹאמַר אָדָם, אַךְ-פְּרִי לַצַּדִּיק; אַךְ יֵשׁ-אֱלֹהִים, **שֹׁפְטִים בָּאָרֶץ.**

58:12 And men shall say: 'Verily there is a reward for the righteous; verily there is **a G-d that judgeth** in the earth.'

58:12 καὶ ἐρεῖ ἄνθρωπος· εἰ ἄρα ἐστὶ καρπὸς τῷ δικαίῳ, ἄρα ἐστὶν **ὁ Θεὸς κρίνων** αὐτοὺς ἐν τῇ γῇ.

58:12 And a man shall say, Verily, then there is a reward for the righteous: verily there **is a God [singular] that judges** them in the earth.

It is true that in the Hebrew the subjects and verbs are in the plural tense. However, in the Greek, we find that for each of these first four verses the subjects (God, ὁ Θεὸς) and the verbs (ἐξήγαγέ, ἐφάνη, λυτρώσασθαι, and κρίνων) are all in the singular tense. However, the JfJ authors take this line of argue further.

III-4.1.2 Alleged references of G-d's plurality

> **JfJ: God not only speaks of Himself in the plural, but many authors of Scripture also refer to God's plurality**. Out of the Hebrew, we

find that nouns and adjectives describing God are in the plural form.

#5-JfJ: Ecclesiastes 12:1: "Remember now your **Creator**." [Literally: creators.]

יב:א וּזְכֹר, אֶת-**בּוֹרְאֶיךָ**, בִּימֵי, בְּחוּרֹתֶיךָ:
12:1 Remember then **thy Creator** in the days of thy youth,

12:1 Καὶ μνήσθητι **τοῦ κτίσαντός** [singular] σε ἐν ἡμέραις νεότητός σου,
12:1 And remember **thy Creator [singular]** in the days of thy youth,

#6-JfJ: Psalm 149:2: "Let Israel rejoice in **their Maker**." [Literally: makers.]

קמט:ב יִשְׂמַח יִשְׂרָאֵל **בְּעֹשָׂיו**; בְּנֵי-צִיּוֹן, יָגִילוּ בְמַלְכָּם.
149:2 Let Israel rejoice **in his Maker**; let the children of Zion be joyful in their King.

149:2 εὐφρανθήτω Ἰσραὴλ **ἐπὶ τῷ ποιήσαντι** [singular] αὐτόν, καὶ οἱ υἱοὶ Σιὼν ἀγαλλιάσθωσαν ἐπὶ τῷ βασιλεῖ αὐτῶν.
149:2 Let Israel rejoice **in him [singular] that made him**; and let the children of Sion exult in their king.

#7-JfJ: Joshua 24:19: "**holy God**" [Literally: holy Gods.]

בד:יט וַיֹּאמֶר יְהוֹשֻׁעַ אֶל-הָעָם, לֹא תוּכְלוּ לַעֲבֹד אֶת- ה'--כִּי-אֱלֹהִים קְדֹשִׁים, הוּא:
24:19 And Joshua said unto the people: '**Ye cannot serve the LORD; for He is a holy G-d**;

24:19 καὶ εἶπεν Ἰησοῦς πρὸς τὸν λαόν· **οὐ μὴ δύνησθε λατρεύειν Κυρίῳ** [singular], **ὅτι ὁ Θεὸς ἅγιός ἐστι**,

24:19 And Joshua said to the people, **indeed, ye will not be able to serve the Lord, for G-d is holy**;

#8-JfJ: <u>Isaiah</u> **54:5**: "For **your Maker is your husband.**"
[Literally: makers, husbands.]

נד:ה כִּי **בֹעֲלַיִךְ עֹשַׂיִךְ**, ה' **צְבָאוֹת שְׁמוֹ**; וְגֹאֲלֵךְ קְדוֹשׁ יִשְׂרָאֵל, אֱלֹהֵי כָל-
הָאָרֶץ יִקָּרֵא.

54:5 For thy **Maker is thy husband, the LORD of hosts is His name**; and the Holy One of Israel is thy Redeemer, the G-d of the whole earth shall He be called.

54:5 ὅτι Κύριος ὁ ποιῶν σε, Κύριος σαβαὼθ ὄνομα [all singulars] αὐτῷ· καὶ ὁ ῥυσάμενός σε αὐτὸς Θεὸς Ἰσραήλ, πάσῃ τῇ γῇ κληθήσεται.
54:5 For [it is] the Lord that made thee; the **Lord of hosts is his name**: and he that delivered thee, he is the God of Israel, [and] shall be called [so] by the whole earth.

The evidence gleamed from last four verses reinforce that from the first four. We must conclude that those who translated these verses from Hebrew to Greek 2300 years ago, understood their correct connotation – that the Hebrew text expresses the "royal we" and, thus, translated them properly into the Greek in the singular. Even the JfJ authors admit that, before entering into this line of argument, they were aware that Rashi and his descendants, the Tzfornot, confirm that "the Deity is referred to in the plural as a sign of respect, similar to להבדיל, the royal "we".[145]

III-4.1.3 Accusation against the Shema

JfJ: The Shema and God's Plural Nature:

> The resounding and profound words throughout all generations: "Hear, O Israel: The LORD our God, the LORD is one!" (Deuteronomy 6:4). This has always been Israel's great confession. This verse is used more than any other to affirm the fact that God is one and to deny the possibility of plurality in the Godhead. On the one hand, it should be noted that the very words "our God" are in the plural in the Hebrew text and literally mean "our Gods." However, the main argument lies in the word "one," which is a Hebrew word, *echad*. A glance through the Hebrew text where the word is used elsewhere can quickly show that the word *echad* does not mean an "absolute one" but a "compound one."

ו:ד שְׁמַע, יִשְׂרָאֵל: ה' אֱלֹהֵינוּ, ה' אֶחָד.
Duet. 6:4 Hear, O Israel: the LORD our G-d, the LORD is **one**.

---

[145] Meir Zlotowitz, trans., *Koheles / Ecclesiastes: a New Translation with a commentary anthologized from Talmudic, Midrashic and Rabbinic Sources* (Brooklyn: Mesorah Publications, Ltd., 2010), Commentary 1., p.194.

6:4 Ἄκουε, Ἰσραήλ· Κύριος ὁ Θεὸς ἡμῶν Κύριος
εἷς ἐστι·
6:4 Hear, O Israel, The Lord our G-d **is one** Lord.

Sorry but, the word אֶחָד *eḥad* does mean an "absolute one". Its literally meaning is "the first among the whole numbers" and is the term used in the majority of the Biblical Scriptures where an absolute one is meant. The term אֲחָדִים *eḥadim* either means "some or few" or it is used as an adjective of a plural noun.

The Greek terms for "one" are: εἷς, ἑνός (*heis, henos*) – a single person or thing, with focus on quantitative aspect of one – in contrast to more than one. Another form is ἕν, ἑνός (*hen, henos*) – a single entity, with focus on uniformity or quality, *one – one and the same*. (ἕν *hen* must not be confused with ἐν *en*, which generally means "in".) Also, the irregular feminine form of one is μία, μίας (*mia, mias*) – one, someone, first or *the first one*. You will find this to be consistently true in the following examples.

#1. Duet. 6:4

ו:ד שְׁמַע, יִשְׂרָאֵל: ה' אֱלֹהֵינוּ, ה' אֶחָד.
Hear, O Israel: the LORD our G-d, the **LORD** is **one**.
6:4 Ἄκουε, Ἰσραήλ· Κύριος ὁ Θεὸς ἡμῶν **Κύριος εἷς** ἐστι·
6:4 Hear, O Israel, The Lord our God is **one Lord**.

#2. 2 Sam. 7:22

ז:כב עַל-כֵּן גָּדַלְתָּ, ה' אֱלֹהִים: **כִּי-אֵין כָּמוֹךָ, וְאֵין אֱלֹהִים זוּלָתֶךָ**, בְּכֹל אֲשֶׁר-
שָׁמַעְנוּ, בְּאָזְנֵינוּ. **כג** וּמִי כְעַמְּךָ כְּיִשְׂרָאֵל, גּוֹי **אֶחָד** בָּאָרֶץ--אֲשֶׁר הָלְכוּ-אֱלֹהִים
לִפְדּוֹת-לוֹ לְעָם

7:22 Therefore Thou art great, O LORD G-d; for **there is none
like Thee, neither is there any G-d beside Thee,** according to all
that we have heard with our ears.

7:22 ἕνεκεν τοῦ μεγαλῦναί σε, Κύριέ μου Κύριε, **ὅτι οὐκ ἔστιν ὡς
σὺ καὶ οὐκ ἔστι Θεὸς πλὴν σοῦ** ἐν πᾶσιν, οἷς ἠκούσαμεν ἐν τοῖς
ὠσὶν ἡμῶν.

7:22 that he may magnify thee, O my Lord; **for there is no one
like thee, and there is no G-d,** but thou among all of whom we
have heard with our ears.

#3. <u>Isaiah 51:2</u>

נא:ב הַבִּיטוּ אֶל-אַבְרָהָם אֲבִיכֶם, וְאֶל-שָׂרָה תְּחוֹלֶלְכֶם: **כִּי-אֶחָד** קְרָאתִיו, וַאֲבָרְכֵהוּ
וְאַרְבֵּהוּ.

51:2 Look unto Abraham your father, and unto Sarah that bore
you; **for when [he was but] one I called him,** and I blessed him,
and made him many.

51:2 ἐμβλέψατε εἰς Ἀβραὰμ τὸν πατέρα ὑμῶν καὶ εἰς Σάρραν τὴν
ὠδίνουσαν ὑμᾶς· **ὅτι εἷς ἦν,** καὶ ἐκάλεσα αὐτὸν καὶ εὐλόγησα
αὐτὸν καὶ ἠγάπησα αὐτὸν καὶ ἐπλήθυνα αὐτόν.

51:2 Look to Abraam your father, and to Sarrha that bore you: **for
he was alone** when I called him, and blessed him, and loved him,
and multiplied him.

#4. <u>Zechariah. 14:9</u>

יד:ט וְהָיָה ה' לְמֶלֶךְ, עַל-כָּל-הָאָרֶץ; בַּיּוֹם הַהוּא, יִהְיֶה ה' **אֶחָד**--וּשְׁמוֹ **אֶחָד**.

14:9 And the LORD shall be King over all the earth; in that day
shall the **LORD be One,** and **His name one.**

14:9 καὶ ἔσται Κύριος εἰς βασιλέα ἐπὶ πᾶσαν τὴν γῆν· ἐν τῇ ἡμέρᾳ
ἐκείνῃ ἔσται **Κύριος εἷς** καὶ **τὸ ὄνομα αὐτοῦ ἕν.**

14:9 And the Lord shall be king over all the earth: in that day there
shall be **one** Lord, and **his name one,**

#5. <u>Malachi 2:10</u>

בְּי הֲלוֹא אָב אֶחָד לְכֻלָּנוּ, הֲלוֹא אֵל אֶחָד בְּרָאָנוּ; מַדּוּעַ, נִבְגַּד אִישׁ בְּאָחִיו--לְחַלֵּל, בְּרִית אֲבֹתֵינוּ.

2:10 Have we not all **one** father? Hath not **one** G-d created us? Why do we deal treacherously every man against his brother, profaning the covenant of our fathers?

2:10 Οὐχὶ **πατὴρ εἷς** πάντων ὑμῶν; οὐχὶ **Θεὸς εἷς** ἔκτισεν ὑμᾶς; τί ὅτι ἐγκατέλιπε ἕκαστος τὸν ἀδελφὸν αὐτοῦ τοῦ βεβηλῶσαι τὴν διαθήκην τῶν πατέρων ὑμῶν;

2:10 Have ye not all **one father**? Did not **one G-d** create you? why have ye forsaken every man his brother, to profane the covenant of your fathers?

#6. Psalms 14:3

ידְג הַכֹּל סָר, יַחְדָּו נֶאֱלָחוּ: אֵין עֹשֵׂה-טוֹב--אֵין, גַּם-אֶחָד.

14:3 They are all corrupt, they are **together** become impure; there is none that doeth good, no, not **one [=single person]**.

13:3a πάντες ἐξέκλιναν, ἅμα ἠχρειώθησαν, οὐκ ἔστι ποιῶν χρηστότητα, οὐκ ἔστιν ἕως **ἑνός**.

13:3a They are all gone out of the way, they are together become good for nothing, there is none that does good, no not **one**.

#7. Psalms 53:4

נגד כֻּלּוֹ סָג, יַחְדָּו נֶאֱלָחוּ: אֵין עֹשֵׂה-טוֹב; אֵין, גַּם-אֶחָד.

53:4 Every one of them is unclean, they are **together** become impure; there is **none** that doeth good, **no, not one.**

52:4 They have all gone out of the way, they are together become unprofitable; there is **none** that does good, there is **not** even **one**.

52:4 πάντες ἐξέκλιναν, ἅμα ἠχρειώθησαν, **οὐκ** ἔστι ποιῶν ἀγαθόν, **οὐκ** ἔστιν ἕως **ἑνός**.

As you can see, the JfJ authors are completely off-base here. In all of the example above, **one** means *one* – in Hebrew, Greek, and English. The argument that they have chosen is hollow; yet, they continue with it.

JfJ: For instance, in Genesis 1:5, the combination of evening and morning comprise one (*echad*) day.

#8. Genesis 1:5

א:ה וַיִּקְרָא אֱלֹהִים לָאוֹר יוֹם, וְלַחֹשֶׁךְ קָרָא לָיְלָה; וַיְהִי-עֶרֶב וַיְהִי-בֹקֶר, **יוֹם אֶחָד**.

1:5 And G-d called the light Day, and the darkness He called Night. And there was evening and there was morning, **one day**.

1:5 καὶ ἐκάλεσεν ὁ Θεὸς τὸ φῶς ἡμέραν καὶ τὸ σκότος ἐκάλεσε νύκτα. καὶ ἐγένετο ἑσπέρα καὶ ἐγένετο πρωΐ, **ἡμέρα μία**.

1:5 And G-d called the light Day, and the darkness he called Night, and there was evening and there was morning, **the first day**.

> **JfJ:** In Genesis 2:24, a man and a woman come together in marriage and the two "shall become **one [echad] flesh**."

#9. Genesis 2:24

ב:כד עַל-כֵּן, יַעֲזָב-אִישׁ, אֶת-אָבִיו, וְאֶת-אִמּוֹ; וְדָבַק בְּאִשְׁתּוֹ, **וְהָיוּ לְבָשָׂר אֶחָד**.

2:24 Therefore shall a man leave his father and his mother, and shall cleave unto his wife, **and they shall be one flesh.**

2:24 ἕνεκεν τούτου καταλείψει ἄνθρωπος τὸν πατέρα αὐτοῦ καὶ τὴν μητέρα καὶ προσκολληθήσεται πρὸς τὴν γυναῖκα αὐτοῦ, **καὶ ἔσονται οἱ δύο εἰς σάρκα μίαν**

2:24 Therefore shall a man leave his father and his mother and shall cleave to his wife, **and they two shall be one flesh.**

Nu? By having children, the genetic material of two individuals unite to create a uniquely new individual. Thus, the two become one. Also, we understand a "day" to be 24 hours, which, of course, includes the hours of night time. The first verse, obviously, relates a more primitive concept of a "day" as including only daylight hours. It simply expresses a

314

period of time from the first ray of light in the morning to the last rays of visible light in the evening twilight. The next "day" begins with the next slighting of the first light. Here it is not necessary to mention the hours of darkness. The verse is still correct.

> **JfJ:** In Ezra 2:64, we are told that the whole assembly was as one (*echad*), though of course, it was composed of numerous people.

#10. Ezra 2:64

ב:סד כָּל-הַקָּהָל, כְּאֶחָד--אַרְבַּע רִבּוֹא, אַלְפַּיִם שְׁלֹשׁ-מֵאוֹת שִׁשִּׁים.

2:64 The whole congregation **as one** was forty and two thousand three hundred and threescore.

2:64 πᾶσα δὲ ἡ ἐκκλησία ὁμοῦ ὡσεὶ τέσσαρες μυριάδες δισχίλιοι τριακόσιοι ἑξήκοντα,

2:64 And all the congregation **together** were about forty-two thousand three hundred and sixty;

Sorry, JfJ authors, even though you translated the כְּ before אֶחָד correct "as one", still you ignored this when you interpreted it as an absolute one. The כ makes this a simile, meaning **as one**. The LXX translates it as "together". But we must give them credit for persistence.

> **JfJ:** Ezekiel 37:17 provides a rather striking example where two sticks are combined to become one (*echad*). The use of the word *echad* in Scripture shows it to be a compound unity and not an absolute unity.

#11. Ezekiel 37:17

לז:יז וְקָרַב אֹתָם אֶחָד אֶל-אֶחָד, לְךָ--לְעֵץ אֶחָד; וְהָיוּ לַאֲחָדִים בְּיָדֶךָ.

37:17 and join them **one to one** for thee **for one stick**, that **they will be some (one plural)** in thy hand.

37:17 καὶ συνάψεις αὐτὰς **πρὸς ἀλλήλας** σαυτῷ εἰς **ῥάβδον μίαν** τοῦ δῆσαι αὐτάς, καὶ ἔσονται ἐν τῇ χειρί σου.

37:17 And thou shalt join them **together** for thyself, so as that they should bind themselves into **one stick**; and they shall be in thine hand.

#12. Genesis 11:1

יא:א וַיְהִי כָל-הָאָרֶץ, שָׂפָה אֶחָת, וּדְבָרִים אֲחָדִים.

11:1 And the whole earth was of one language and of **one speech**.

11:1 Καὶ ἦν πᾶσα ἡ γῆ χεῖλος ἕν, καὶ **φωνὴ μία** πᾶσι.

11:1 And all the earth was one lip, and there was **one language** to all.

#13. Genesis 27:44

מד וְיָשַׁבְתָּ עִמּוֹ, יָמִים אֲחָדִים--עַד אֲשֶׁר-תָּשׁוּב, חֲמַת אָחִיךָ.

27:44 and tarry with him **a few days**, until thy brother's fury turn away.

27:44 Καὶ οἴκησον μετ᾽ αὐτοῦ **ἡμέρας τινάς**, ἕως τοῦ ἀποστρέψαι τὸν θυμὸν καὶ τὴν ὀργὴν τοῦ ἀδελφοῦ σου ἀπὸ σοῦ

27:44 And dwell with him **certain days**, until thy brother's anger,

#14. Genesis 29:20

כ וַיַּעֲבֹד יַעֲקֹב בְּרָחֵל, שֶׁבַע שָׁנִים; וַיִּהְיוּ בְעֵינָיו כְּיָמִים אֲחָדִים, בְּאַהֲבָתוֹ אֹתָהּ.

29:20 And Jacob served seven years for Rachel; and they seemed unto him but **a few days**, for the love he had to her.

29:20 Καὶ ἐδούλευσεν Ἰακὼβ περὶ Ῥαχὴλ ἑπτὰ ἔτη, καὶ ἦσαν ἐναντίον αὐτοῦ ὡς **ἡμέραι ὀλίγαι**, παρὰ τὸ ἀγαπᾶν αὐτὸν αὐτήν.

29:20 And Jacob served for Rachel seven years, and they were before him as **a few days**, by reason of his loving her.

Again, in their enthusiasm to make a point, the JfJ authors are missing the bigger-picture. The term אֲחָדִים is the plural of אֶחָד "one". Usually, it means "some, a few", except when it is used as an adjective modifying a plural noun. Here each of the single sticks retains its individual characteristics but they interact and behave as one.

III-4.1.4 Accusations against David

The JfJ authors embarrass themselves to an equally humiliating extent in their next misstep.

> **JfJ:** The case for God's plurality becomes stronger when we encounter the term Elohim applied to two personalities in the same verse, such as in Psalm 45:7. "Your throne, O God, is forever and ever. The scepter of your kingdom is a scepter of uprightness; **8.** you have loved righteousness and hated wickedness. Therefore God, your God, has anointed you with the oil of gladness beyond your companions."

The missionaries make a great fuss over a few of David's psalms. What they have forgotten is that they were composed to be sung and that is how we should read them – as

317

a song. Perhaps, if we add graphics, it would help to visualize
a better translation.

Psalm 45:7

מה:ז-ח כִּסְאֲךָ, אֱלֹהִים, עוֹלָם וָעֶד – ♪ ♪ – ♪ ♪ – שֵׁבֶט מִישֹׁר, שֵׁבֶט
מַלְכוּתֶךָ – ♪ ♪ – ♪ ♪ – אָהַבְתָּ צֶּדֶק, וַתִּשְׂנָא-רֶשַׁע –♪ ♪ – עַל-כֵּן מְשָׁחֲךָ,
אֱלֹהִים, –♪, (to the audience) ♪ – אֱלֹהֶיךָ,– ♪♪ – שֶׁמֶן
שָׂשׂוֹן ♪–♪ ♪ ♪ – מֵחֲבֵרֶךָ. – ♪ ♪ ♪ .

45:7-8 (*Strumming a melody ♪ while singing:*)
Thy throne, G-d, is for ever and ever – (*strumming ♪ on his lyre
♪, then singing:*) –
a sceptre of equity is the sceptre of Thy kingdom – (*strumming
♪ on his lyre ♪, then singing:*) –
**Thou hast loved righteousness, and hated
wickedness;** (*strumming ♪ on his lyre ♪, then singing:*) –
even now, Your anointed-one, G-d, (*strumming ♪ on his lyre
♪ & then, looking directly at his audience, he stresses:*) **your G-d,**
(*strumming ♪ on his lyre ♪ & singing:*)
an oil of gladness (*strumming ♪ on his lyre ♪ & singing:*)
among your companions. (*Strumming the melody ♪*)

<u>**Psalm 110:1**</u>

1. **A Psalm of David** – (*Strumming a melody ♪ while
    singing:*) –
    "Hashem uttered [a prophecy] – **'Unto my nobleman
    [David]: 'Sit thou to My right until I make thine
    enemies thy footstool'** – (*Strumming ♪ while singing:*) –
2. **The rod of your [David's] strength** – (*Strumming ♪
    while singing:*) – **will Hashem stretch out from Zion** –
    (*Strumming ♪ while singing:*) – **'Rule thou [David's] in
    the midst of thine enemies [the Philistines]'.** –
    (*Strumming the melody ♪ then singing:*) –
3. **Thy [Hashem's] people offer themselves willingly in the
    day of thy [Hashem's] warfare;** – (*Strumming ♪ while

singing:) – **'In the majestic holiness, –** (*Strumming* ♪ *while singing*:) – **from the womb, from the dawn, a morning-dew He will bring forth for you.'** – (*Strumming a melody* ♪ *then singing*:)

4. **The LORD hath sworn, and will not repent:** – (*Strumming* ♪ *while singing*:) – **'Thou [David] art a priest for ever after the manner of a melchizedek [a king of righteousness].** – (*Strumming* ♪ *while singing*:) –

5. **My Lord [Hashem]** – (*Strumming* ♪ *while singing*:) – **at Thy [Hashem's] right hand, he [David] doth crush kings in the day of His [Hashem's] wrath.** (*Strumming* ♪ *while singing*:)

6. **He [Hashem] will judge among the nations;** – (*Strumming* ♪ *while singing*:) – **He [David] filleth it with dead bodies,** – (*Strumming* ♪ *while singing*:) – **He [David] crusheth a head over a wide land.** – (*Strumming* ♪ *while singing*:) –

7. **He [David] will drink of the brook in the way; therefore, will he lift up the head.'** – (*Strumming the melody* ♪)

Psalm 2:1-12

א לָמָּה, רָגְשׁוּ גוֹיִם;   וּלְאֻמִּים, יֶהְגּוּ-רִיק.

1. Why are the nations in an uproar? And why do the peoples mutter in vain?

ב יִתְיַצְּבוּ, מַלְכֵי-אֶרֶץ-- וְרוֹזְנִים נוֹסְדוּ-יָחַד: עַל- ה',   וְעַל-מְשִׁיחוֹ.

2. The kings of the earth stand up, and the rulers take counsel together, against the LORD, and against His anointed:

ג נְנַתְּקָה, אֶת-מוֹסְרוֹתֵימוֹ;   וְנַשְׁלִיכָה מִמֶּנּוּ עֲבֹתֵימוֹ.

3. 'Let us break their bands asunder, and cast away their cords from us.'

ד יוֹשֵׁב בַּשָּׁמַיִם יִשְׂחָק: אֲדֹנָי, יִלְעַג-לָמוֹ.

4. He that sitteth in heaven laugheth, the Lord hath them in derision.

ה אָז יְדַבֵּר אֵלֵימוֹ בְאַפּוֹ;   וּבַחֲרוֹנוֹ יְבַהֲלֵמוֹ.

5. Then will He speak unto them in His wrath, and affright them in His sore displeasure:

ו וַאֲנִי, נָסַכְתִּי מַלְכִּי: עַל-צִיּוֹן, הַר-קָדְשִׁי.

6. 'Truly it is I that have established My king upon Zion, My holy mountain.'

ז אֲסַפְּרָה, אֶל-חֹק: ה', אָמַר אֵלַי בְּנִי אַתָּה--אֲנִי, הַיּוֹם יְלִדְתִּיךָ.

7. I will tell of the decree: the LORD said unto me: 'Thou art My son, this day have I borne thee.

ח שְׁאַל מִמֶּנִּי--וְאֶתְּנָה גוֹיִם, נַחֲלָתֶךָ;   וַאֲחֻזָּתְךָ, אַפְסֵי-אָרֶץ.

8. Ask of Me, and I will give the nations for thine inheritance, and the ends of the earth for thy possession.

ט תְּרֹעֵם, בְּשֵׁבֶט בַּרְזֶל: כִּכְלִי יוֹצֵר תְּנַפְּצֵם.

9. Thou shalt break them with a rod of iron; thou shalt dash them in pieces like a potter's vessel.'

י וְעַתָּה, מְלָכִים הַשְׂכִּילוּ;   הִוָּסְרוּ, שֹׁפְטֵי אָרֶץ.

10. Now therefore, O ye kings, be wise; be admonished, ye judges of the earth.

יא עִבְדוּ אֶת- ה' בְּיִרְאָה;   וְגִילוּ, בִּרְעָדָה.

11. Serve the LORD with fear, and rejoice with trembling.

יב נַשְּׁקוּ-בַר, פֶּן-יֶאֱנַף וְתֹאבְדוּ דֶרֶךְ--   כִּי-יִבְעַר כִּמְעַט אַפּוֹ:
אַשְׁרֵי,   כָּל-חוֹסֵי בוֹ.

12. Do homage in purity, lest He be angry, and ye perish in the way, when suddenly His wrath is kindled. Happy are all they that take refuge in Him.

JfJ: 2:7 I will proclaim the decree of the LORD: He said to me, 'You are my **Son**; today I have **become your Father**.

ז אֲסַפְּרָה, אֶל-חֹק: ה' אָמַר אֵלַי: **בְּנִי אַתָּה--אֲנִי הַיּוֹם יְלִדְתִּיךָ.**

7. I will tell of the decree: the LORD said unto me: '**Thou art My son, this day have I begotten thee.**
Or a more direct translation it could be: '**Thou art My son, I, this day, have borne thee.'**

יב **נַשְּׁקוּ-בַר,** פֶּן-יֶאֱנַף וְתֹאבְדוּ דֶרֶךְ-- כִּי-יִבְעַר כִּמְעַט אַפּוֹ:

Ps. 2:12. Do homage in purity [join/unite purely (imperative-you pl.)], lest He be angry, and ye perish in the way, when suddenly His wrath is kindled.

LXX: 2:12 δράξασθε παιδείας, μήποτε ὀργισθῇ Κύριος καὶ ἀπολεῖσθε ἐξ ὁδοῦ δικαίας.

2:12 **Accept correction** [*i.e.* Grasped instruction/guidance], lest at any time the Lord be angry, and ye should perish from the righteous way:

NIV: 2:12 Kiss his son, or he will be angry and your way will lead to your destruction, for his wrath can flare up in a moment.

KJV: 2:12 Kiss the Son, lest he be angry, and ye perish *from* the way, when his wrath is kindled but a little.

JfJ: 2:12 Kiss the Son, lest he be angry and you be destroyed in your way, for his wrath can flare up in a moment.

The JPS translation uses the Biblical Hebrew term בר, meaning "clean or purify". Stating that a righteous live is one lived according to the laws of purity. The Septuagint has branched out somewhat, viewing education as the key to maintaining a righteous life. The three Christian translations migrate to the Aramaic word, בר, which means "son". This, of course, is in keeping with their ancestral focus on the notion of gods begetting demi-gods.

> **JfJ: Hosea 1:7**: "I will have mercy on the house of Judah, and I will save them by the LORD their G-d. I will not save them by bow or by sword or by war or by horses or by horsemen." The speaker is Elohim who says He will have mercy on the house of Judah and will save them by the

instrumentality of YHVH, their Elohim. So, Elohim number one will save Israel by means of Elohim number two.

The JfJ authors are often confused as to who is speaking when reading prophetic texts. Here in **Hosea**, it seems to be a simple issue of punctuation.

א:ו וַתַּהַר עוֹד, וַתֵּלֶד בַּת, וַיֹּאמֶר לוֹ, קְרָא שְׁמָהּ לֹא רֻחָמָה: כִּי לֹא אוֹסִיף עוֹד, אֲרַחֵם אֶת-בֵּית יִשְׂרָאֵל--כִּי-נָשֹׂא אֶשָּׂא, לָהֶם. ז וְאֶת-בֵּית יְהוּדָה אֲרַחֵם וְהוֹשַׁעְתִּים בַּה', **אֱלֹהֵיהֶם**; וְלֹא אוֹשִׁיעֵם, בְּקֶשֶׁת וּבְחֶרֶב וּבְמִלְחָמָה, בְּסוּסִים, וּבְפָרָשִׁים.

And she [Hosea's wife] conceived again, and bore a daughter. And He [Hashem] said unto him [Hosea]: 'Call her name Lo-ruhamah; for I will no more have compassion upon the house of Israel, that I should in any wise pardon them. 7. But I will have compassion upon the house of Judah, and will save them **by the LORD, their G-d**, and will not save them by bow, nor by sword, nor by battle, nor by horses, nor by horsemen.'

1:6 καὶ συνέλαβεν ἔτι καὶ ἔτεκε θυγατέρα, καὶ εἶπεν αὐτῷ· κάλεσον τὸ ὄνομα αὐτῆς, Οὐκ-ἠλεημένη, διότι οὐ μὴ προσθήσω ἔτι ἐλεῆσαι τὸν οἶκον Ἰσραήλ, ἀλλ᾽ ἢ ἀντιτασσόμενος ἀντιτάξομαι αὐτοῖς. 7 τοὺς δὲ υἱοὺς Ἰούδα ἐλεήσω καὶ σώσω αὐτοὺς **ἐν Κυρίῳ Θεῷ αὐτῶν** καὶ οὐ σώσω αὐτοὺς ἐν τόξῳ οὐδὲ ἐν ῥομφαίᾳ οὐδὲ ἐν πολέμῳ οὐδὲ ἐν ἵπποις οὐδὲ ἐν ἱππεῦσι.

1:6 And she conceived again, and bore a daughter. And he said to him, Call her name, Unpitied: for I will no more have mercy on the house of Israel, but will surely set myself in array against them. 7 But I will have mercy on the house of Juda, and will save them **by the Lord, their G-d**, and will not save them with bow, nor with sword, nor by war, nor by horses, nor by horsemen.

322

Here Hashem is emphasizing that He, who is their G-d, will save Judaea by the power of his Name. The anti-Jewish missionaries are simply too eager to force their beliefs upon us. They should have read more carefully. Then they would have noticed that Hosea, as the other prophets, uses phrasing to indicate that these are the words of Hashem and not the prophet's own thoughts.

In addition, they employ our high esteem of Solomon by taking words from Proverbs out of context and employ them for their purpose.

> **JfJ:** Proverbs paints a mysterious picture of a figure who bears the name of God's son and asks the reader to identify him. But is the idea of God having a son actually Jewish?
>
> Who has gone up to heaven and come down?
> Who has gathered up the wind in the hollow of his hands?
> Who has wrapped up the waters in his cloak?
> Who has established all the ends of the earth?
> What is his name, and the name of his son?
> Tell me if you know! (Proverbs 30:4)

But, when we read the entire text, we find that these questions were not even written by King Sholmo! Also, **Proverbs 30:6** contain an admonition not to do precisely what the JfJ authors are doing – adding to the message that Hashem actually sent to the prophets!

א דְּבְרֵי, אָגוּר בִּן-יָקֶה--הַמַּשָּׂא: נְאֻם הַגֶּבֶר, לְאִיתִיאֵל; לְאִיתִיאֵל וְאֻכָל.

1. The words of Agur the son of Jakeh; the burden. The man saith unto Ithiel, unto Ithiel and Ucal:

ב כִּי בַעַר אָנֹכִי מֵאִישׁ;   וְלֹא-בִינַת אָדָם לִי.

2. *Surely I am brutish, unlike a man, and have not the understanding of a man;*

ג וְלֹא-לָמַדְתִּי חָכְמָה;   וְדַעַת קְדֹשִׁים אֵדָע.

3. *And I have not learned wisdom, that I should have the knowledge of the Holy One.*

ד מִי עָלָה-שָׁמַיִם וַיֵּרַד, מִי אָסַף-רוּחַ בְּחָפְנָיו מִי צָרַר-מַיִם בַּשִּׂמְלָה-- מִי, הֵקִים כָּל-אַפְסֵי-אָרֶץ: מַה-שְּׁמוֹ וּמַה-שֶּׁם-בְּנוֹ, כִּי תֵדָע.

4. Who hath ascended up into heaven, and descended? Who hath gathered the wind in his fists? Who hath bound the waters in his garment? Who hath established all the ends of the earth? What is his name, and what is his son's name, if thou knowest?

ה כָּל-אִמְרַת אֱלוֹהַּ צְרוּפָה;   מָגֵן הוּא, לַחֹסִים בּוֹ.

5. Every word of G-d is tried; He is a shield unto them that take refuge in Him.

ו **אַל-תּוֹסְףְּ עַל-דְּבָרָיו: פֶּן-יוֹכִיחַ בְּךָ וְנִכְזָבְתָּ.**

6. Add thou not unto His words, lest He reprove thee, and thou be found a liar.

ז שְׁתַּיִם, שָׁאַלְתִּי מֵאִתָּךְ;   אַל-תִּמְנַע מִמֶּנִּי, בְּטֶרֶם אָמוּת.

7. Two things have I asked of Thee; deny me them not before I die:

ח *שָׁוְא וּדְבַר-כָּזָב, הַרְחֵק מִמֶּנִּי-- רֵאשׁ וָעֹשֶׁר, אַל-תִּתֶּן-לִי; הַטְרִיפֵנִי, לֶחֶם חֻקִּי.*

8. *Remove far from me falsehood and lies; give me neither poverty nor riches; feed me with mine allotted bread;*

ט פֶּן אֶשְׂבַּע, וְכִחַשְׁתִּי-- וְאָמַרְתִּי, מִי ה' : וּפֶן-אִוָּרֵשׁ וְגָנַבְתִּי; וְתָפַשְׂתִּי, שֵׁם אֱלֹהָי.

9. Lest I be full, and deny, and say: 'Who is the LORD?' Or lest I be poor, and steal, and profane the name of my G-d.

III-4.1.5 Accusation against the Rambam

Their next adventurous attempt at translating Hebrew really upset me when I first read it. Since the Rambam's teachings are so well documented and known, this depth to which the JfJ authors have plunged is unconscionable. It is unscrupulous to imply that the Rambam, the great Rabbi Moshe ben Maimon – who wrote an entire chapter in his *Guide of the Perplexed* (Part I, 35) entitled: "The Incorporeality of G-d should be made known to all" – would ever consider endorsing their ill-conceived notions. However, since they have published it and are teaching this to uneducated Jews, we are forced to answer them.

> **JfJ:** There is a Hebrew word that does mean an absolute unity and that is the word *yachid*, which is found in many Scripture passages,[2] with the emphasis being on the meaning of "only." If Moses intended to teach God's absolute oneness instead of as a compound unity, *yachid* would have been a far more appropriate word. In fact, Maimonides noted the strength of "*yachid*" and chose to use that word in his "Thirteen Articles of Faith" in place of *echad*. However, Deuteronomy 6:4 (the Shema) does not use "*yachid*" in reference to God.

Again, their unfamiliarity of the Hebrew language is at the heart of their misinterpretations. In ancient Ugaritic *yhd* meant "only one" and, thus, we find in Biblical Hebrew the term יָחִיד *yachid* meaning "only or solitary", as in these examples.

#1. Judges 11:34

יא:לד וַיָּבֹא יִפְתָּח הַמִּצְפָּה, אֶל-בֵּיתוֹ, וְהִנֵּה בִתּוֹ יֹצֵאת לִקְרָאתוֹ, בְּתֻפִּים
וּבִמְחֹלוֹת: וְרַק הִיא **יְחִידָה**, אֵין-לוֹ מִמֶּנּוּ בֵּן אוֹ-בַת.

11:34 And Jephthah came to Mizpah unto his house, and, behold, his daughter came out to meet him with timbrels and with dances; and she was **his only** child; beside her he had neither son nor daughter

11:34 Καὶ ἦλθεν Ἰεφθάε εἰς Μασσηφὰ εἰς τὸν οἶκον αὐτοῦ, καὶ ἰδοὺ ἡ θυγάτηρ αὐτοῦ ἐξεπορεύετο εἰς ὑπάντησιν ἐν τυμπάνοις καὶ χοροῖς· καὶ αὕτη ἦν **μονο**γενής, οὐκ ἦν αὐτῷ ἕτερος υἱὸς ἢ θυγάτηρ.

11:34 And Jephthae came to Massepha to his house; and behold, his daughter came forth to meet him with timbrels and dances; and she was his **only**-child, he had not another son or daughter.

#2. Psalm 22:21

כב:כא הַצִּילָה מֵחֶרֶב נַפְשִׁי; מִיַּד-כֶּלֶב, **יְחִידָתִי**.

22:21 Deliver my soul from the sword; mine **only one** from the power of the dog

21:21 ῥῦσαι ἀπὸ ῥομφαίας τὴν ψυχήν μου, καὶ ἐκ χειρὸς κυνὸς τὴν **μονο**γενῆ **μου**

21:21 Deliver my soul from the sword; my **only**-begotten **one** from the power of the dog.

#3. Psalm 25:16

כה:טז פְּנֵה-אֵלַי וְחָנֵּנִי: **כִּי-יָחִיד וְעָנִי אָנִי**.

25:16 Turn Thee unto me, and be gracious unto me; **for I am solitary** and afflicted

25:16 ἐπίβλεψον ἐπ᾽ ἐμὲ καὶ ἐλέησόν με, ὅτι **μονο**γενὴς καὶ πτωχός εἰμι ἐγώ.

25:16 Look upon me, and have mercy upon me; for I am an **only**-child and poor.

Those who are interested can also turn to Jeremiah

6:26; Amos 8:10; Zechariah 12:10 for more examples of the

same. It must be kept in mind that word usage changes from generation to generation and region to region. The term יָחִיד *yachid* is derived from the verb יחד "to become one, to make one, to unite". In Aramaic we find יַחֵד meaning "he united". In Syriac שׁוּחַד it means "he sat alone", and in Arabic *waḥada* meaning "he was alone" As the JfJ authors point out, in Old South Arabic וחד means "one". Of course, all of the forms are related to אֶחָד, since they are all from the same root אח. However, the JfJ authors have once again missed-the-mark. In Hebrew, the usage of יָחִיד *yachid* morphed during the Babylonian exile. In Post Biblical Hebrew (PBH), it means "he set apart, singled out"; "he devoted"; "he caused to be alone", "left alone"; "he professed or proclaimed the *oneness or unity of*".

III-4.1.6 Accusations against the Zohar

In addition to their insults to the Rambam above, JfJ authors are guilty of making a terrible, insolent accusations against the Zohar.

> **JfJ:** The author of the Zohar sensed plurality in the Tetragrammaton. and wrote:
> Come and see the mystery of the word YHVH: there are three steps, each existing by itself: nevertheless, they are One, and so united that one

cannot be separated from the other. The Ancient
Holy One is revealed with three heads, which are
united into one, and that head is three exalted.
The Ancient One is described as being three:
because the other lights emanating from him are
included in the three. But how can three names be
one? Are they really one because we call them
one? How three can be one can only be known
through the revelation of the Holy Spirit.

Personally, I cannot understand how the JfJ authors can
possibly consider themselves to be at the level of interpreting the
Zohar, if they cannot understand who is speaking and who is being
spoken about in well-known Hebrew verses from the Tanak? Such
ḥutzpanim חֻצְפָּנִים! Below is an excerpt from Wikipedia. I
encourage the JfJ authors to either set their arrogance aside and
study these subjects in much greater depth or, better yet, simply
move on to other topics.

The relationship between God's absolute Unity and
Divine manifestations may be compared to a man in
a room - there is the man himself, and his presence
and relationship to others in the room. In Hebrew,
this is known as the Shekhinah. It is also the concept
of God's Name - it is His relationship and presence
in the world towards us. The Wisdom (literally
written as Field of Apples) in kabbalistic terms refers
to the Shekhinah, the Divine Presence. The
Unknowable One (literally written as the Miniature
Presence) refers to events on earth when events can
be understood as natural happenings instead of God's
act, although it is actually the act of God. This is

known as perceiving the Shekhinah through a blurry, cloudy lens. This means to say, although we see God's Presence (not God Himself) through natural occurrences, it is only through a blurry lens; as opposed to miracles, in which we clearly see and recognize God's presence in the world. The Holy Ancient **One** refers to God Himself, Who is imperceivable. (see Minchas Yaakov and anonymous commentary in the Siddur Beis Yaakov on the Sabbath hymn of Askinu Seudasa, composed by the Arizal based on this lofty concept of the Zohar).[146]

III-4.2 Original Sin

We dealt with the deification of historic Yeshu by the earlier Christian authors above. Yet, before leaving the discussion of the Trinity, we should explore Paul's rational for why it was *necessary*, even essential, for Yeshu "Ḳristos" to be crucified.

1. Why would G-d do such things (*i.e.* "send one as a human sacrifice")? Paul's answer: as explored in Part 1, a sacrifice was required to atone for sins.

2. What sin could be so great as to require the death of a deity? Paul's answer: "When Adam and Eve sinned, all of their descendants were stained by that transgression. Also, Cain murdered Abel, and his sin left him with a mark of sin on his forehead.

3. Why should this necessitate a sacrifice? Paul's answer: Since all of mankind is stained by this sin, then all are

---

[146] https://en.wikipedia.org/wiki/Zohar

destined to burn for eternity in the inextinguishable fires of Hell, unless an acceptable sacrifice should be made as an atonement.

4. How does one benefit from this great atonement? Paul's answer: Only by accepting this guilt and solution as proposed by Paul, which through him became a central theme in Christianity, can mankind hope to be acceptable to G-d and return to the Garden of Eden.

Paul's argument stands on the premise that everyone is doomed because of mistake of two very inexperience young people. Therefore, we must reexamine these two accounts in Genesis and test Paul's hypothesis. The story of the "Fall of Man" is found in chapter three. There we find:

Genesis 4:6-7

ו וַיֹּאמֶר ה׳, אֶל-קַיִן: לָמָּה חָרָה לָךְ, וְלָמָּה נָפְלוּ פָנֶיךָ. ז הֲלוֹא אִם-תֵּיטִיב, שְׂאֵת, וְאִם לֹא תֵיטִיב, לַפֶּתַח חַטָּאת רֹבֵץ; וְאֵלֶיךָ, תְּשׁוּקָתוֹ, וְאַתָּה תִּמְשָׁל-בּוֹ.

6. And the LORD said unto Cain: 'Why art thou wroth? and why is thy countenance fallen? **7.** If thou doest well, shall it not be lifted up? and if thou doest not well, sin coucheth at the door; and unto thee is its desire, but thou mayest rule over it.'

7. If thou does well, [By ceasing to harbor rancor and jealousy] shall it [your countenance/self-respect, which has fallen] **not be lifted up** [shalln't you earn forgiveness] **and if thou doest not well.** [If you do not relinquish your grudge and malice,], **sin coucheth at the door.** [You will be ready to lapse into greater sin – as painfully real as if it were lying in wait for you at your door-step to encompass your ruin – unto the door of the grave] **unto thee is its desire,** [The tempter ever seeks to entice thee; but sin is willing to submit to you, if only you put forth the effort] **but thou mayest rule over it.** [You can conquer sin, if you wish, because repentance and forgiveness are always open to you.][147]

Keep in mind that since Hashem is omniscient, then He must have known that Adam and Eve would be tempted and would eat of the fruit of the knowledge of good and evil Therefore, it was always our destiny to leave the "Garden of Eden". We accept on faith that this all happened for our benefit and that of the world. Additionally, we find that Paul was mistaken – we are not condemned to eternal "hell and damnation" because Adam and Eve ate from the Tree or the Knowledge of Good and Evil.

---

[147] Menahem M. Kasher, *Encyclopedia of Biblical Interpretation*, Rabbi Dr. Harry Freedman, ed. (New York: American Biblical Encyclopedia Society, 1953.), pp. 150-152.

III-5 Opposing Ḥillul Hashem

From Sophocles play, *Oedipus Rex,* we learn that among
the Greeks murder, incest, and rape were considered impious acts
that imparted a state of impurity upon the criminal. While awaiting
his trial for impiety. In his case this was demoralizing the youth of
Athens by teaching a lack of proper respect for the gods. In Plato's
dialogue *Euthyphros,* Socrates engages Euthyphros in an dialect
analysis of the meaning of piety. The young man was also waiting
for a trail, since he had brought criminal charges of impiety against
his father for having caused the death of a servant due to callous
neglect. Socrates' inquiry into the meaning of impiety is
inconclusive, exposing an inherent circular-logic. For the Greeks,
deeds were pious if they were of intense concern to or in some
manner associated with a deity; but, since they had many gods,
each with it on concerns, there were as many forms of piety.

The online definition of sacrilege is a violation or injurious
treatment of a sacred object, site or person. This can take the form
of irreverence to sacred persons, places, and things. When the
sacrilegious offence is verbal, it is called blasphemy, and when
physical, it is often called desecration. In a less proper sense, any
transgression against what is seen as the virtue of religion would
be a sacrilege, and so is coming near a sacred site without
permission. This is essentially Christianity's concept of
sacrilegious. The greatest degree of impiety for Christians is

blatant derogation of any aspect of the Trinity with special sensitivity for disrespect of "God's manifestation as the Son". Catholics hold the Holy Mother in great esteem as well and are very protective of her honor.

In Judaism, impiety is referred to as *Hillul Hashem,* the "Desecration of G-d's Name", which is any deed or expression that demeans the beliefs and practices taught in the Torah – in either the written or oral format. Since Judaism maintains that there is only one G-d, whose concerns and mode of worship are outlined in His Law, the issues that plagued Socrates and sealed his fate were non-issues. Christians and Jews both revere G-d and abhor all forms of sacrilege. However, we have very different understandings of what constitute desecration.

The purpose of following this analysis is intended as an explanation of what constitutes Desecration of the Name of G-d in Judaism and why we cannot accept Christian doctrines. It should not be misconstrued as an attack on Christian beliefs. The Ten Commandments are sacred to both Christians and Jews and, therefore, should be an appropriate median for this portion of our study. Though they are not in effect today, the Torah stipulated four forms of capital punishment for various crimes. They are strangulation, the sword, fire, and stoning.[148]

---

[148] Abraham Chill, *The Mitzvots: The Commandments and Their Rationale* (Jerusalem: Keter Books, 1974), pp. 67-68.

III-5.1.1 The Unity of Hashem

כ:ב‎ אָנֹכִי ה' אֱלֹהֶיךָ, אֲשֶׁר הוֹצֵאתִיךָ מֵאֶרֶץ מִצְרַיִם מִבֵּית עֲבָדִים

I am the LORD thy G-d, who brought thee out of the land
of Egypt, out of the house of bondage. (Ex. 20:2a)

מ:כה‎ וְאֶל-מִי תְדַמְּיוּנִי, וְאֶשְׁוֶה--יֹאמַר, קָדוֹשׁ... כח‎ הֲלוֹא יָדַעְתָּ אִם-לֹא
שָׁמַעְתָּ, אֱלֹהֵי עוֹלָם ה' בּוֹרֵא קְצוֹת הָאָרֶץ--לֹא יִיעַף, וְלֹא יִיגָע: אֵין חֵקֶר,
לִתְבוּנָתוֹ.

**Isaiah 40:25, 28. To whom then will ye liken Me, that I should
be equal?** saith the Holy One... 28 Hast thou not known? hast
thou not heard that the **everlasting G-d, the LORD, the Creator
of the ends of the earth, fainteth not, neither is weary? His
discernment is past searching out.**

מה:כא‎ הַגִּידוּ וְהַגִּישׁוּ, אַף יִוָּעֲצוּ יַחְדָּו: מִי הִשְׁמִיעַ זֹאת מִקֶּדֶם מֵאָז הִגִּידָהּ,
הֲלוֹא אֲנִי ה' וְאֵין-עוֹד אֱלֹהִים מִבַּלְעָדַי--אֵל-צַדִּיק וּמוֹשִׁיעַ, אַיִן זוּלָתִי.
כב‎ פְּנוּ-אֵלַי וְהִוָּשְׁעוּ, כָּל-אַפְסֵי-אָרֶץ: כִּי אֲנִי-אֵל, וְאֵין עוֹד. כג‎ בִּי נִשְׁבַּעְתִּי-
-יָצָא מִפִּי צְדָקָה דָּבָר, וְלֹא יָשׁוּב: כִּי-לִי תִּכְרַע כָּל-בֶּרֶךְ, תִּשָּׁבַע כָּל-לָשׁוֹן.
כד‎ אַךְ בַּה' לִי אָמַר, צְדָקוֹת וָעֹז; עָדָיו יָבוֹא וְיֵבֹשׁוּ, כֹּל הַנֶּחֱרִים בּוֹ. כה‎ בַּה'
יִצְדְּקוּ וְיִתְהַלְלוּ, כָּל-זֶרַע יִשְׂרָאֵל.

Isaiah 45:21-25. Declare ye, and bring them near, yea, let them
take counsel together: Who hath announced this from ancient time,
and declared it of old? Have not I the LORD? **And there is no G-d
else beside Me**, a just G-d and a Saviour; **there is none beside
Me. 22 Look unto Me, and be ye saved**, all the ends of the earth;
for **I am G-d, and there is none else.** 23 By Myself have I sworn,
the word is gone forth from My mouth in righteousness, and shall
not come back, that unto Me every knee shall bow, every tongue
shall swear. **24 Only in the LORD, shall one say of Me, is**

victory and strength; even to Him shall men come in confusion, all they that were incensed against Him. 25 **In the LORD shall all the seed of Israel be justified, and shall glory**.

Therefore, there is **no** evidence supporting the JfJ authors' claim that the Hebrew Scriptures is the source for the Christian belief in the Trinity. The answer is a very definite: No – **there is no room for plurality of the "Godhead" in either the Hebrew Texts or Judaism.**

With the sin of the Golden Calf, the Children of Israel turned to the Egyptian worship of the sacred Apis Bull, whose worship was primarily in the region of Memphis, near the Hebrew settlement in Goshen. He was the son of Hathor (goddess of music, dance, joy, love, sexuality, and maternal care) who was sacrificed and reborn. In later dynasties, the Apis was also an intermediary between humans and the gods. Likewise, Christian doctrine teaches that their god was born to die and was to then become an intermediary between humans and the divine – thus, violating this first commandment.

The punishment for a religious leader who encouraged anyone of the Children of Israel to turn away from the required total commitment to the One G-d by acknowledging others was death by strangulation. The Christian Text repeatedly states that their god insisted that Jews must incorporate the belief in a divine son as part of our worship. Are we to believe them (*has v'halilah*) when they insist that such an unthinkable crime could ever be

335

committed? According to the Torah, anyone who promotes the belief in other gods should be condemned to death by strangulation.

III-5.1.2 No other Deities

כ:בb לֹא-יִהְיֶה לְךָ אֱלֹהִים אֲחֵרִים, עַל-פָּנָי.

Thou shalt have no other gods before Me. (Ex. 20:2c)

You shall revere no other אֱלֹהִים gods/powers/forces within/about my Presence. To say that Hashem is One teaches us much more than that he is simply a single, solitary deity. Of course, One also indicates that He is not two or three or four in number. However, it is also stating that He is whole, complete, balanced, and awesomely independent. In contrast to being inconsistent, erratic, fractured, splintered, schizophrenic, or composed of multiple personalities.

Note that all verbs referring to Hashem are singular

לב:לט רְאוּ עַתָּה, כִּי אֲנִי אֲנִי הוּא, וְאֵין אֱלֹהִים, עִמָּדִי;
Deut. 32:39. See now that **I, even I, am He, and there is no G-d with Me**;

מג:י אַתֶּם עֵדַי נְאֻם- ה', וְעַבְדִּי אֲשֶׁר בָּחָרְתִּי: לְמַעַן תֵּדְעוּ וְתַאֲמִינוּ לִי
וְתָבִינוּ, כִּי-אֲנִי הוּא--לְפָנַי לֹא-נוֹצַר אֵל, וְאַחֲרַי לֹא יִהְיֶה.
Isaiah 43:10. Ye are My witnesses, saith the LORD, and My servant whom I have chosen; that ye may know and believe Me,

and understand that **I am He; before Me there was no G-d formed, neither shall any be after Me**.

מד:ו כֹּה-אָמַר ה' מֶלֶךְ-יִשְׂרָאֵל וְגֹאֲלוֹ, ה' צְבָאוֹת: אֲנִי רִאשׁוֹן וַאֲנִי אַחֲרוֹן, וּמִבַּלְעָדַי אֵין אֱלֹהִים.

Isaiah 44:6. Thus saith the LORD, the King of Israel, and his Redeemer the LORD of hosts: **I am the first, and I am the last, and beside Me there is no G-d.**

מה:ה אֲנִי ה' וְאֵין עוֹד, זוּלָתִי אֵין אֱלֹהִים; אֲאַזֶּרְךָ, וְלֹא יְדַעְתָּנִי. ו לְמַעַן יֵדְעוּ, מִמִּזְרַח-שֶׁמֶשׁ וּמִמַּעֲרָבָה, כִּי-אֶפֶס, בִּלְעָדָי: אֲנִי ה', וְאֵין עוֹד.

Isaiah 45:5 I am the LORD, and there is none else, beside Me there is no G-d; I have girded thee, though thou hast not known Me; **6.** That they may know from the rising of the sun, and from the west, **that there is none beside Me; I am the LORD; and there is none else.**

מו:ט זִכְרוּ רִאשֹׁנוֹת, מֵעוֹלָם: כִּי אָנֹכִי אֵל וְאֵין עוֹד, אֱלֹהִים וְאֶפֶס כָּמוֹנִי.

Isaiah 46:9. Remember the former things of old: **that I am G-d, and there is none else; I am G-d, and there is none like Me;**

ט:ו אַתָּה-הוּא ה', לְבַדֶּךָ--

Nehemiah 9:6. Thou art the LORD, **even Thou alone;**

With the sin of the Golden Calf, the Children of Israel created a graven image specifically to replace G-d. Likewise, Christian doctrine teaches that their god created a graven image of himself of flesh and bone in the form of his son – thus, violating the second commandment. In addition, they state that Yeshu conversed with demons, which is punishable with death by stoning. When will the anti-Jewish missionaries acknowledge their sins and seek His forgiveness?

III-5.2 No Idols

כ:ג לֹא-תַעֲשֶׂה לְךָ פֶסֶל, וְכָל-תְּמוּנָה, אֲשֶׁר בַּשָּׁמַיִם מִמַּעַל, וַאֲשֶׁר בָּאָרֶץ מִתָּחַת--וַאֲשֶׁר בַּמַּיִם, מִתַּחַת לָאָרֶץ. ד לֹא-תִשְׁתַּחֲוֶה לָהֶם, וְלֹא תָעָבְדֵם: כִּי אָנֹכִי ה' אֱלֹהֶיךָ, אֵל קַנָּא--פֹּקֵד עֲוֹן אָבֹת עַל-בָּנִים עַל-שִׁלֵּשִׁים וְעַל-רִבֵּעִים, לְשֹׂנְאָי. ה וְעֹשֶׂה חֶסֶד, לַאֲלָפִים--לְאֹהֲבַי, וּלְשֹׁמְרֵי מִצְוֹתָי.

Thou shalt not make unto thee a graven image, nor any manner of likeness, of anything that is *in heaven above, or that is in the earth beneath*, or that is in the water under the earth; *thou shalt not bow down unto them, nor serve them*; for I the LORD thy G-d am a jealous G-d, visiting the iniquity of the fathers upon the children unto the third and fourth generation of them *that hate Me*; And showing mercy unto the thousandth generation *of them that love Me and* **keep My commandments**. (Ex. 20:3-5)

With the sin of the Golden Calf, the Children of Israel created an idol of gold. Likewise, Christian doctrine teaches that their god created a graven image of himself of flesh and bone as the form of his son specifically for not only the descendant of Abraham to worship but for all of mankind. Thus, according to Christianity, God himself violated this second commandment. The punishment for inciting an individual to worship idols death by stoning. Since it is inconceivable that the Creator would commit such a crime everything stated as a prophecy in the Christian Texts

338

brought their authors under punishment of death by strangulation, since these concepts are promoting the belief in false gods.

III-5.3 Blasphemy

כ:ו לֹא תִשָּׂא אֶת-שֵׁם- ה' אֱלֹהֶיךָ **לַשָּׁוְא**: כִּי לֹא יְנַקֶּה ה', אֵת אֲשֶׁר-יִשָּׂא אֶת-שְׁמוֹ **לַשָּׁוְא**.

Thou shalt not take the name of the LORD thy G-d in vain; for the LORD will not hold him guiltless that taketh His name in vain. (Ex. 20:6)

The term לַשָּׁוְא is derived from the root שָׁוְא and means a "lie, falsehood, nothingness, worthlessness, and vanity". Therefore, we can translate this commandment as "Do not make (use) the Name of Hashem your G-d "to lie", "to create a falsehood", "to make it as nothingness or worthlessness", or "for any vanity purpose". All such utterances or actions are blasphemous. Examples are cursing either the name of G-d with another appellation customarily used to denote Him or demeaning G-d by word or deed. The sin of the Golden Calf was a fourfold negation of Hashem.

1. They created a graven image specifically to replace G-d.

    Likewise, Christian doctrine teaches that "God the Father" created a graven image of himself from flesh and bone to form a physical image of himself – thus violating the second commandment.

2. They sacrificed their gold in order to make. Likewise, Christian doctrine teaches that in their concept of G-d, he sacrificed himself in to form of this idol/son .

3. They led all of the Children of Israel in bowing down and worshipping their idol of gold. Likewise, Christian doctrine teaches that in their concept of God he demands that all people, individually and collectively, must worship this idol or endure eternal punish in Hell. Here God, as they imagine him, is following the example set by Nebuchadnezzar, who condemned to death anyone who would not bow down and worship the golden idol he made of himself.

4. They lied by announcing to all of the people: "This is your G-d, O Israel, that brought you out of the land of Egypt." Likewise, Christian doctrine teaches that God, as they imagine him, misrepresented the true meaning of the Torah by saying that this scenario was the only means by which mankind could be saved from their collective and personal sins.

The punishment for committing blasphemy and inciting an entire community to worship idols was death by stoning. The Children of Israel repented of their transgression regarding the Golden Calf and were forgive on the first Yom Kippur almost

3500 years ago. Yet, the anti-Jewish missionaries constantly, daily still promote these base accusations.

III-5.4 Keep Shabbat

כ:ז זָכוֹר אֶת-יוֹם הַשַּׁבָּת לְקַדְּשׁוֹ .ח שֵׁשֶׁת יָמִים תַּעֲבֹד, וְעָשִׂיתָ כָּל-

מְלַאכְתֶּךָ .ט וְיוֹם הַשְּׁבִיעִי--שַׁבָּת לַה' אֱלֹהֶיךָ: לֹא-תַעֲשֶׂה כָל-מְלָאכָה

אַתָּה וּבִנְךָ וּבִתֶּךָ, עַבְדְּךָ וַאֲמָתְךָ וּבְהֶמְתֶּךָ, וְגֵרְךָ אֲשֶׁר בִּשְׁעָרֶיךָ. אֲשֶׁר י כִּי

שֵׁשֶׁת-יָמִים עָשָׂה ה' אֶת-הַשָּׁמַיִם וְאֶת-הָאָרֶץ, אֶת-הַיָּם וְאֶת-כָּל-אֲשֶׁר-בָּם,

וַיָּנַח בַּיּוֹם הַשְּׁבִיעִי; עַל-כֵּן, בֵּרַךְ ה' אֶת-יוֹם הַשַּׁבָּת--וַיְקַדְּשֵׁהוּ.

Remember the sabbath day to keep it holy. 8 Six days shalt thou labour, and do all thy work, 9 but the seventh day is a sabbath unto the LORD thy G-d, in it thou shalt not do any manner of work, *thou, nor thy son, nor thy daughter, nor thy man-servant, nor thy maid-servant, nor thy cattle, nor thy stranger that is within thy gates*; **10** for in six days the LORD made heaven and earth, the sea, and all that in them is, and rested on the seventh day; wherefore **the LORD blessed the sabbath day, and hallowed it**. (Ex. 20:7-10)

We are commanded to remember (זָכוֹר) to separate out/sanctify/consecrate/hallow (לְקַדְּשׁוֹ) the Day of Shabbat ("day of ceasing or desisting from"). We are specifically informed that we will complete all of our *malakah* (כָּל-מְלָאכָה), our work/occupation/services/missions, within six days, but the seventh day is a שַׁבָּת (a cessation) day for Hashem your G-d. It is interesting that *malakah* is from the same root as *malak*, an "angel" – *i.e.* anyone or anything that is sent on a mission to accomplish a task for G-d. Therefore, the Shabbat is a time set aside for us to rejuvenate ourselves physically while we regenerate ourselves spiritually. Hence, the Shabbat is a very sacred, consecrated time. Now we will examine how the CT handles the sanctity of this holy day.

> At that time **Jesus went through the grainfields on the sabbath; his disciples were hungry**, and **they began to pluck heads of grain and to eat**. [2]When the Pharisees saw it, they said to him, "Look, your disciples are doing what **is not lawful to do on the sabbath**." [3]He said to them, "Have you not read **what David did when he and his companions were hungry**? [4]He entered the house of God and ate the bread of the Presence, which **it was not lawful for him** or his companions **to eat**, but only for the priests. [5]Or have you not read in the law that **on the sabbath the priests in the temple break the sabbath** and yet are guiltless? [6]I tell you, something greater than the temple is here. [7]But if you had known what this means, 'I desire mercy and not sacrifice,' **you would not have condemned the guiltless**. [8]For the **Son of Man is lord of the sabbath**." (Matt. 12:1-8)

This story is repeated almost word-for-word in Mark 2:23-28 and Luke 6:1–5. It is not found in *John*. The JfJ website gives us this explanation.

> **JfJ:** The *P'rushim* obviously had a rule that one could glean on Shabbat but not "thresh". If you "threshed", you were working, and they considered the *talidim*'s rubbing the grains in their hands similar to how we would shell a peanut to be "threshing". **He corrected the *P'rushim* that their**

342

rule added to Torah and violated the spirit of Torah. His *talmidim* were all orthodox-trained Jews, so they knew what was lawful.

By "P'rushim", they mean Pharisees, and *talmidim* is used for his disciples. They have misinterpreted the issue.

And when the layer of dew was gone up, behold upon the face of the wilderness a fine, scale-like thing, fine as the hoar-frost on the ground. And when the children of Israel saw it, they said one to another: 'What is it?'--for they knew not what it was. And Moses said unto them: 'It is the bread which the LORD hath given you to eat. This is the thing which the LORD hath commanded: **Gather ye of it every man according to his eating**; an omer a head, according to the number of your persons, shall ye take it, every man for them that are in his tent.' And **they gathered it morning by morning**, every man according to his eating; and as the sun waxed hot, it melted. And it came to pass that **on the sixth day they gathered twice as much bread**, two omers for each one; and all the rulers of the congregation came and told Moses. And he said unto them: 'This is that which the LORD hath spoken: **To-morrow is a solemn rest, a holy Sabbath unto the LORD.** Bake that which ye will bake, and seethe that which ye will seethe; and **all that remaineth over lay up for you to be kept until the morning**.' And they laid it up till the morning, as Moses bade; and it did not rot, neither was there any worm therein. **Six days ye shall gather it; but on the seventh day is the Sabbath, in it there shall be none.'** See that the LORD hath given you the Sabbath; therefore, He giveth you on the sixth day the bread of two days; abide ye every man in his place, let no man go out

of his place on the seventh day.' So the people rested on the seventh day. (Ex. 16:14-30)

I am certain that whoever wrote this passage from the Synoptic Texts had never experienced a Shabbat, which is spent with family and/or friends. To begin with, why were thirteen adult men walking through a field of standing grain on Shabbat? They were trespassing on someone's property, trampling his crop to the ground, and stealing his produce – all on the Shabbat! Why? But even worst, they have failed to זָכוֹר אֶת-יוֹם הַשַּׁבָּת לְקַדְּשׁוֹ "remember the Shabbat and to "make it holy". We "remember" the Shabbat by preparing food and everything else need for the day in advance or by arranging to be hosted by family are friends before it begins. We consecrate it by refraining from mundane activities on it, which includes those that his followers were doing in this passage. If his "*talmidim* were all orthodox-trained Jews," who "knew what was lawful", then why were they not aware of the instructions given in the above excerpt from *Exodus*, specifying the part where gathering and preparing food on Shabbat is strictly forbidden.

However, we should give them the benefit of the doubt. Let's say that they were simply walking at the edge of a field, deeply in preoccupied in discussion of Torah precepts. Absentmindedly, his students, who were uneducated Jews, stripped a handful of grains each and ate them. Others, who were passing

344

by, were shocked and instinctively reprimanded them – as anyone naturally would do. A righteous teacher would thank that person for bringing the transgression to his attention. He would have rebuked his students and directed them to return to proper Torah observance; and, in those day, he would have instructed them to take a sin-offering to the Temple – asap.

Why does he response instead by attacking these who protested the offense? "Have you not read what David did when he and his companions were hungry?" Really?! David and his men were fleeing for their lives and were actually, physically starving. Where does it say that the priests *ate* the לֶחֶם פָּנִים (Ex. 25:30, 35:13, 39:36, 40:4 and 23)? Neither David nor the priests violated the law. In addition, this incident occurred on the sixth day (Friday), since the priests had just replaced the old bread with the new. Also, it should also be noted that, then as now, it is mandatory to save a life, even if it involves breaking the Shabbat.

The next accusation clearly demonstrates that the author's lacks Torah knowledge. "Or have you not read in the law that on the sabbath the priests in the temple break the sabbath and yet are guiltless?" Read where? In both the MS text and the LXX, the priests are required to perform prescribed duties in the Temple on Sabbath that include tending fire, slaughtering and burning two lambs. This was their job-description; therefore, they were not violating the Shabbat. Outside of this service, when they were at

345

home with their families, they were under the same laws as all other Jews.

What does he mean by "the 'Son of Man' is lord of the sabbath"? I'm sorry, but this account is so ignorant of Judaism and the Torah laws, that no one can convince me that the author was Jewish, much less an Orthodox Jew. Therefore, I am certain that this story never happened. It is a literal device inserted to belittle our laws in the minds of the non-Jews.

In the original law, breaking the Sabbath and inciting an entire community to do so incurred a penalty of death by stoning. According to this text, which is accepted as the absolute truth by a large proportion of the world's population, the CT-Yeshu and his followers were guilty of desecrating the Shabbat and of teaching this transgression to Jews first and also to the Gentiles.

III-5.5 Honor Your Parents

כ:יא כַּבֵּד אֶת-אָבִיךָ, וְאֶת-אִמֶּךָ--לְמַעַן, יַאֲרִכוּן יָמֶיךָ, עַל הָאֲדָמָה,
אֲשֶׁר-ה׳ אֱלֹהֶיךָ נֹתֵן לָךְ.

Honour thy father and thy mother, that thy days may be
long upon the land which the LORD thy G-d giveth thee.
(Ex. 20:11)

There are many ways to honor one's parents – positive family interactions, showing love, respect and concern, care-giving, and any number of other thoughtful kindnesses.

Conversely, one also honors a parent by refraining from doing those things that would demean or disparage a parent, especially in public. There is a troubling incident where the CT-Yeshu publicly disrespects his mother.

> And they went into a house. And the multitude cometh together again, so that they could not so much as eat bread... There came then his brethren and his mother, and, standing without, sent unto him, calling him. And the multitude sat about him, and they said unto him, Behold, thy mother and thy brethren without seek for thee. And he answered them, saying, "Who is my mother, or my brethren? And he looked round about on them which sat about him, and said, Behold my mother and my brethren! For whosoever shall do the will of God, the same is my brother, and my sister, and mother." (Mark 3:19b-20, 31-35)

If we are discussing Yeshu-Ḳristos, his mother and brothers could have come to warn him that people were spreading fantastic rumors about him. Since stories of him as the Mashiaḥ would have attracted the attention of the authorities, they would naturally have feared for his life.

The CT informs us that their version of Yeshu (Matt. 12:46-50; Mark 3:31-35; Luke 8:19-21) was so pressed by a large crowd that he and his disciples could not eat in peace, so they entered a house probably for lunch. Pushed about and suffering during the heat of the day, his mother and brothers have succeeded in work their way through the crowd. They manage to get word to him that they needed to speak with him. Perhaps they only wanted to sit with him for a few minutes to make sure that he is alright and in good health. But the CT-Yeshu refuses to let them inside the house and callously belittles them before his followers. "Who is my mother or my brethren?" This is a cold, heartless response.

Thus, the CT-Yeshu, broke the fifth commandment. He not only did not honor his mother, but he also publicly demeaned her. Of course, this behavior would not in itself be a capital offence. However, if it had resulted in her death of serious injury, especially if deliberate intent could be proven, then the CT-Yeshu would have faced death by strangulation for having inflicted an injury upon one of his parents.

III-5.6 Don't Commit Murder

כ:יבא לֹא תִרְצָח,

Thou shalt not murder. (Ex. 20:12a)

In Leviticus 18:21, we are given a very serious commandment: "And thou shalt neither cause any of thy seed to crossover to the Molek̟, nor shalt thou desecrate the name of thy G-d [by doing this] – I am Hashem." Reference is made to the Molek̟ or it's worship twenty-two times in the Tanak̟. Our G-d, the G-d of

348

Abraham, Isaac, and Jacob irrevocably condemns anyone who participates in human sacrifice.

Think for a moment how you would feel if someone accused you of ritual murdering your only child. You would of course be out raged. Yet, the CT patently accuse our G-d of having done exactly that. This is precisely what the famous Christian declaration of faith found in John 3:16 is stating about G-d. Christians are perfectly free to believe whatever the wish. However, for us this is so sacrilegious that it is extremely difficult for us to comprehend. The penalty for sacrifice one's children on the altar of the Molek was death by stoning. For murder in general, it was death by the sword.

III-5.7 Don't Commit Adultery

כ:יבב לֹא תִנְאָף;

Thou shalt not commit adultery. (Ex. 20:12b)

This is another very sensitive point – for one of Christianity's most cherished doctrines is to us a most serious example of sacrilege. In most traditions, a couple are betrothed before they are married. However, in Jewish tradition, the betrothal was part of the marriage ceremony. Between the betrothal and the second stage when they actually began to share their lives together, the bride and groom continued to live with their parents until they had everything necessary to create a home. During this time, they were legally husband and wife and, even though the marriage had not yet been consummated, they would still need a *get*, divorce document, to dissolve the marriage. Thus, the following excerpts from the CT was a much more serious matter than it would have been for most non-Jewish couples.

> Now the birth of Jesus Christ was on this wise: When as his mother Mary was espoused to Joseph, before they came together, she was found with child of the Holy Ghost. Then Joseph her husband, being a just *man*, and not willing to make her a public example, was minded to put her away privily. But while he thought on these things, behold, the angel of the Lord appeared unto him in a dream, saying, "Joseph, thou son of David, fear not to take unto thee Mary thy wife: for that which is conceived in her is of the Holy Ghost." (Matthew 1:18-20)

> And in the sixth month the angel Gabriel was sent from God unto a city of Galilee, named Nazareth, to a virgin espoused to a man whose name was Joseph, of the house of David; and the virgin's name *was* Mary. And the angel came in unto her, and said, "Hail, *thou that art* highly favoured, the Lord *is* with thee: blessed *art* thou among women." And when she saw *him*, she was troubled at his saying, and cast in her mind what manner of salutation this should be. And the angel said unto her, "Fear not, Mary: for thou hast found favour with G-d. And, behold, thou shalt conceive in thy womb, and bring forth a son, and shalt call his name Jesus." (Luke 1:26-30)

Again, the CT are accusing our G-d of committing a terrible crime. The penalty for engaging in sexual relations or any other activity that would result in a betrothed virgin becoming pregnant by anyone other than her lawful husband was death by stoning for both partners.

III-5.8 Don't Commit Theft

כ:יב‍ג לֹא תִגְנֹב,

Thou shalt not steal. (Ex. 20:12c)

The CT teaches that there is nothing more righteous than to bring a non-believer to the Christian doctrine, since this is the only path to God, as they imagine him, and eternal life. Thus, the ends – saving the souls of non-believers – justifies the means. Throughout the long, dark days of the past two millennium, countless Jewish children have been stolen and reared by despotic missionaries. Our Torah teaches that stealing a person from his or her family is very great evil. The penalty for this crime was death by strangulation. Today, I wonder if stealing the hearts of our young people and turning them against their family and heritage isn't just as sinister as stealing them physically.

III-5.9 Don't Bear False Witness

כ:יבד לֹא-תַעֲנֶה בְרֵעֲךָ עֵד שָׁקֶר.

Thou shalt not bear false witness against thy neighbour. (Ex. 20:12d)

These are examples of the false witness that the authors of the Christian Texts have borne against us for 2000 years. Whenever an anti-Jewish missionary meets a Jew, these are the characteristics they anticipate.

- And he (the CT-Yeshu) said unto them, Full well ye (Jews) reject the commandment of God, that ye may keep your own tradition. (Mark 7:9)
- And when thou prayest, thou (his disciples) shalt not be as the hypocrites *are*: for they love to pray standing in the synagogues and in the corners of the streets, that they may be seen of men. (Matt. 6:5)
- Woe unto you, scribes and Pharisees, hypocrites! for ye devour widows' houses, and for a pretense make long prayer: therefore, ye shall receive the greater damnation. (Matt. 23:14)
- *Ye* serpents, *ye* generation of vipers, how can ye escape the damnation of hell? (Luke 23:33)
- Let them alone: they be blind leaders of the blind. And if the blind lead the blind, both shall fall into the ditch. (Luke 15:14)

- *Ye* blind guides, which strain at a gnat, and swallow a camel. (Luke 23:24)
- Ye are of *your* father the devil, and the lusts of your father ye will do. He was a murderer from the beginning, and abode not in the truth, because there is no truth in him. When he speaketh a lie, he speaketh of his own: for he is a liar, and the father of it. (John 8:44)

When is theft not theft, rape not rape, murder not murder? Answer: When the victim is a Jew. Such is the results of canonized slander. It is time that the world acknowledges that Jews are just as human as any other people. Jews have faults like everyone else but, we strive to improve our characteristics. Thus, I can say in all honesty that Jews on the whole are better than the majority of other people encountered in life.

"And the judges shall inquire diligently; and, behold, if the witness be a false witness, and hath testified falsely against his brother; then shall ye do unto him, as he had purposed to do unto his brother; so shalt thou put away the evil from the midst of thee." (Deut. 19:18-19) Hence, the penalty for bearing false witness is that the evil witness will incur the same punishment that he was hoping to see his would-be victim endure.

III-5.10 Don't Harbor Envy

כ:יג לֹא תַחְמֹד, בֵּית רֵעֶךָ; {ס} לֹא-תַחְמֹד אֵשֶׁת רֵעֶךָ, וְעַבְדּוֹ וַאֲמָתוֹ וְשׁוֹרוֹ
וַחֲמֹרוֹ, וְכֹל, אֲשֶׁר לְרֵעֶךָ.

Thou shalt not covet thy neighbour's house; thou shalt not covet

thy neighbour's wife, nor his man-servant, nor his maid-servant,

nor his ox, nor his ass, nor any thing that is thy neighbour's. (Ex.

20:13)

Paul cautions his readers, "For the love of money is the root

of all evil." (Timothy 6:10) I might suggest that envy is the root of

all evil, because if one were not envious, he wouldn't become

consumed with excessive greed. There more on this topic below.

In Closing

We, Jews, wholeheartedly support the right of every individual to live life guided by their own ancestral beliefs. Paul and his followers combined primal Southwest Asian and Egyptian mysticism with the Greek philosophers' concept of God and select elements of Jewish spiritualism. Thus, they produced a perfect blend of religious concepts from the first three centuries of the Common Era. The text that they produced was a "New Testament" honoring Classical Mythology not Hashem's Torah. The raw hedonism of the pagan world was modified by the sanctifying waters of Torah teachings. Even though Christianity is a beautiful bud, its development has been restrained by the continuous impalement of Jews upon its pagan thorns. In my humble opinion, Christianity cannot achieve full bloom until it sheds these pagan thorns. Isn't it time for them to take us down from their crucifix?

We ask nothing more than to be allowed to follow our traditions and spiritual heritage, passed to us by our ancestors and sages over those same millennia – free of harassment, degradation, and heartless attacks on our persons and families. The Jewish People are to the world as Joseph was to Egypt. We are always ready and willing to assist when lives can be saved. Like Joseph, we desire only to be a "father to pharaoh" not to usurp him.

To Jews who have been misguided, please do not be so hasty to toss aside your own rich birthright. To Christians who are disguising themselves as Jews, please understand that Hashem does not respect those who practice deceit; therefore, you have more to loss than to gain from this charade. Remember the lesson of I Samuel 5 – Dagon/Dionysos will again fall before the Holy Ark of the Covenant. I believe with perfect faith that Hashem will inaugurate a great age of peace and brotherhood guided by His promised Mashiaḥ. May it be soon and in our days.

With heartfelt sincerity,

רבנית מיכל סימני   טו-אב תשפ"ב
Rabbanit Michal Simani   12-August, 2022

Bibliography

Albright, William F. *The Biblical Period: From Abraham to Ezra.* Baltimore: John Hopkins Press, 1949.

_____. *From the Stone Age to Christianity.* Baltimore: The John Hopkins Press, 1940.

Bosworth, A. B. and E. J. Baynham, eds. *Alexander the Great in Fact and Fiction.* New York: Oxford University Press, 1999.

Braude, Wm. G. *Jewish Proselyting in the First Five Centuries of the Common Era: the Age of the Tannaim and Amoraim.* Providence: Brown University Press, 1940.

Burkert, Walter. *Greek Religion.* John Rafin, trans. Cambridge: Harvard University Press, 1985.

Chill, Abraham *The Mitzvots: The Commandments and Their Rationale.* Jerusalem: Keter Books, 1974.

Choksy, Jamsheed K. *Triumph over Evil: Purity and Pollution in Zorastrianism.* Austin: University of Texas Press, 1989.

Cordovero, Moses, *The Palm Tree of Deborah,* Louis Jacobs, trans. New York: Sepher-Hermon Press, 1974.

Croix, Horst de la and Richard G. Tansey, *Gardner's Art Through the Ages.* Fifth Edition. New York; Harcourt, Brace World, Inc., 1970.

Danker, Frederick William, ed. *A Greek-English Lexicon of the New Testament and other Early Christian Literature,*3rd Edition. University of Chicago Press, 2000.

Demandt, Alexander. *Pontius Pilatus.* Munich: C. H. Beck, 2012.

Ehrman, Bart D. *The Orthodox Corruption of Scripture: The Effect of Early Christological Controversies on the Text of the New Testament.* Oxford: Oxford University Press, 1993.

Elsner, Jaś. "Orpheus as David. Orpheus as Christ?" *Biblical Archaeology Review*, Vol. 35 No. 2, March/April, 2009.

Thackeray, H. St. J. and Louis H. Feldman, trans. *Flavius Josephus: Complete Works.* Harvard University Press, 1966.

Fisher, Mary Pat. *Living Religions,* 5th edition. New Jersey: Prentice-Hall, 2002.

Forchheimer, Paul, trans. *Moses Maimonides, The Mishna of Avoth: Living Judaism.* Jerusalem: Feldheim Publishing, 1974.

France, R.T. The Gospel of Mark: A Commentary on the Greek Text. Wm. B. Eerdmans Publishing, 2002.

Frazer, James George. *The Golden Bough: a Study in Magic and Religion*, a new abridgement from the second and third editions. Oxford University Press, 2009.

Fredricksmeyer, Ernst. "Alexander's Religion and Divinity." *Brill's Companion to Alexander the Great.* Joseph Roisman, ed. Boston: Leiden, 2003.

Fredriksen, Paula. *From Jesus to Christ.* Second ed. New Haven: Yale University Press, 2000.

Michael Friedländer, trans., *Guide of the Perplexed of Maimonides.* New York: Hebrew Publishing Co. 1881.

Gordon, Cyrus H. *Ugaritic Textbook.* Rome: Pontifical Biblical Institute, 1965.

358

Hadley, P. L. "Pilate's Arrival in Judaea" *Journal of Theological Studies,* XXXV, 1934.

Hamilton, Joel R. *Alexander the Great.* Pittsburgh: University of Pittsburgh Press, 1982.

Holt, Frank L. *Alexander the Great and the Mystery of the Elephant Medallions.* Los Angeles: University of California Press, 2003.

Kasher, Menahem M. and Harry Freedman, eds. *Encyclopedia of Biblical Interpretation.* New York: American Biblical Encyclopedia Society, 1953.

Klein, Ernest. *A Comprehensive Etymological Dictionary of the Hebrew Language for Readers of English.* Jerusalem Carta: University of Ḥaifa, 1987.

Leon, Harry J. *The Jews of Ancient Rome.* Philadelphia: Jewish Publication Society of America, 1960.

Malandra, William W. *An Introduction to Ancient Iranian Religion: Readings from the Avesta and Achaemenid Inscriptions.* Minneapolis: University of Minnesota Press, 1983.

Milns, R. D. *Alexander the Great.* New York: Pegasus, 1965.

Chanan Morrison, Gold from the Land of Israel: A New Light on the Weekly Torah Portion – From the Writings of Rabbi Abraham Isaac HaKohen Kook. Jerusalem: Urim Publications, 2006.

Pomeroy, Sarah B. Stanley, M. Burstein, Walter Donlan, and Jennifer Tolbert Roberts, *Ancient Greece: A Political, Social, and Cultural History.* New York: Oxford UP, 1999.

Rawlinson, George. *Seven Great Monarchies of the Ancient Eastern World.* New York: John B. Alden, Publisher, 1885.

Redford, Donald B. *The History and Chronology of the Eighteenth Dynasty of Egypt.* Toronto University Press, 1967.

Saunders, N. K. *The Epic of Gilgamesh.* London: Penguin Books, 1960.

Scherman, Nosson ed. *Tanach – the Torah, Prophets, Writings: the twenty-four books of the Bible Newly translated and annotated,* Second edition. New York: Mesorah Publications, ltd., 1997.

Schiffman, Lawrence H. *Reclaiming the Dead Sea Scrolls.* Philadelphia: Jewish Publication Society, 1994.

Smith, Mark S. *The Early History of God: Yahweh and the Other Deities in Ancient Israel,* 2nd ed. Grand Rapids: Eerdmans, Dearborn, Dove, 2002.

Smith, Stephen H, "A Divine Tragedy: Some Observations on the Dramatic Structure of Mark's Gospel", *Novum Testamentum* 37 (3). Leiden: E.J. Brill, 1995.

Hutton, M. W. Petterson, John Jackson, C. H. Moore, R.M. Ogilvie, E.H. Warmington & M. Winterbottom, trans. *Tacitus: Complete Works.* Harvard University Press, 2000.

Tarn, W.W. *Alexander the Great: Narrative.* New York: Cambridge University Press, 1947.

Weingreen, J. *A Practical Grammar for Classical Hebrew.* Oxford: Oxford University Press, 1959.

Wilson, John A. *The Culture of Ancient Egypt*. Chicago: University of Chicago Press, 1963.

Worthington, Ian. *Alexander the Great: A Reader*. New York: Routledge Taylor & Francis Group, 2003.

Zlotowitz, Meir, trans. *Koheles / Ecclesiastes: a New Translation with a commentary anthologized from Talmudic, Midrashic and Rabbinic Sources*. Brooklyn: Mesorah Publications, Ltd., 2010.

Index:

Christian Text (CT), 9, 18,
21, 41, 44, 48, 53, 56, 59,
60, 70, 72, 80, 81, 85, 87,
140, 212, 215-219, 222,
227, 230, 231-233, 243-
261, 264, 279, 281, 286,
288, 292, 295-297, 300,
304, 308, 313, 317, 318,
320, 321, 324-327, 330,
331-335, 338, 370, 376,
381-387
Christianity, 3-7, 13, 17, 18,
21, 67, 85-87, 109, 118,
135, 197, 207, 208, 230,
233, 155, 243, 244, 250,
254, 260, 261, 294, 299,
315, 317, 329, 364, 366,
373, 384, 390, 392
Chronicles, 129, 245, 263
Clemens, 195, 226, 229
Constantine, 21, 232, 317
Coponius, 203
CT-Yeshu, 53, 60, 80, 85, 87,
212, 218, 219, 230-233,
245, 249-252, 255-260,
264, 281, 292, 295, 300,
304, 308, 313, 317-321,
326, 330-334, 381-383,
387
Curtius, 162, 167
Cyrene, 230
Da Vinci Code, 59
Dagon, 101, 391
Damascus, 221, 283, 306-
308, 317
damsel, 251-253; *see also*
maiden
Darius, 137-139, 153, 156,
159, 162, 165
Dasius, 290-292

David, 39, 56, 59, 65, 119,
127, 129, 176, 197, 198,
233, 245, 248-250, 261,
263, 272, 275-279, 287,
296, 298, 302, 303, 313,
321, 350-352, 376, 380,
385, 393
Dead Sea Scrolls, 62, 182,
191, 395
Demetrius, 171-173
demons, 117, 155, 372
Deuteronomy, 58, 115, 116,
205, 262, 271, 302, 329,
343, 359, 371, 389
Devil, 139, 140
Dio Cassius, 195, 217, 330
disciples, 192, 198, 205, 206,
273, 281, 292, 293, 300,
303, 306, 308, 323, 324,
330, 331, 376, 377, 382,
387
Domitian, 14, 195, 196, 228,
229
doomsday doctrine, 325
Durostorum, 290, 291
Ebionites, 300, 301, 304
Eden, 364, 365
EDH *Comprehensive
Etymological Dictionary
of the Hebrew Language*,
22, 24, 27, 30, 34, 35, 39,
42, 44, 49, 53, 60, 63, 69
Egypt, 21, 87-90, 99, 112-
114, 117-119, 130, 148,
156, 162-167, 170-173,
178, 187, 255, 257, 262,
266, 316, 334, 338, 368,
375, 390, 395, 396
eḥad, 344

El, 99, 100, 106, 108, 114, 339
Elamites, 122, 124
El-Shaddai, 107, 109-113
Epistles, 315, 327
Esarhaddon, 126
Esau, 110, 161
Essenes, 175, 178-181, 184, 219
Eucharistía, 325, 326
Eupator, 190
Euripides, 151, 318, 319
Eusebius, 145, 207, 208
Euthyphros, 366
evil spirits, 149
evil-inclination, 117
Exodus,Book of (Ex.*)*, 52, 108, 180, 251, 253, 262, 274, 333, 368, 370, 372, 373, 376, 378, 379-389
Exodus, 8, 111, 114,
Fulvia, 215-217
Galilee, 219, 224, 225, 230, 281, 283, 294, 298, 314, 385
Gamaliel, 224, 226, 309, 310
Gaugamela, 162, 164, 170
G-d~fearers, ~worshipers, 194, 195, 201, 212, 226, 309, 313, 316, 317
genealogies, CT-Yeshu, 245, 249, 250
gnostic, 298, 317
Golden Calf, 333, 369, 372-375
Gospels, 227
grain, 90, 93, 94, 101, 326, 376, 378
Gratus, 204-206

Greece, 90, 135, 145, 150, 153, 156, 157, 395
guilt-offering, 56, 82, 83, 87
Habakkuk, 42
Habiru, 110
Hadrian, 197, 228, 230
Ḥalakhic Letter, 182-184, 279
Ḥananiah, 206
haNazir, Yeshus, 298, *see also nazir*
Ḥannah, 248
haNotzi, Yeshu, 268-271, 275-280, *see also netzer*
Ḥaran, 109, 269
Hashem, 15, 24, 26, 32, 38-42, 46, 48, 51-58, 65, 74-79, 83-86, 97, 112, 114, 119, 120, 123, 128-133, 139, 140, 174, 189, 226, 259, 263, 287, 298, 313, 329, 333, 334, 337, 352, 356, 357, 365-373, 376, 383, 390, 391
Ḥasmonean, 191, 193
Hebrew, 3, 11, 15, 21, 22, 26, 29, 30, 38, 41, 63, 69, 72, 80, 96, 97, 101, 108, 112, 114, 116, 123, 140, 160, 161, 173, 179-181, 185, 189, 243-245, 251, 281, 287, 295, 297, 306, 309, 337-343, 347, 355, 358-362, 369, 394, 396
Hebrews, 108, 309
Hera, 90, 94, 166
ḥerem, 268
Herod, 193, 200, 203, 219-221, 255, 256, 290
Herodias, 219, 220

Sabbatical, 123

Ṣadducees, 175-177, 182, 192, 279

Salome, 191, 192, 222, 267, 278, 279

Samaria, 37, 121, 129, 172

Samaritans, 162, 218, 220, 222

Samuel, 62, 101, 127, 184, 340, 391

Sanhedrin, 17, 186, 199, 202, 205, 206, 226, 264-267, 270, 274, 278, 298

Sassanids, 137

Satan, 18, 140

Saturnalia, 290, 291

Saturninus, 216, 217

Saʿadya, 26

Seleucid, 172, 190, 191

Seleucus, 171, 172, 187

Semele, 91, 102, 318, 319

Semitic, 25, 29, 69, 100, 102, 108, 109

Sennacherib, 37, 46, 76, 122-126

Septuagint LXX, 21, 62, 69, 24, 27, 31, 34, 36, 40-45, 48, 50, 54, 61, 64, 68-73, 173, 245, 248, 251, 260, 276, 279, 297, 313, 339, 349, 354, 355, 380

Seth, 87, 88, 98, 205

Shabbat, 8, 172, 179, 193-195, 199-202, 206, 301, 313, 375-380, 381

Shalmaneser, 37, 121

Shamesh, 101

Shammai, 197, 199, 200-206, 223-226, 230, 285, 286, 291, 310

Shammai, Yeshivat, 197, 202, 283-286

Shekhinah, 362

Shema, 266, 302, 343, 359

Shimon, haTzadek, 177, 200, 266, 268, 279

sin-offering, 82, 326, 379

Sion, 297, 342; *see also Zion*

Siwah, 147, 163, 164

Socrates, 135, 152, 366, 367

Solomon, 41, 57, 58, 127, 128, 131, 135, 160, 176, 183, 245, 250, 357

Son of Man, 314, 377, 380

Song of Songs, 251

sorcery, 267, 270, 278

Spitamenes, 167

Stephen, 305, 306, 314, 396

Suetonius, 14, 196, 217, 225

Suffering Servant, 17-20, 26, 28, 38, 44, 47, 51, 53, 60, 77, 87, 113, 119, 264, 271, 314

Sumerian, 102, 106, 110

Tacitus, 214-217, 315, 396

Talmud, 161, 162, 177, 199, 201, 205, 264, 269, 270, 278, 281, 318

Tammuz, 102, 188, 330

Tanach, 13, 20, 52, 76, 86, 395

targums, 21

Teacher of Righteousness, 183

Temple, 41, 129-135, 160, 175-177, 183, 185, 188, 190, 193, 196, 199, 211, 216, 217, 225, 226, 229, 281, 314-317, 379, 380